GYPSIES

FREE SPIRITS OF THE OPEN STEPPE

Ljalja Kuznetsova

GYPSIES

FREE SPIRITS OF THE OPEN STEPPE

Introduction by Inge Morath
Afterword by Marina Rasbeshkina

THAMES AND HUDSON

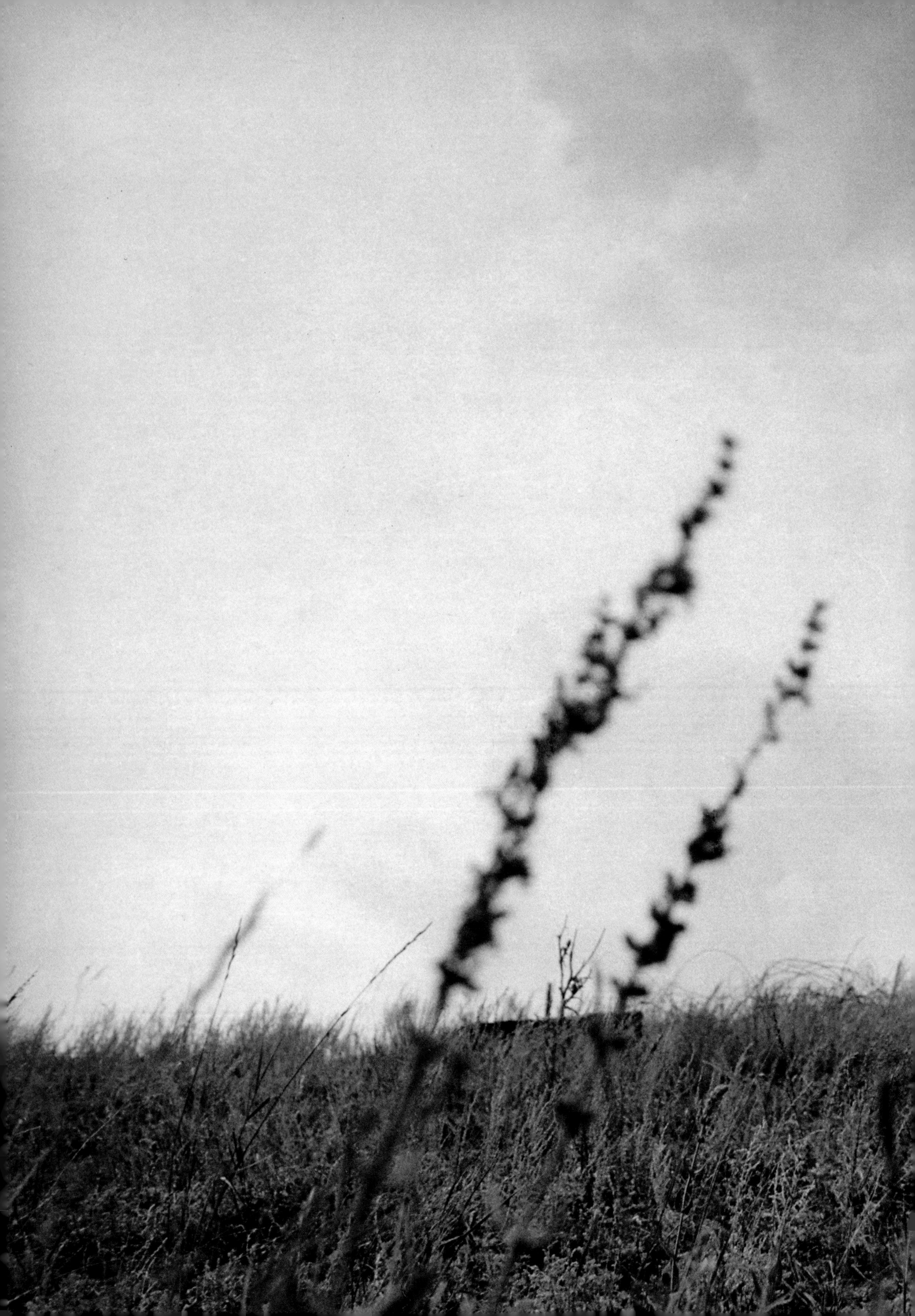

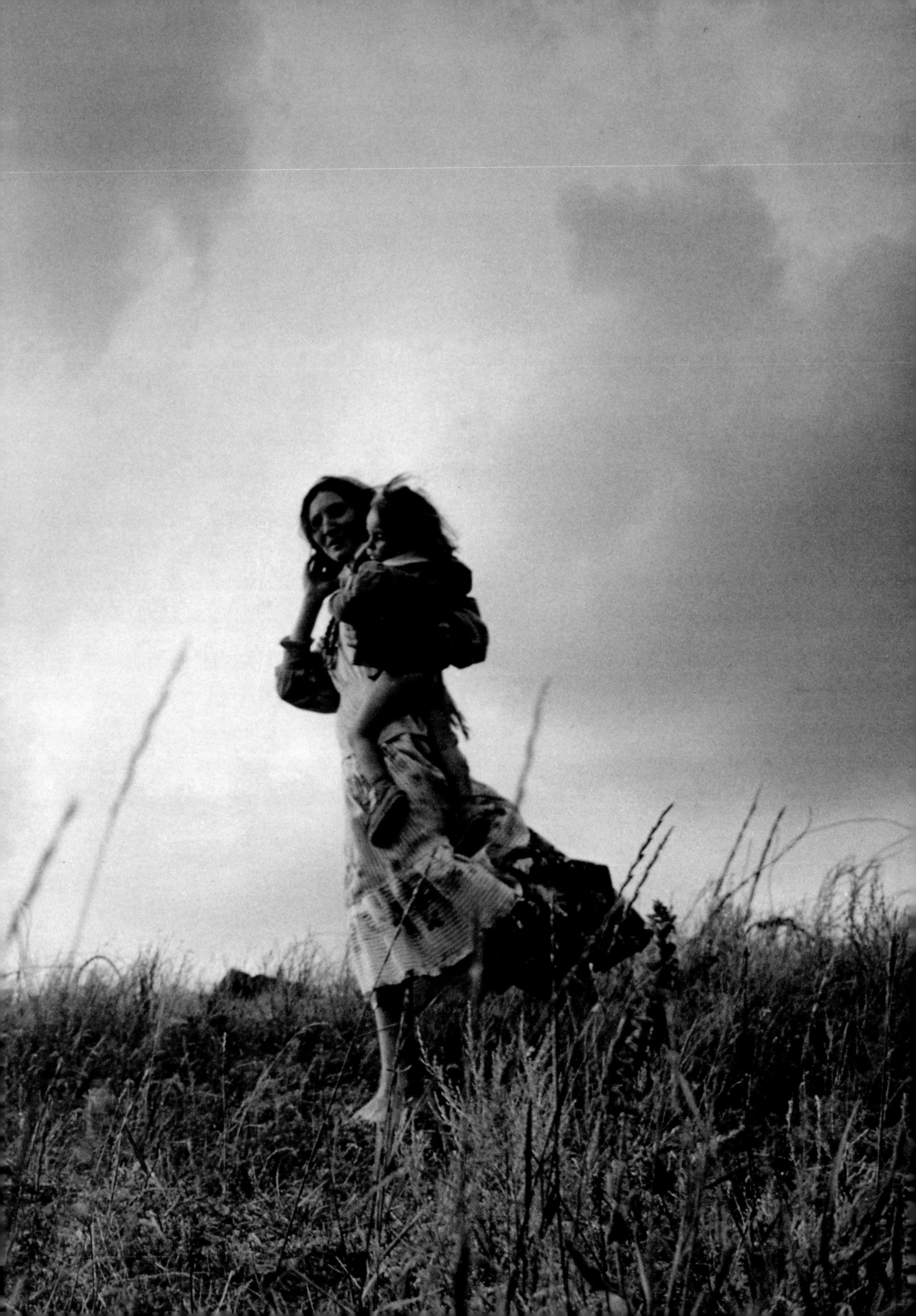

TO MY DEAR FAMILY—
MY PARENTS, MY BROTHER,
AND MY BELOVED HUSBAND,
WHO HAVE LEFT ME AND
MY WORLD MUCH TOO SOON—
AND TO MY DAUGHTER WLADA,
FOR WHOM I THANK GOD.

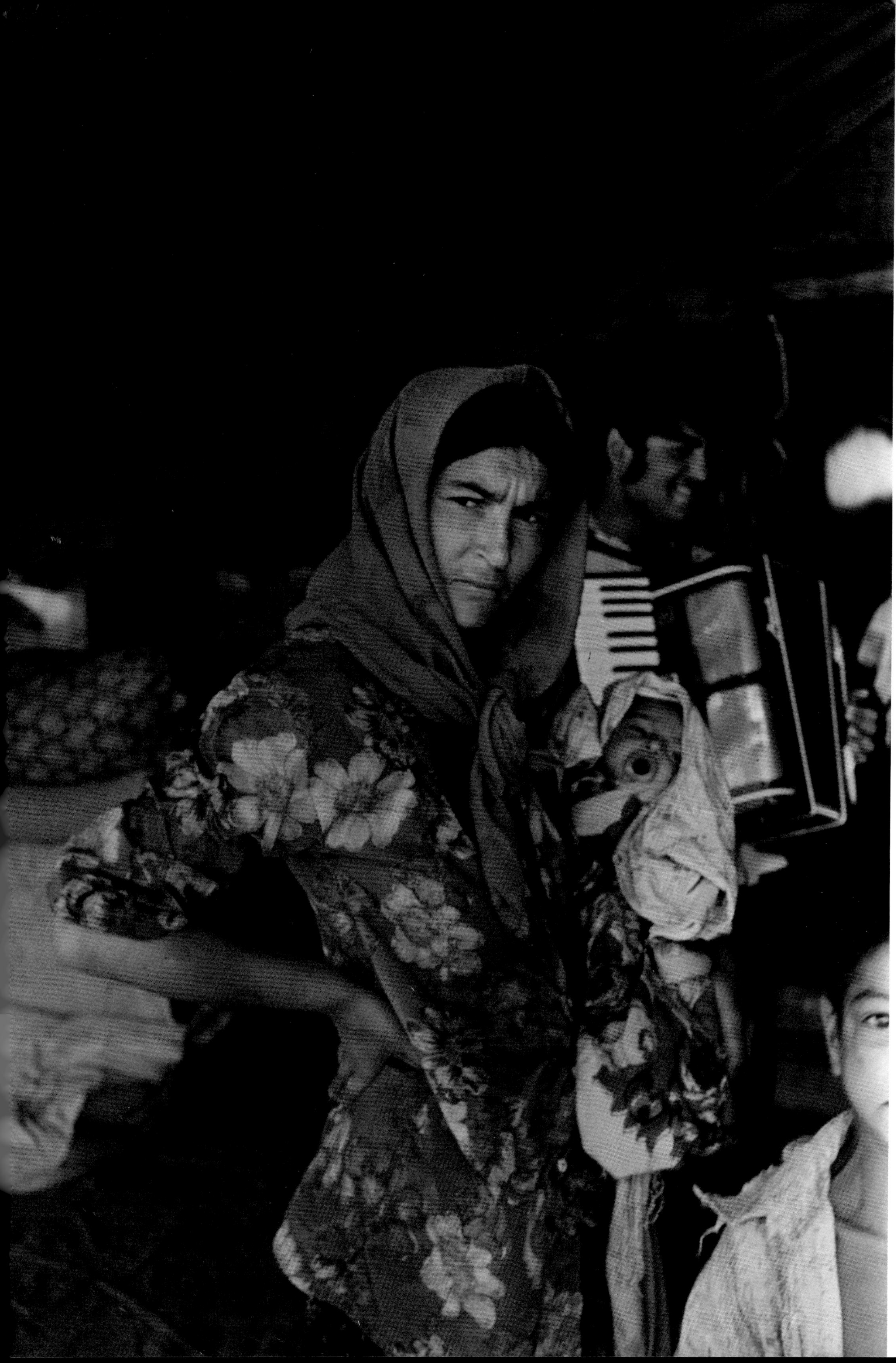

Inge Morath

Introduction

IN 1989 I EXHIBITED some of my photographs in Moscow. A few days after the opening, my interpreter, Svetlana Makurenkova, told me that several photographers wanted to meet me and show me their work in a studio that belonged to one of the artists. The studio was in one of those Moscow neighborhoods where mostly tradesmen and artisans seem to live–part of an older Moscow, where entranceways lead to multifamily flats with peeling paint, through courtyards, and over dark and narrow stairs.

When I arrived, I was struck by the absence of professional jealousy among the artists. Their main complaint was their restricted communication with the West–they so wanted to get their pictures out there, to be seen and published. As travel abroad was still banned, except to other socialist countries, a profound feeling of "Russian-ness" pervaded the work. The artists' individual styles differed but were not as diversified as they might have been among this kind of loose collective in, say, New York. They were also less imitative of Western art-historical precedents, with a refreshing absence of trendiness.

Toward the end of our little meeting, they brought out an envelope which contained the work of Ljalja Kuznetsova, a Kazakhstan-born photographer who was living in Kazan and was unable to come to Moscow for our meeting. At once, I was taken with her work, which displayed a rare combination of visual and emotional perceptiveness, an unusual degree of wisdom, and a lack of sentimentality. She was apparently drawn to the more vulnerable members of human society, to those whose strength resides not in forcefulness but in the capacity to produce a sort of magic existence in the margins of civilization. Most of the images featured gypsies from the steppe region of Kazakhstan. They seemed to let her get close enough to watch them in their own space, in the way that birds may let you watch them as long as you don't disturb their ways. There were pictures of circus performers as well, leading fringe existences outside the big city. There was also a wonderful series of women photographed while dressing for key events in their lives: a beauty contest, a performance, a date.

On my next visit to Moscow I met Kuznetsova herself. She was just as I had imagined her on the basis of her work. Her features were fine, and she moved with the grace of a girl. Beyond her occasional smile or a rare burst of laughter at some human frailty–a laughter that was never mocking but full of comprehension–her face was possessed of a vulnerability, a suffering that is present in her photographs. Her eyes were forever watching. Even when she did not move, an urgency seemed to animate her. She was anxious to return to her daughter and her work and anticipated a long train ride back to Kazan. I sensed that her life was still very difficult.

Born in 1946 in the small town of Uralsk, in western Kazakhstan near the Russian border, Kuznetsova was reared by Tatar parents of modest means in the Muslim tradition: to be a good housewife, a faithful spouse, and a loving mother. At first it seemed that her life would follow this course, albeit a slightly modernized version of it. Kuznetsova finished school and straightaway went to work and study at an aviation institute. She fell in love, got married, and had a daughter. Her job as an aviation engineer guaranteed a comfortable income, so she continued to work after giving birth. Then in 1976, Kuznetsova's husband died suddenly, leaving her alone with her little daughter. In this time of crisis, through some unfathomable strength, she decided to follow an old dream and she picked up a camera, never to put it down again. It was especially difficult then to earn a living as a photographer, and her choice meant exchanging a secure existence for a life of wandering and uncertainties. Yet not only did Kuznetsova, newly widowed, manage to secure a job as a photographer for the Kazan State Museum of Fine Art, she decided soon after to test fate again and work as an independent.

It seems fitting that even before Kuznetsova picked up a camera, her profession had to do with space and air, two elements that later were to play such an important part in her photography of the Central Asian steppe. In 1976, on a drive into this vast, flat, air-filled expanse with her brother, Kuznetsova found, encamped on a riverbank, the gypsies who would become her favorite subjects for the next couple of decades. As a child, with avid curiosity, she'd watched the mysterious comings and goings of "these graceful, sunburned people" from a small window in a hayloft at her aunt's house on the steppes. She saw their fires burn in the night and listened to their songs. She saw their painted wagons on the road, but there was no way to follow them, for no outsiders were allowed to go into the camp. On this particular trip with her brother, gypsy children ran out to look at the new strangers, and Kuznetsova and her brother dared to follow them back to their tents. After presenting the children with little presents, Kuznetsova started photographing the men and women sitting on the floor. Gypsies dislike being photographed, and winning their confidence isn't easy. But in the Central Asian Roma she knew that she had discovered the subjects she had been searching for–a kindred people whose strange familiarity moved her. Slowly the gypsies let this young woman, whose appearance somewhat resembled theirs, to enter into their world, and she continued to document them over the years. With the instinct of a cat, she found her gypsies again and again on the steppe. At times she seemed to make herself almost invisible as she photographed the gypsies' pursuits. At other times she let them squarely face her camera as they chose, with good humor, seriousness, ostentation, or even a withdrawn remoteness.

It is Kuznetsova's way with the space through which her gypsies move that is so wonderful. They are rarely at the center of her compositions, but they show up everywhere–high up in corners, way down, at all kinds of distances. She portrays them where she finds them, and so we seem to discover them with her. Her touch is so light that we might forget the determination and even toughness required to get each image. Kuznetsova's gypsy series is like a huge novel, each photo holding its place as the big picture unfolds.

Over time, Kuznetsova's photographs have moved from the wandering gypsies living in tents on the steppe into the gypsy settlements outside bigger towns like Odessa. There we find houses, accompanied by a feeling of confinement in the photographs. It is no longer only the world of the Roma. Other people enter the work–Uzbeks and Tatars, performers in wandering circuses–the people who keep themselves, or are kept by fate, away from the big road that tempts millions to move into the cities. Kuznetsova too stays back in her beloved provinces and continues to photograph life in these places still built to the measure of man.

Kuznetsova has come a long way since I first saw her work. Now a famous photographer in Europe, she has exhibited all over the world, from Berlin to Arles, Paris, and New York. Still, she continues to photograph outsiders. She is not afraid to reveal their weaknesses or vanities, little frailties or idiosyncrasies, but she reveals them with sympathy, occasionally with tenderness. Ljalja Kuznetsova knows her craft and enriches us with the gift of her pictures, filled with the poetry of freedom, suffering and pride. Her images linger in the mind like personal memories.

Ljalja Kuznetsova

Photographer's Notes: Memories of My Time with the Gypsies

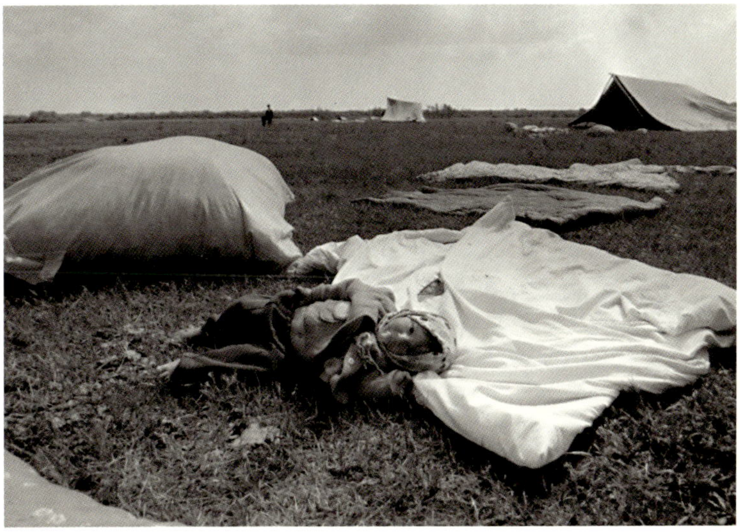

The Steppe Gypsies in Kazakhstan

WHEN I WAS A LITTLE GIRL with black curly hair, the grown-ups used to try to scare me by telling me the gypsies were going to come and steal me. Later on, I lost my fear and became intrigued and enchanted by these beautiful people. There was always something extraordinary about them. The women were so graceful, and their brightly colored skirts swung from side to side as they walked. Their eyes were at once kind, sad, and full of mystery.

As a child, I had the opportunity to witness gypsy life firsthand on my aunt's farm. In the mornings, the gypsy women came to fetch milk. We were not allowed to go to the gypsy camp, but from my aunt's hayloft I could see their campfires burning and food being prepared. On the road, we met brightly painted gypsy caravans with dogs following behind. Sometimes I could hear them singing.

In 1979, I took my first photos of the nomadic gypsies' tents on the endless steppes of the Urals, with their scent of wormwood. My first encounter with this caravan came about purely by chance. They were camping on a riverbank, near where my brother and I were driving along in his car. When we turned off the road and arrived at the camp, the sun was just setting. Children came running toward us, and a few young men rode up on horseback.

Around us, twelve or thirteen white tents were arranged in a circle. Small children were romping around nearly naked. The ten-year-old girls were already wearing colorful long skirts. We handed out gifts to the children, and they surrounded us as we went over to the big tent.

The gypsies were sitting on the ground with friendly smiles on their faces. Their horses were grazing around the tents and seemed very much in harmony with nature. The gypsies were smiths, so they shod their own horses. They had bellows and a small anvil with which they also made household items out of metal–things like door hinges and tubes for samovars.

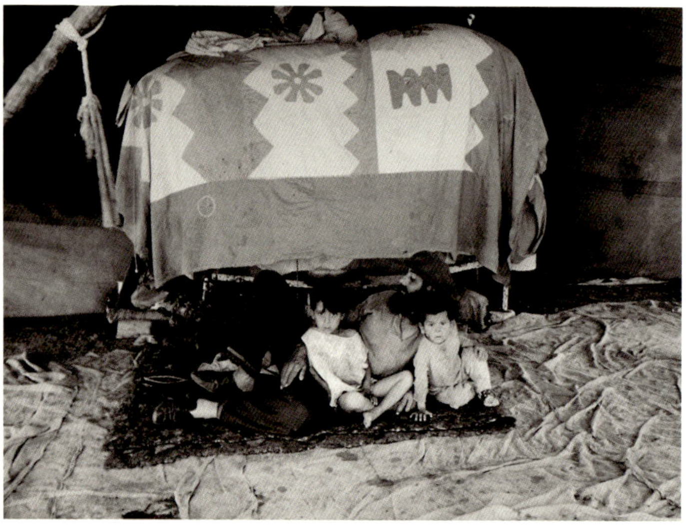

A photographer is an unexpected apparition in a traveling gypsy camp, so they were suspicious of me at first. The gypsies were trying to keep their sons hidden away so that they would not be conscripted into the Soviet Army. Because I was just a slip of a girl, however, their suspicion evaporated quickly. How could I possibly be up to no good? It also helped that I look like a gypsy–apart from the fact that I was a woman wearing trousers.

I was very excited that they accepted me and tried to take some photos of them to carry back with me to my other life. Much to my surprise, they agreed to let me photograph them the following day when the gypsy baron was to arrive for a summer festival.

THE SUMMER FESTIVAL

The festival took place on Sunday morning, so the gypsies first went to church and had their honey-coated apples blessed by the priest. Then they caught fish from the river for the festive meal.

A gypsy caravan stood in the middle of a huge tent. Quilts covered a large bed on the caravan, topped by a beautiful decorated rug and an icon of Saint Nicholas, the camp's patron saint. The men were sitting around in a circle on carpets. A feast of melons, watermelons, tomatoes, bread, and vodka was laid out on the ground. The honey-coated apples were arranged on large dishes; other dishes contained fish baked on the fire. My brother was invited to sit down and eat. The gypsy baron poured glasses of vodka and handed them around to the guests. Before they drank, each of them gave a toast and wished the others well.

The women and children were also sitting on the ground–but at a much more modest table outside the tent. Because I was still young, it was difficult to establish a relationship with the women, especially the young ones. They were very jealous of me because they saw me as a rival for the men's attention. Once one of the women lashed out and hit me on the head with a stick while I was taking a photograph.

All the smaller tents had been cleared for the party. The quilts and rugs on display in the middle of the big tent were spread out at night and a curtain was hung over each bed to keep out mosquitoes and flies.

WORK AND LIVELIHOOD OF THE KAZAKHSTAN GYPSIES

The gypsies kept horses, chickens, and turkeys. The camp swarmed with dogs, and they were always milling around the children. The horses whinnied close to the camp; at that time the horses were the gypsies' main source of wealth. A dove was looping the loop. The themes I was exploring in my work at that time are epitomized by a photograph I took on the festival day of a boy playing with this dove, freeing it into the open air.

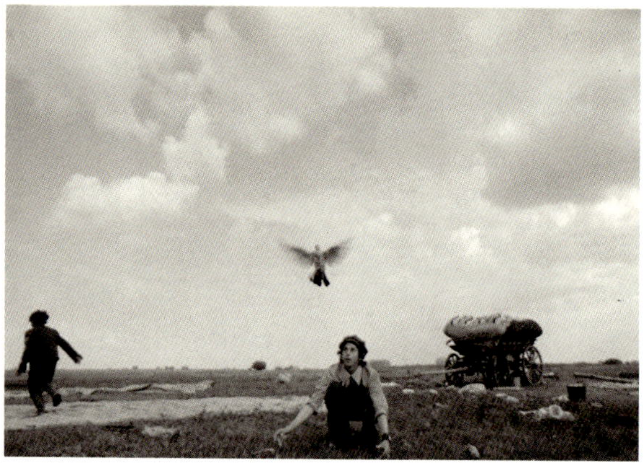

Gypsies in Russia

A few years later I met gypsies at the bazaar in Uralsk, the town where I was born and raised. The women were telling fortunes and asking for fruit and vegetables. The men were selling and exchanging horses, and after they closed a deal they would go to a beer kiosk to discuss it. They were all sunburned, and most of them, except for the younger ones, had beards. They were speaking their own language, Romani, sometimes with a few Russian words thrown in.

Outside of Kazan, Russia, which is still my home, the gypsies had a house which they would all move into and share in the winter. In the summer, they lived outdoors, and the house remained perfectly clean and tidy. When I first entered the courtyard of this house I saw a big tent with a lot of quilts in it. The matriarch, a stout gypsy woman, was sitting on top. Her young daughter-in-law brought the samovar to boil water, and soon we were sitting in the tent drinking tea.

These gypsies belonged to the Orthodox faith and kept religious icons in a corner of the room. In the yard they cultivated a small vegetable garden. Russians were living nearby, and the gypsy family was friendly with their neighbors.

The husband worked as a watchman at the factory. The daughter-in-law and daughters went from house to house collecting clothes and money, and some of them told fortunes. They often came to my house, to warm up, drink tea, or change their babies' diapers. I once asked a gypsy from Moldavia whether their womenfolk worked anywhere. His reply was, "They have children. They even go on having children when they get old."

In Moscow, I met a family whose surname was Demeter. There, in the city, the women worked in the sciences, on stage, or as fashion designers. The men were professors and writers. I was even introduced to a gypsy who served as a priest in a Moscow church.

I have spent Christmas with gypsy families in Moscow and Kuibyshev, Russia, and seen spacious, beautifully furnished and well-kept houses, but they had no appeal for me. It saddens me that I no longer meet traveling gypsies in their tents.

Gypsies in the Ukraine

I arrived in Odessa in the spring of 1990, just before Easter. In Privos, a big market there, I waited for the bus, and a gypsy family was sitting surrounded by groceries–chickens, sausage, ducks, vodka, beer, vegetables, and fruit. The man was already slightly drunk. The woman, whose name was Tamara, was beautiful with big, sad eyes. The children were playing around them. I went up to them and tried to explain briefly that I wanted to come and visit them with my camera over Easter.

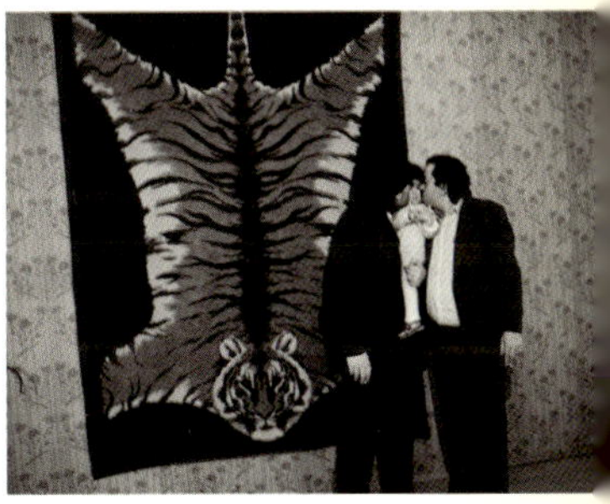

The gypsy husband immediately began issuing a pressing and cordial invitation, while his wife sized me up skeptically. I waited to see what she would say. She smilingly agreed, and he wrote down directions to the gypsy settlement.

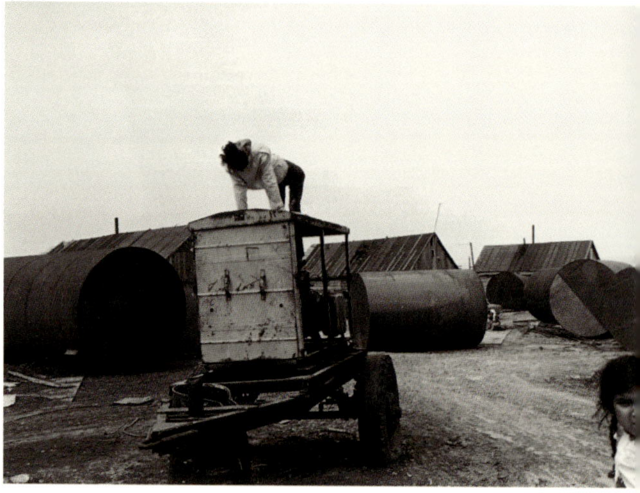

I was staying with the family of my friend Seryosha, who is also a photographer. He grew up in Odessa and knows the gypsies well. Seryosha helped me a great deal with contacts. When Easter Sunday arrived, I set off with him for the village. The gypsy settlement is located at the far end, right near the river and away from the Russian and Ukrainian houses. It is fairly large, with about fifteen houses. The children gave us a boisterous welcome. Among them were Tamara's children, who led Seryosha and me proudly to their house. The other gypsy children accompanied us as well, watching curiously.

They kept peacocks in the yard. The husband hugged the male and told us how he had brought this magnificent pair of birds from Bulgaria. I was just as taken with the peacock's master as I was with the resplendent bird. He took us into the house, and we greeted the owners. The windows were small, and it was dark indoors. The main decorations in the room were large woolen carpets, some with patterns and brightly colored flowers, others with pictures of lions and tigers on them. Happiness welled up inside me as I took in the atmosphere. In that moment I knew that I would keep coming back to these Odessa gypsies, and that every new encounter would bring me pleasure.

In every house a table with a lavish spread awaited the guests. The centerpiece was a plaited dough cake surrounded by eggs painted different colors. Guests helped themselves to roast chickens, vegetables, fruit, beer, vodka, and huge flans.

Groups of men in their best clothes moved from house to house greeting everyone. A musician, in this case an accordion player, accompanied each group. After the greeting, the gypsies split up and either gathered in the houses or carried a table with food and drink on it out onto the street. After a few hours the men were drunk, and my friend Seryosha could take no more of the gypsies' high spirits.

WORK AND LIVELIHOOD OF THE ODESSA GYPSIES

The Odessa gypsies forged huge metal containers in various shapes, mostly cylinders and cubes, and stored them in the center of the settlement and between the little, single-story wooden houses. Nearby they kept the enormous metal sheets they used to make the containers. The gypsies told us that people bought the containers to store fresh water and chemicals. To make them, the gypsies welded the metal plates and bent them into enormous cylinders with a hand winch. Then they welded on the bases and painted each tank with oil paint.

Most of the women at the Odessa gypsy settlement spent all day in the town's streets and markets. They went about in groups and told fortunes, usually earning very little money. The children begged a little or just went around with their mothers. My impression was that this work was simply a sideline for the women, for the sake of tradition, before they did their daily shopping in the stores and markets.

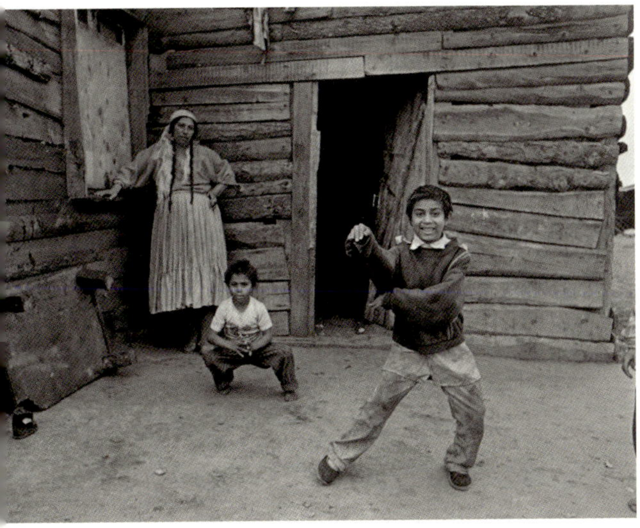

Nowadays most Odessa gypsy families have a television. But a color television is a real luxury, often kept on the table in the middle of the room or on a stand. Every house has religious icons. A large number of small, framed photos, which are a record of the entire family, decorates the walls. Now they also have some of my photos. A table always occupies the center of the room. Sometimes it is round, sometimes square, sometimes oblong; but it is always low. The gypsies sit around it on the floor.

THE GYPSY GRAVEYARD NEAR ODESSA

That Easter Sunday, as evening approached, Tamara's husband showed me the cemetery next to their house, screened by a hedge of wild cherry bushes full of whitish-pink blossoms. The gravestones were an unusual shape, very simple and painted white. There was something mysterious and beautiful about them. The gypsy graves were interspersed with Russian graves with metal fences around them. The gypsy graves were unfenced.

The children were strictly forbidden by their parents to play in the cemetery. As children will, they ignored this restriction. On my next few visits I went to the graveyard with them, and that was how I came to take my series of children among the headstones.

Children were always my main companions. They would all shout at once, tugging on my sleeve and urging me to photograph them. "Take me, take me!" They danced around, picked up their dogs, hugged their little brothers and sisters, and posed for the camera. The first day we met, the gypsy baron's son kept following me around in a King Kong mask. At first I found this annoying, but then I started taking photos. Now when I look back on them I am grateful to him for his persistence.

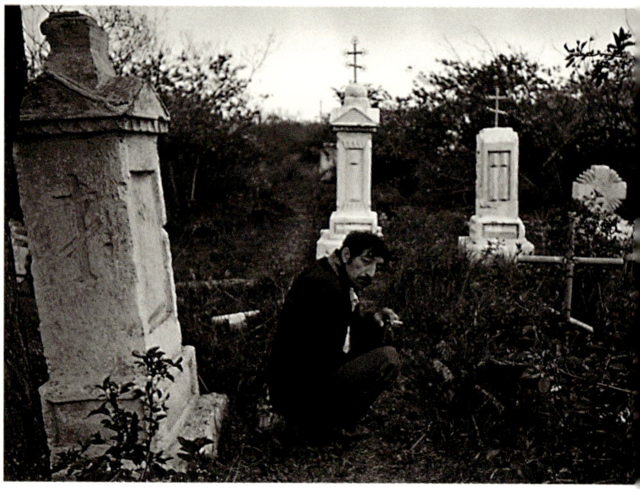

CHRISTMAS NEAR ODESSA

The next time I visited the Odessa gypsies it was Christmas time. By then I had become friendly with the people, and they were very kind to me. Unfortunately, though, I had taken a flash camera with me, something which I later regretted. The gypsies treated it like a new toy. My flash photos did not turn out as I had hoped, because the scenes were no longer so natural.

The gypsies were expecting me for Christmas. They had Christmas trees in their houses, lovingly decorated with silver foil. Under the trees were the usual bottles of champagne, vodka, and wine. All of them were dressed up in their best clothes–the men in brightly-colored shirts and expensive boots, the women in silk skirts with shiny foil in their hair, like the decorations on their Christmas trees. The girls wore light skirts and blouses. The small children had painted their cheeks with lipstick.

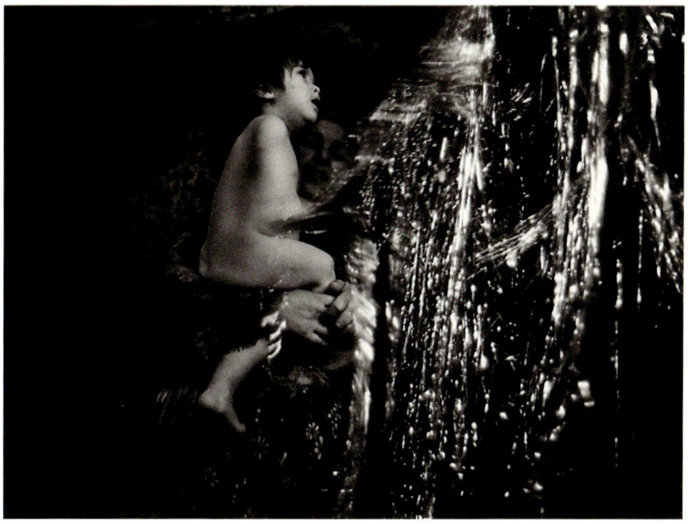

The women had set out on the tables a sumptuous feast for the many guests they were expecting. As they do at Easter, men, women, and children go from house to house in small groups, wishing everyone a happy new year. The masters of the house offer the men drinks to thank them for their new-year greetings.

They eat a little, drink a little, and stay a short while at each house. Then they have a last dance, a last song, and move on to the next home. The dancing and singing continue on the street. In the Odessa settlement the dancing and singing are particularly good. The men dance with great feeling despite their outward restraint.

THE WEDDING NEAR ODESSA

Lastly I will describe a wedding I attended. I had been looking forward to it for some time. The bridegroom was only thirteen years old, the bride fourteen. They both came from the same settlement and were married by their parents–that is to say the children had not given their consent.

I arrived on the day when the fathers of the bride and bridegroom were buying the food and bridal clothes in Odessa. They let me go with them to choose. First we selected the dress and veil. The dress was exquisite. After that we bought a satin bow, to decorate the wedding car, and a bridal doll, to adorn the hood of another car in the bridal party. We bought a bouquet of roses and large quantities of champagne, vodka, and beer. The gypsies loaded everything into the cars and drove back to the settlement in procession. At the edge of the woods we stopped and sat down in a meadow and drank to the couple's health with champagne. The gypsies threw flowers at the bride. We sang songs then got back into the cars.

When we arrived at the settlement the children ran up to the cars with joyful cries. We drove to the bride's house where a gypsy tent had been set up, with long rows of tables in front. In the street the gypsies lit fires under pots and began cooking and roasting in the open air. People with video cameras had been invited from the city to film the wedding. A gypsy singer from an Odessa restaurant was accompanied by a boy on a synthesizer.

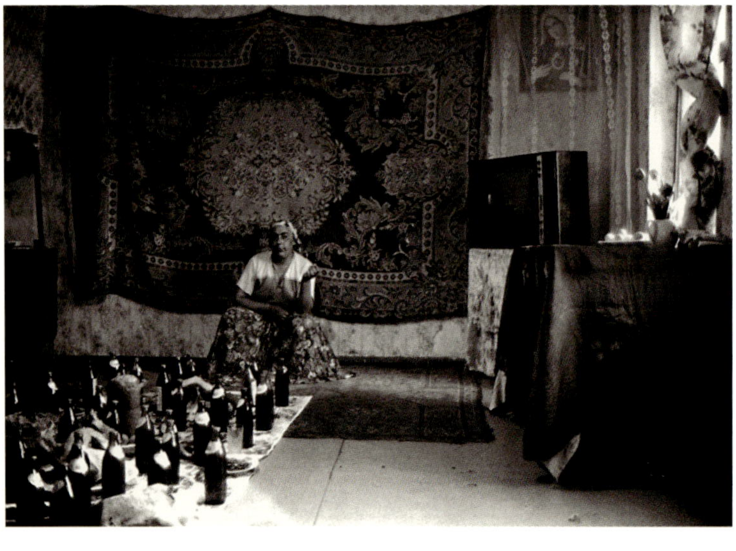

While preparations were made, the bride was dressing at her parents' house. The room was very small, and only the women and girls were allowed in. An old gypsy woman splashed the onlookers with champagne, and they sang songs in Romani. When the bride was ready she was led to a friend's house. In the meantime, the women had been setting the table in the tent, and the guests had taken their seats. Only men sat at the table; the women remained behind the tent.

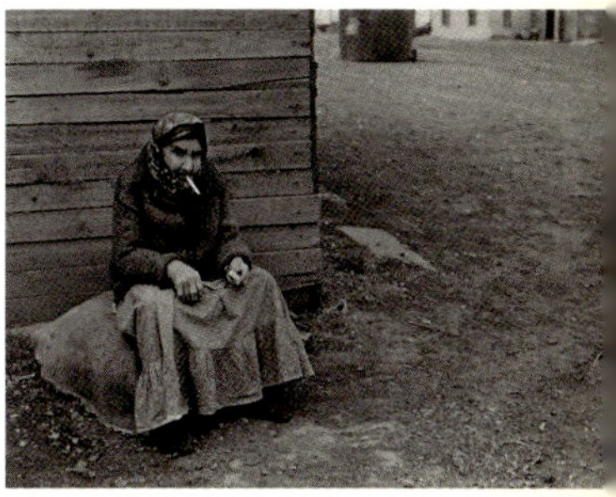

The bride was led into the tent. No priest had been invited, and the newlyweds did not go to church. The guests ate and drank and then began dancing. The bride danced with her girlfriends. Then it was time to buy the bride's freedom from her. She was taken to the bridegroom's house. There was no table, everything was done on the floor. Champagne was poured, and as people finished their drinks, they congratulated the newly married couple and gave the bride money. Next to her she kept a tray, and everyone put their donations there. The following morning the young bride was wearing a head scarf. From now on she would not be allowed to go out without it. All the important tasks in the bridegroom's house now fell to her. This was how she began her married life.

THE OLD FORTUNE TELLER NEAR ODESSA

A very old woman of ninety lived in the gypsy settlement near Odessa. The story of how we met has a mysterious significance for me. I first met the old woman at the home of a rich Moscow family at Christmas. She sat in silence away from the table, smiling quietly to herself. As the only woman at the table, I took it upon myself to look after her and offer her something. Gypsies told me that soon after that meeting, she left her son in Moscow and went back to her other son who lived in a gypsy settlement.

I was to meet her again–but in the completely different atmosphere of the gypsy settlement near Odessa. I had recently lost a few photographic negatives that were very important to me. I thought they had been stolen. My colleagues smiled and advised me to go to the old fortune teller in the gypsy encampment. I was very doubtful, but when I next went to Odessa I called on her. I was surprised to find the same old woman I had met in Moscow. I have no idea if she recognized me. I gave her some money and put out my left hand. She looked at it carefully, stroked it, and started to describe in a low, hoarse voice what had happened. I was amazed by what I heard. The fortune teller ended by telling me that everything I had lost would soon be returned. I did not mention this to anyone in the camp. When I got back to Odessa a few days later, the negatives were sitting on my desk.

I never saw the fortune teller again. She had asked me to bring some cigarettes with me the next time I came; but when I returned, she had died. I shared the cigarettes out among the women, and we sat in the meadow together and reminisced about the old woman. When I went there later to ask if anyone else could tell my fortune, no one was willing, on the grounds that no one wanted to deceive me.

The Fate of the Steppe Gypsies

Ever since I was a child I have had a fondness for gypsies, which is mixed with my memories of the steppe. The view behind the gypsy houses near Odessa reminded me of the wide steppes of my childhood. When my exhibition opened in Berlin, the German photographer Sigrid Neubert said to me, "Your photos are so powerful.

You obviously have a rapport with gypsies." In the summer of 1990, I attended the international gypsy music festival in Nîmes, France, organized by the famous French group the Gipsy Kings, and exhibited my photos there. A group called Bratsh was performing Russian gypsy songs at the festival. The songs spoke to me; they were so full of emotion and came straight from the soul.

But now I have a new feeling toward the gypsies–a feeling of sadness. Encounters with nomadic gypsies in the steppes of the Urals are a thing of the past, never to be experienced again. My regret for this loss is underscored by the sadness I feel toward the situation of gypsies in Odessa, where metal separates them from the steppe, and there is not a horse to be seen.

In the settlement there, gypsy boys pose for me now in karate positions–copied from the American films they have seen on television. Eight-year-old girls put on their mothers' high heels and paint their lips bright red. The Zhigulis parked outside the houses of the more prosperous gypsies often blast music onto the street. But these days it is almost never the songs of the Roma that they play.

Translated from the Russian to German by Elena Gram.
Translated from the German by Lorna Dale.

УРАЛЬСК

Uralsk Ouralsk Uralsk

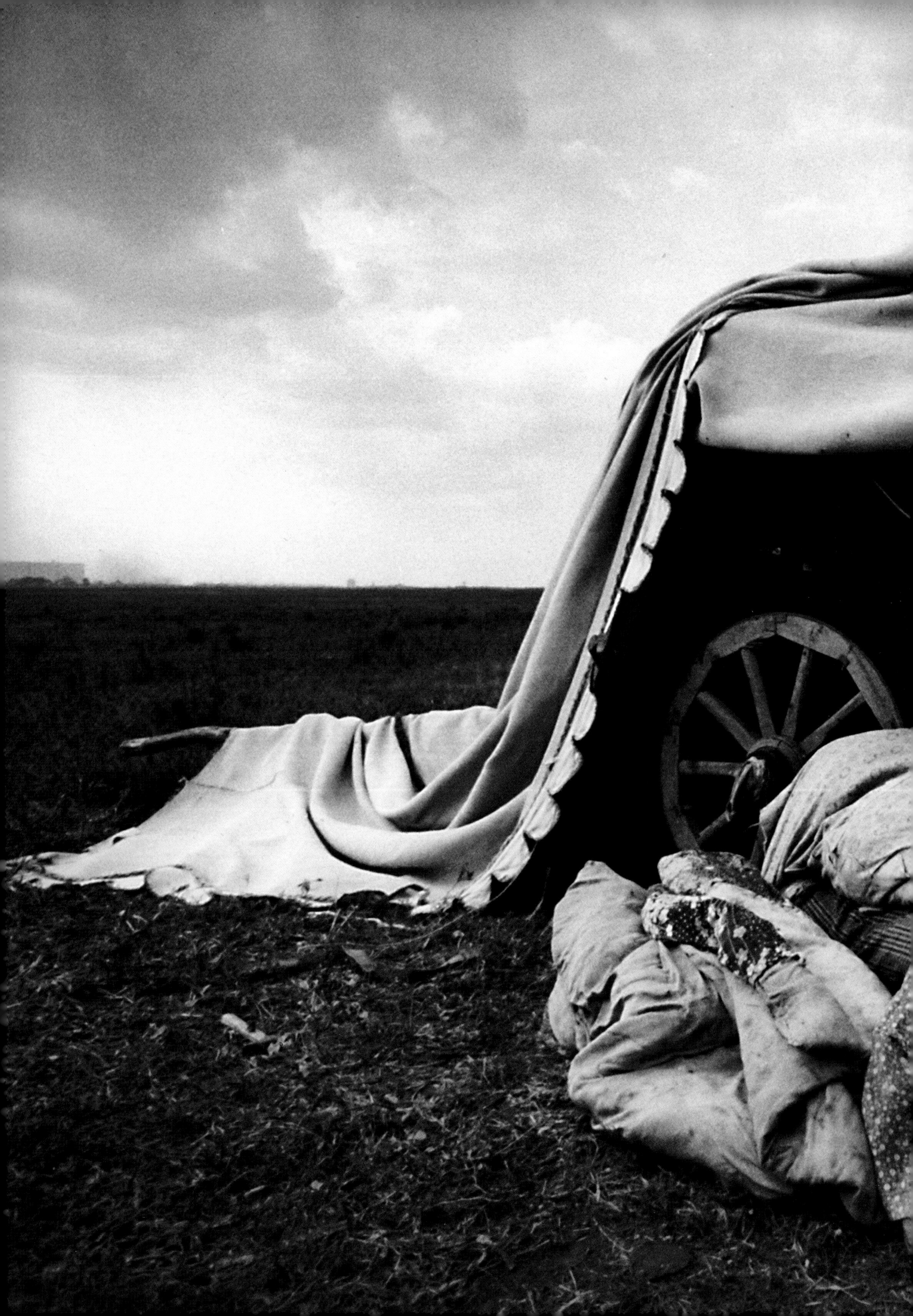

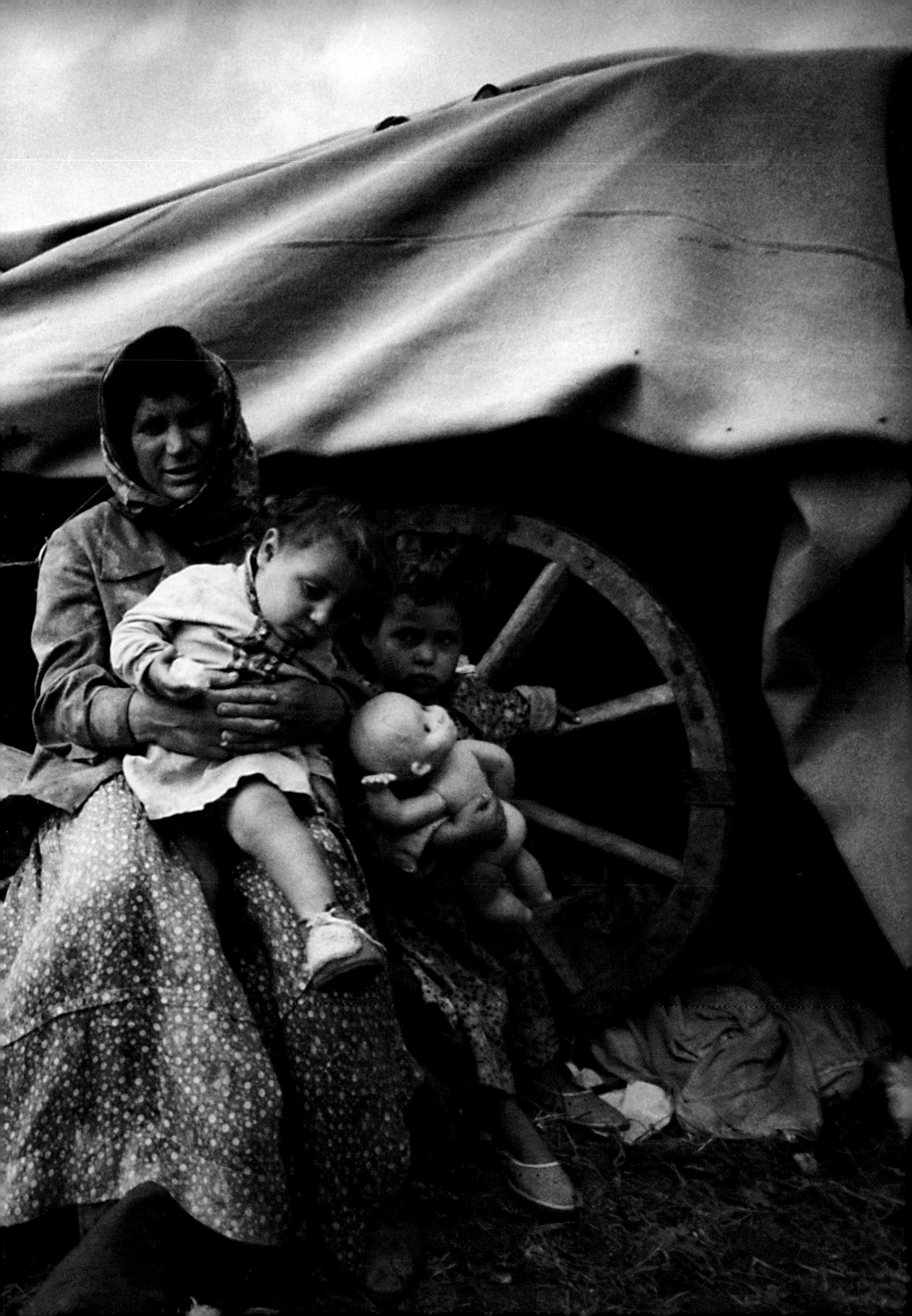

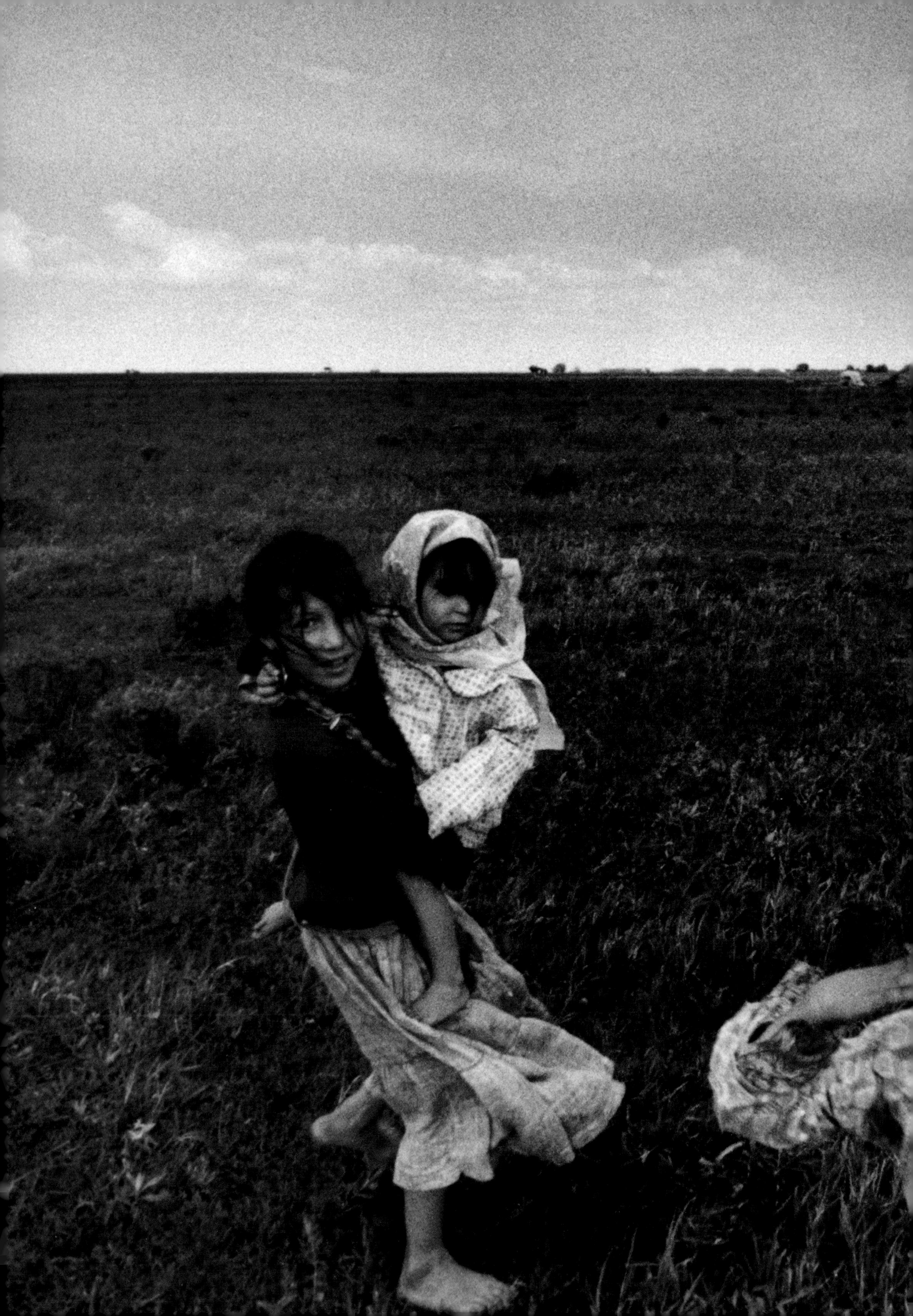

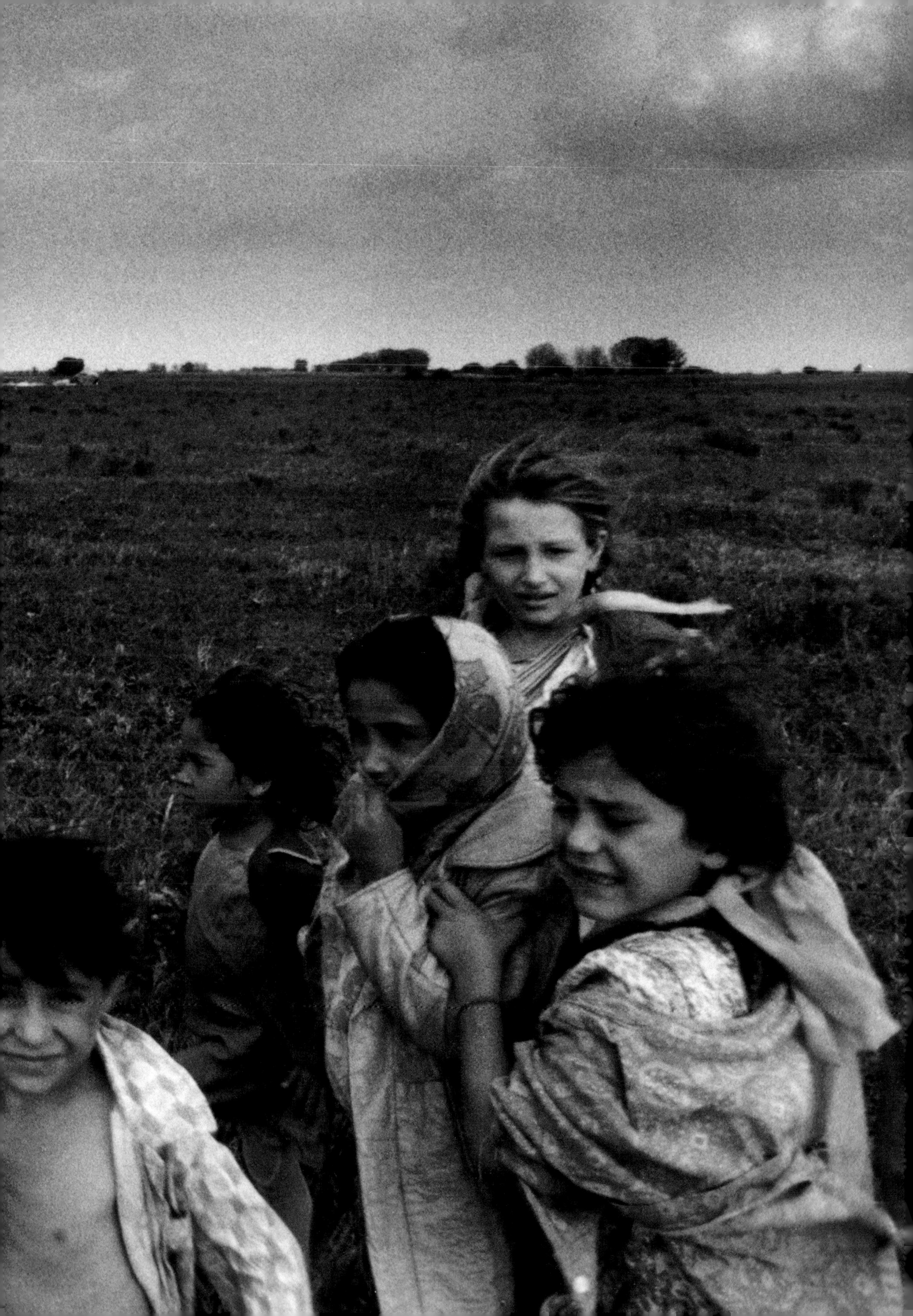

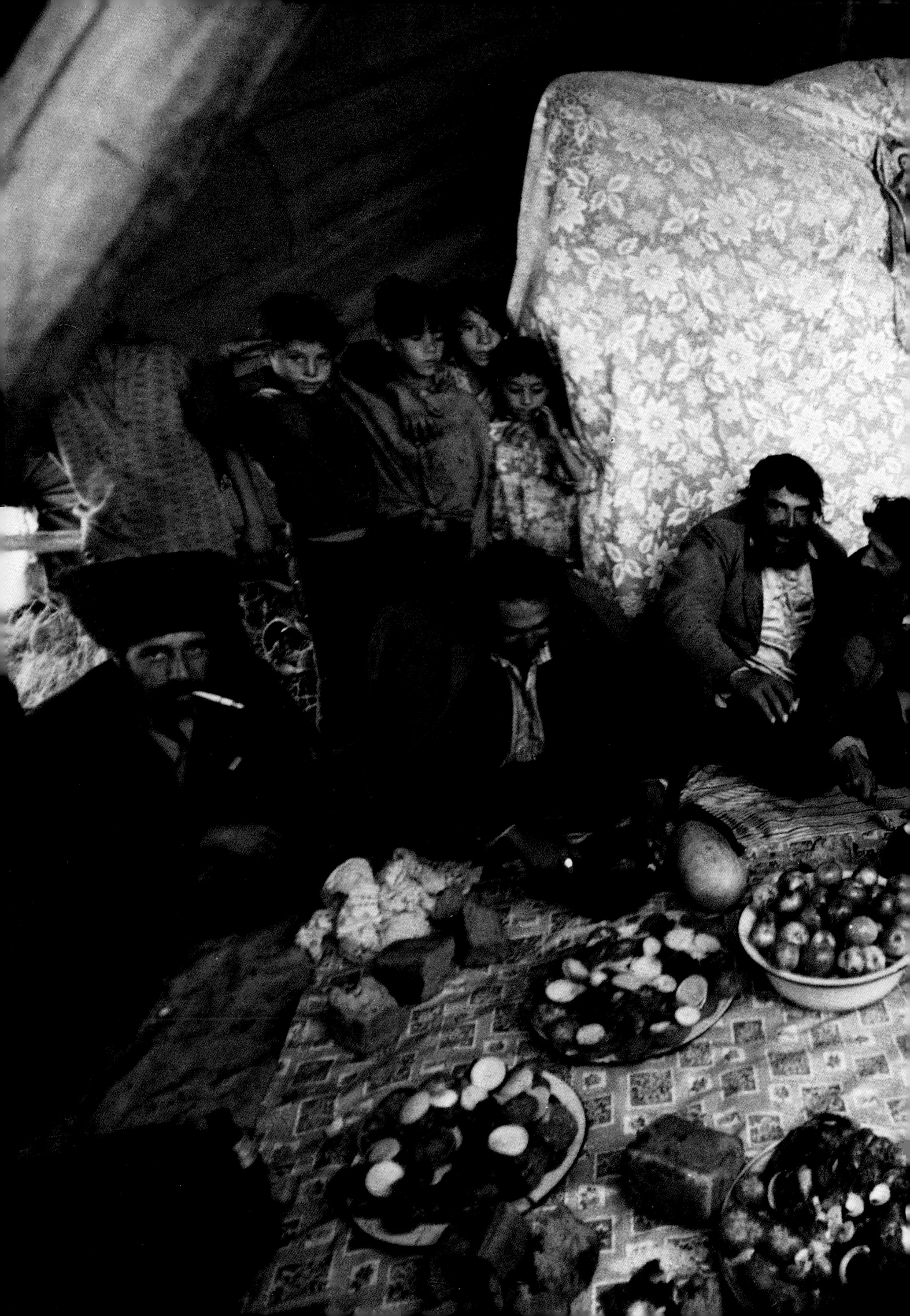

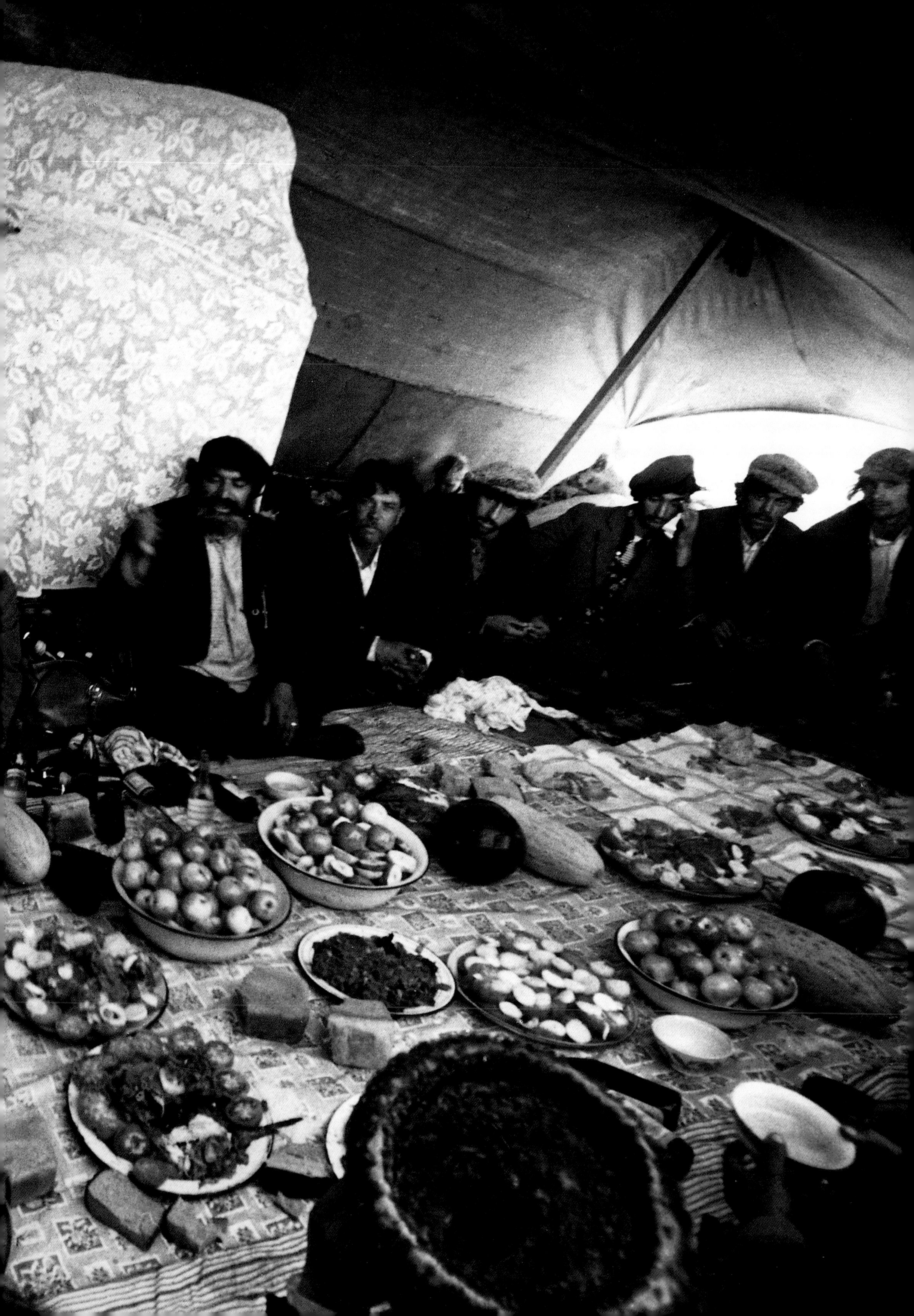

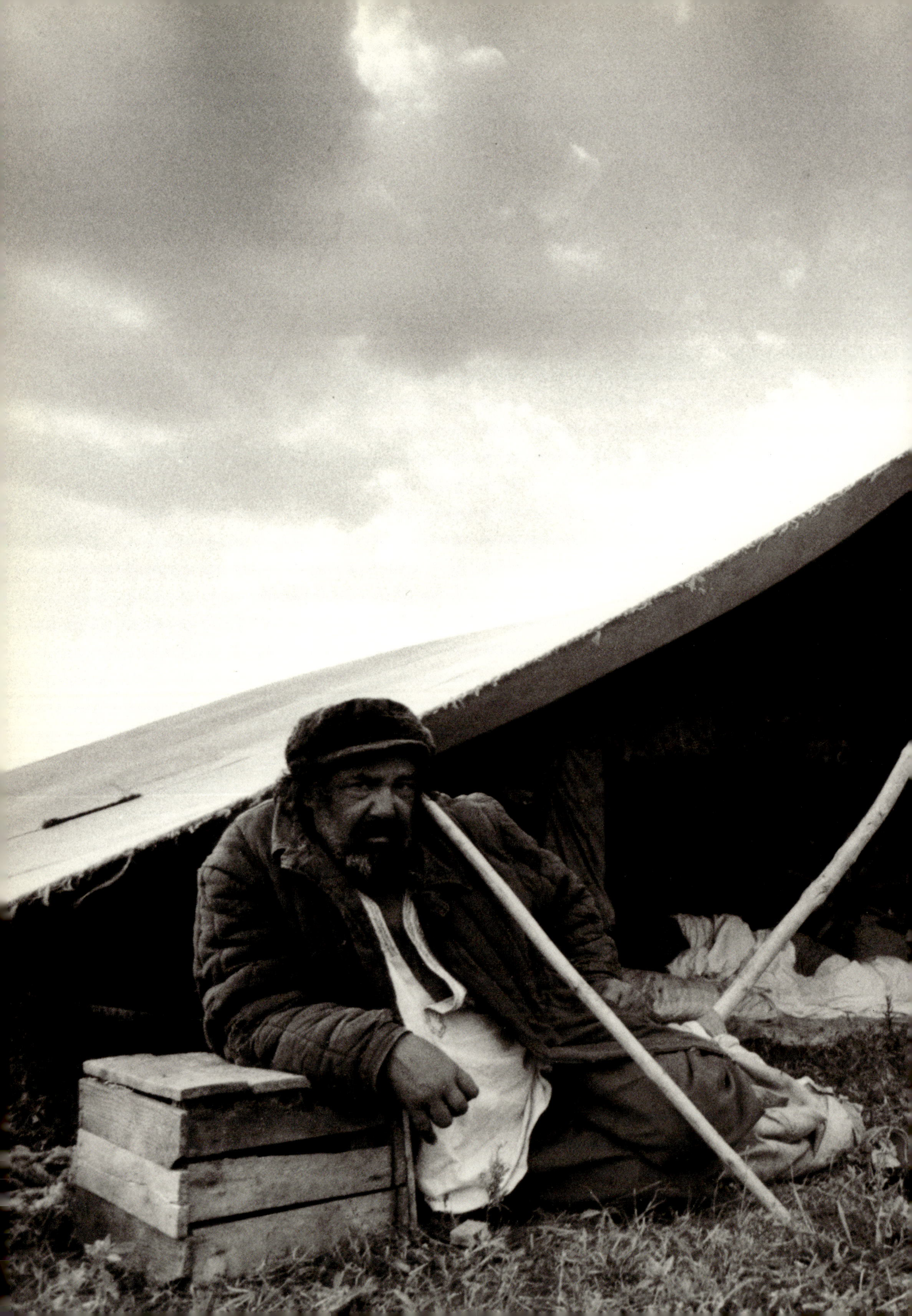

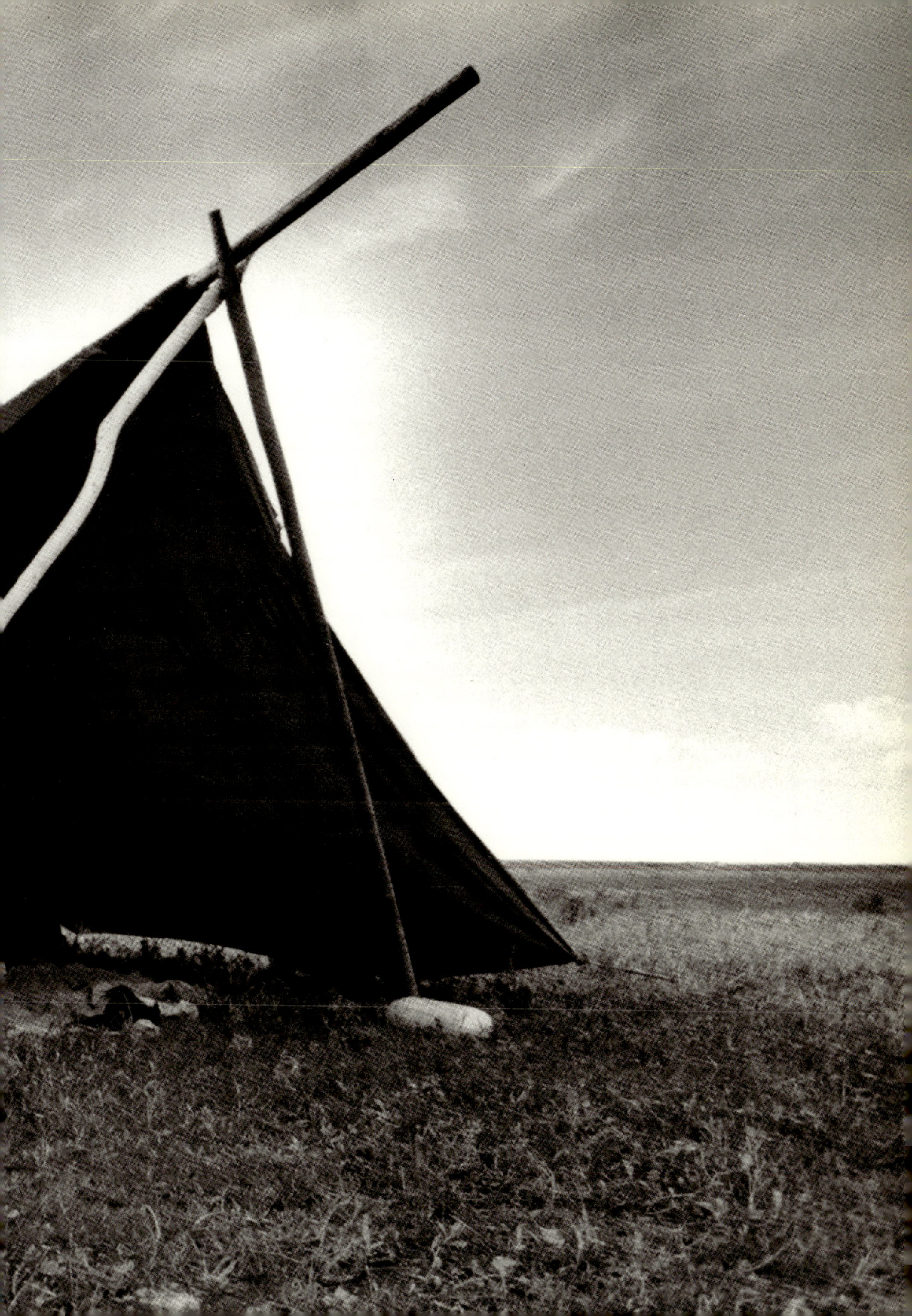

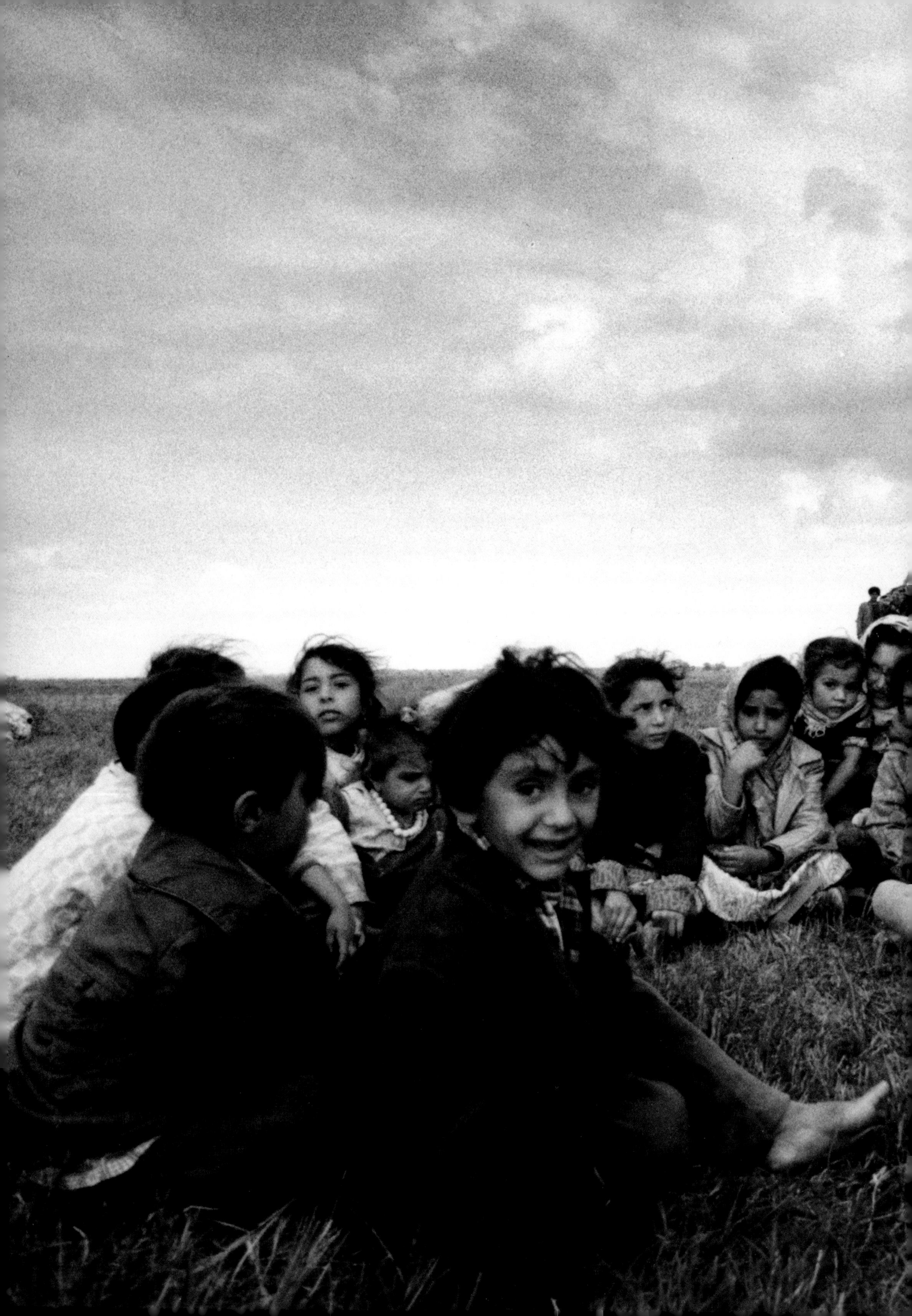

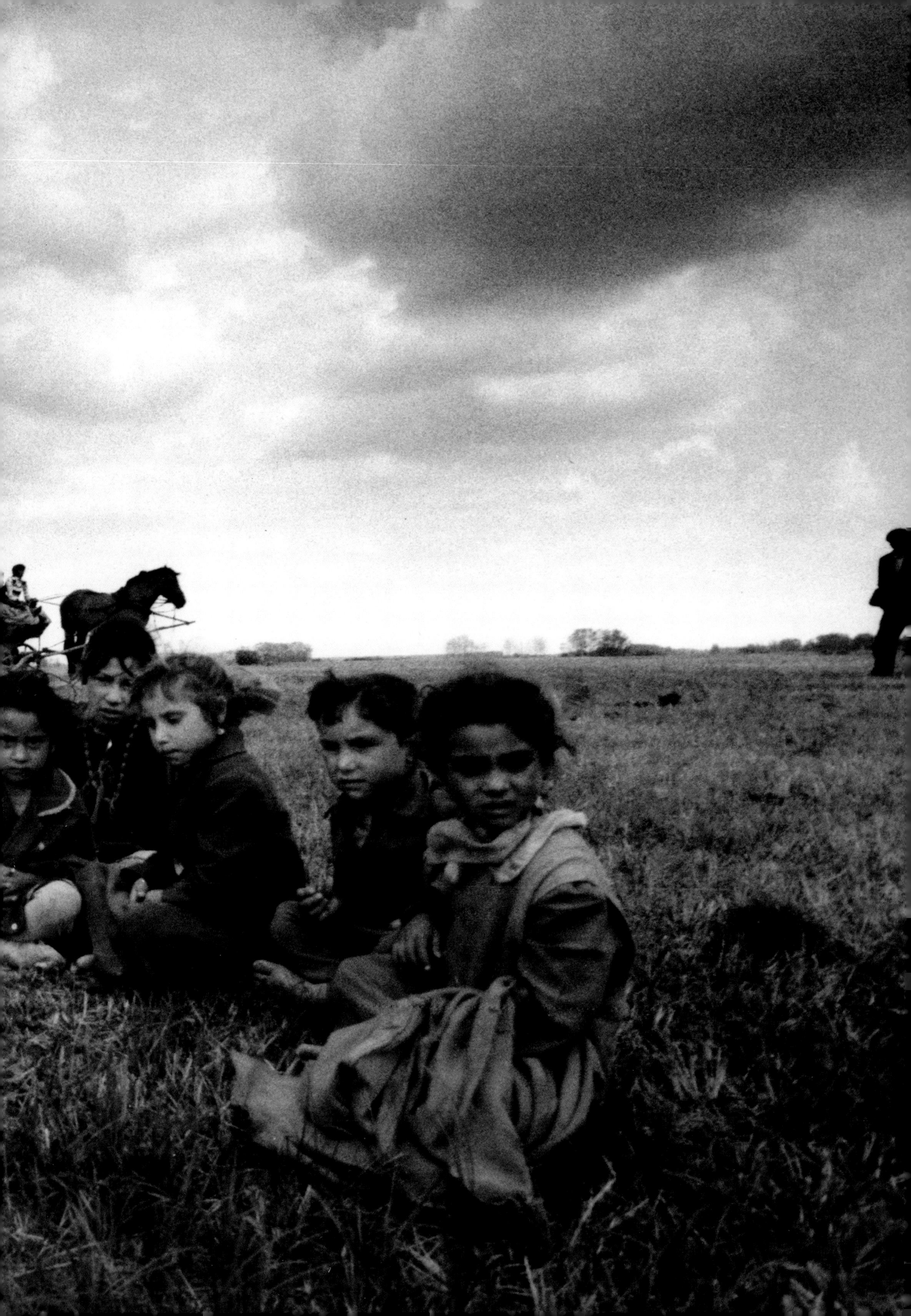

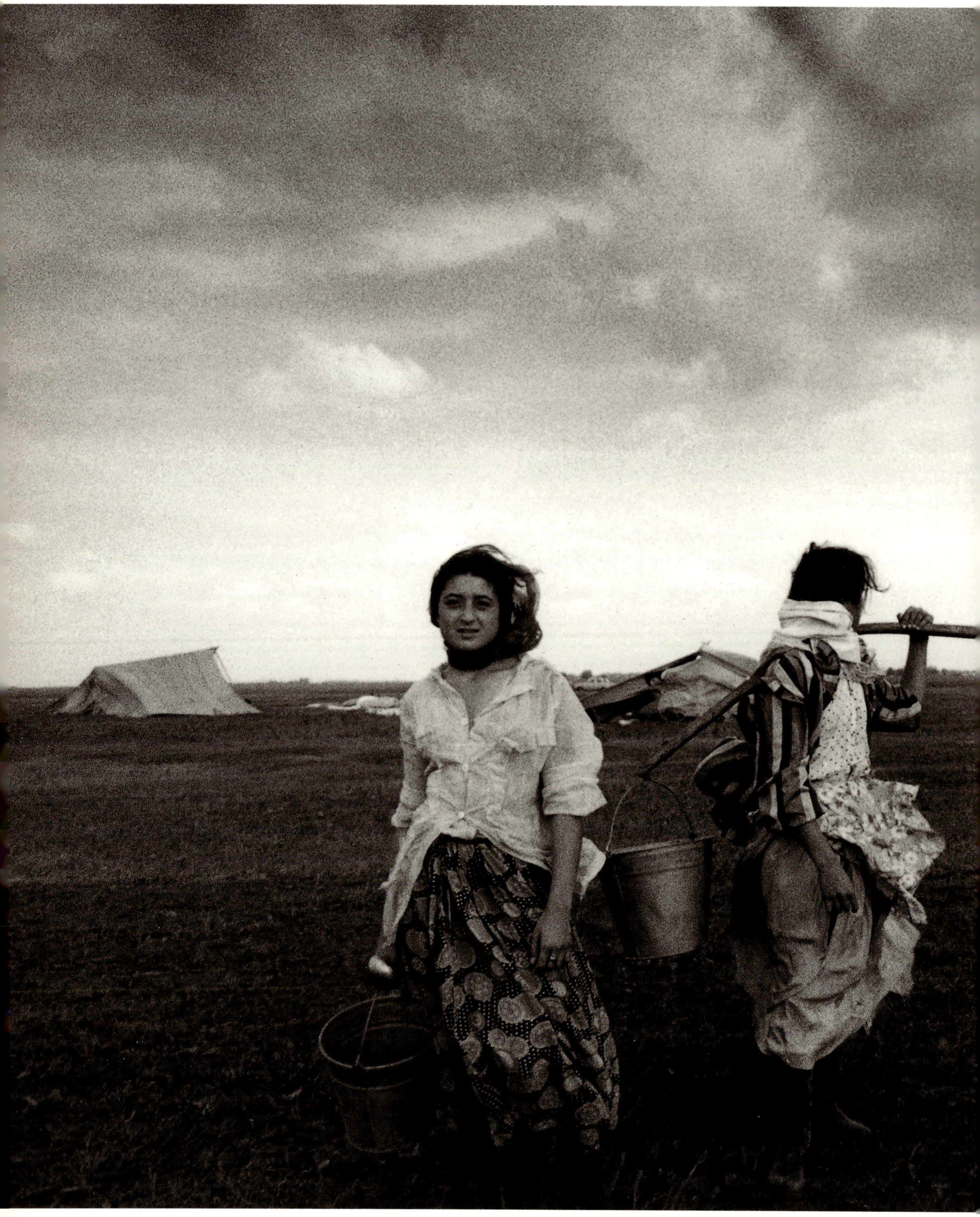

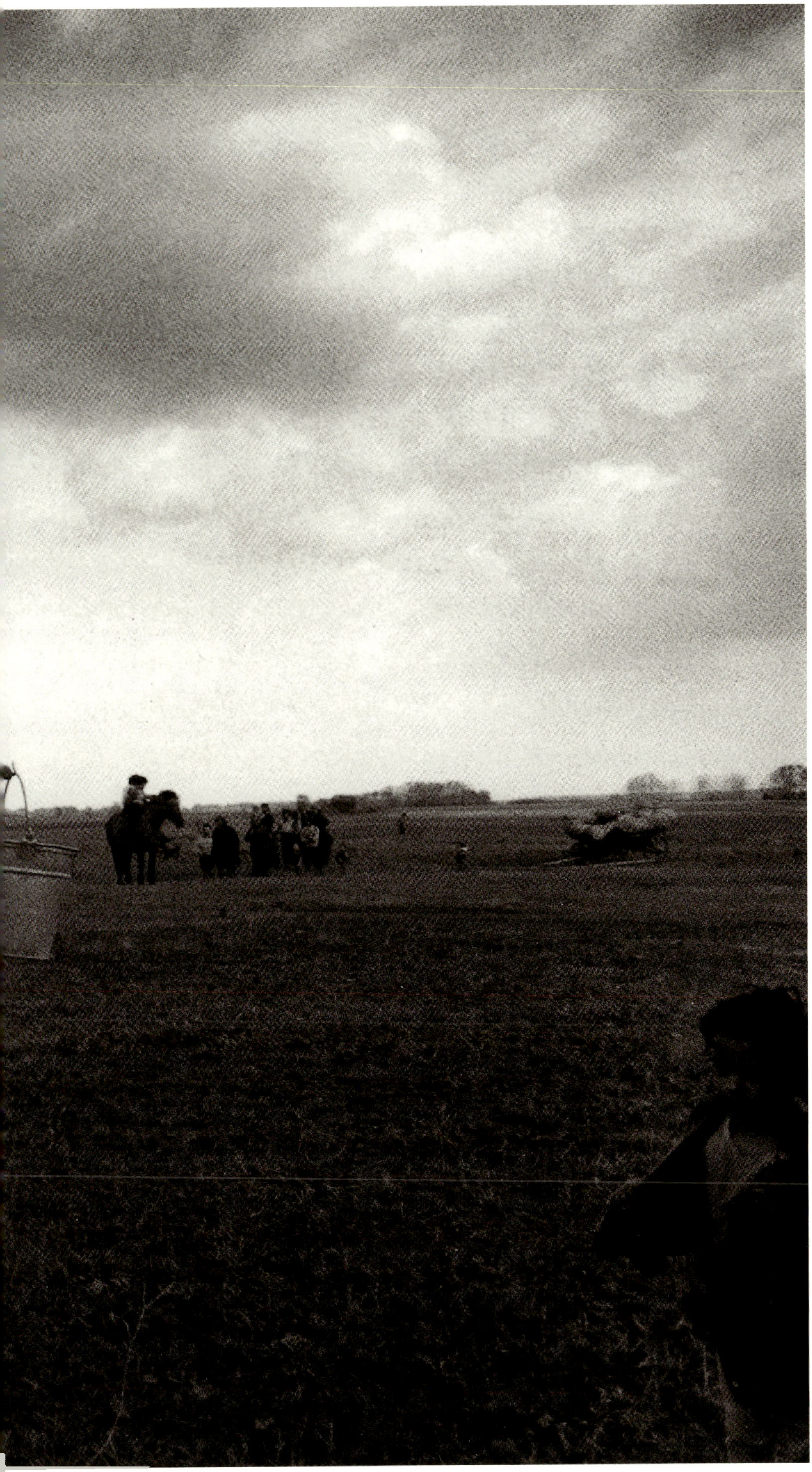

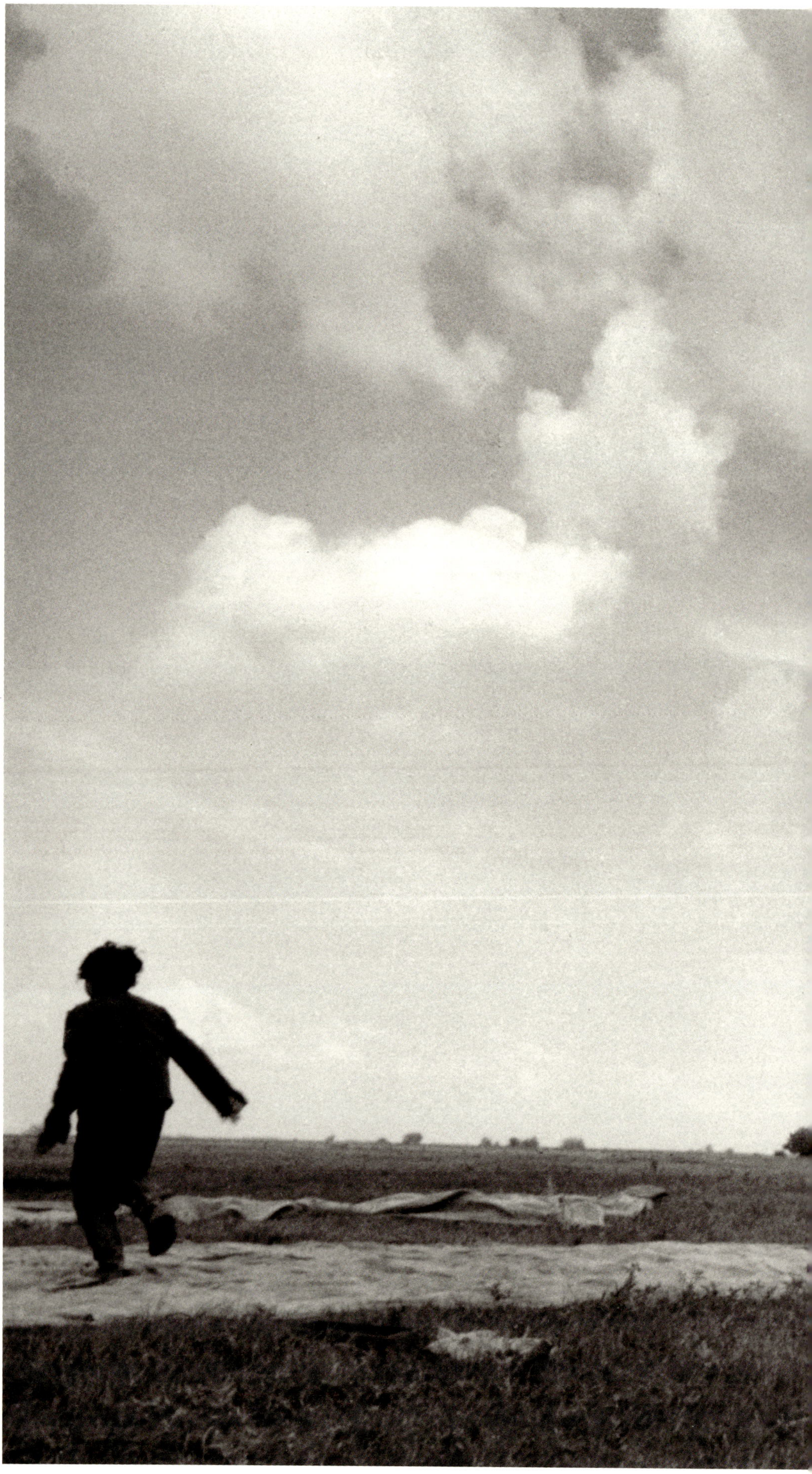

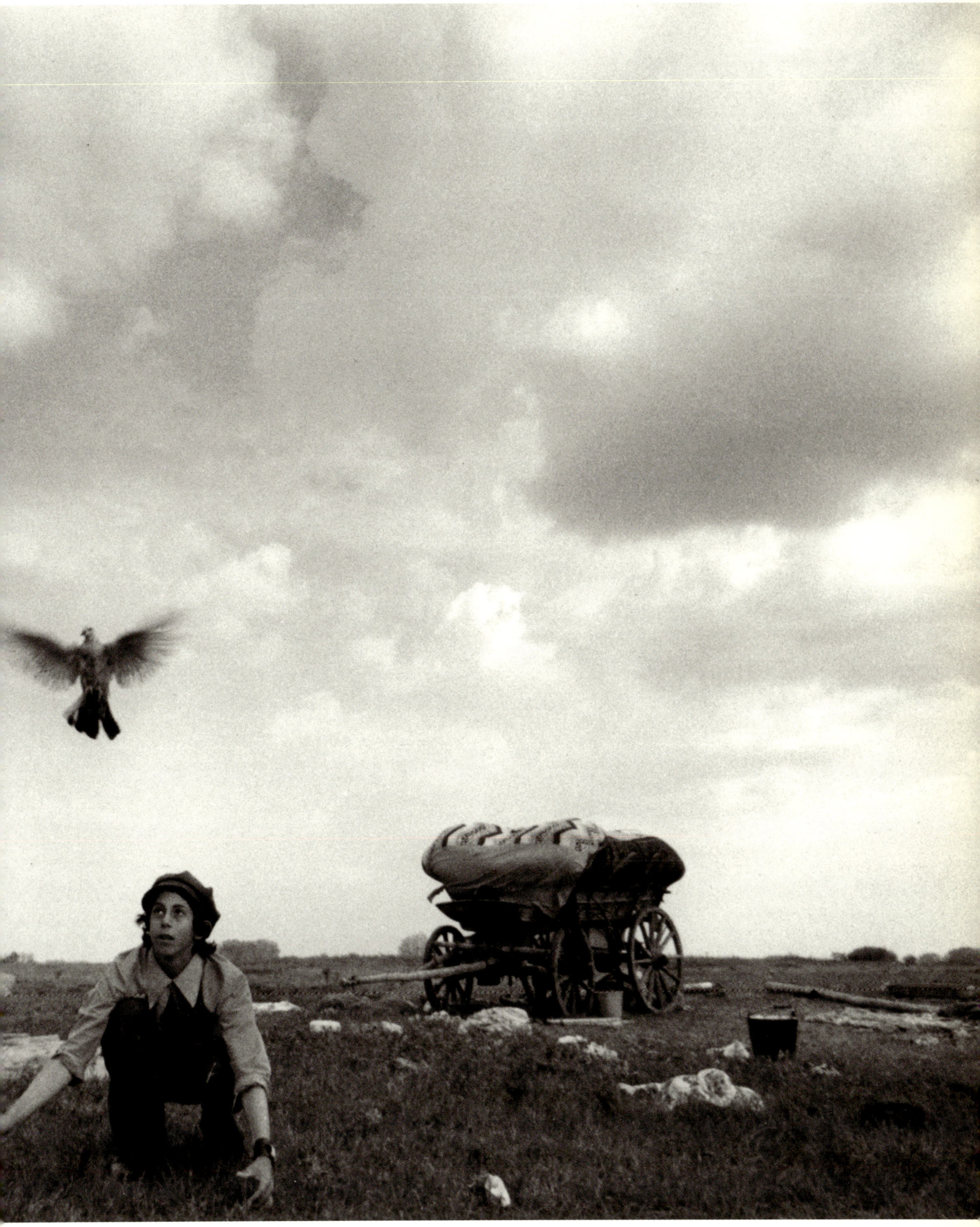

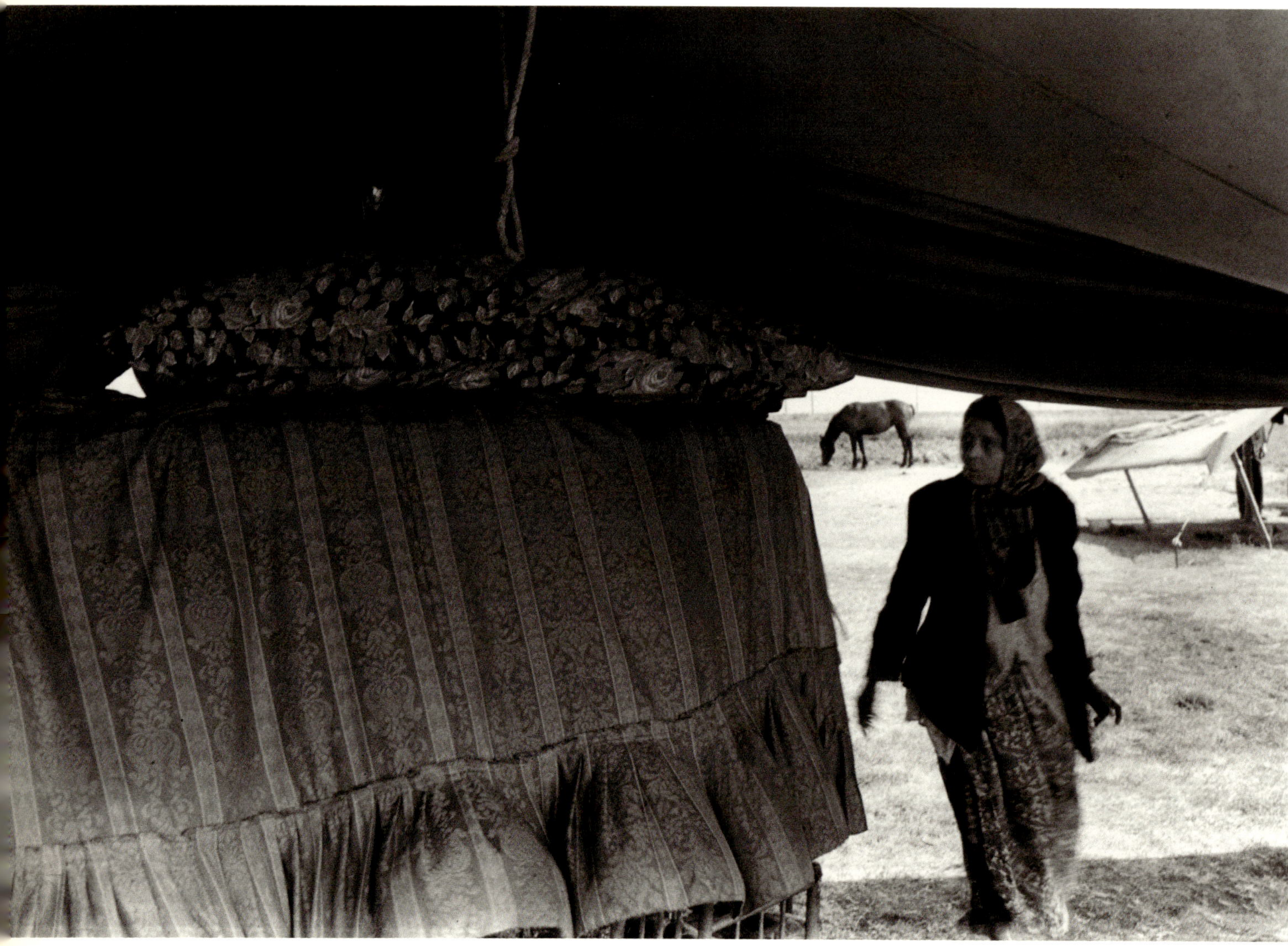

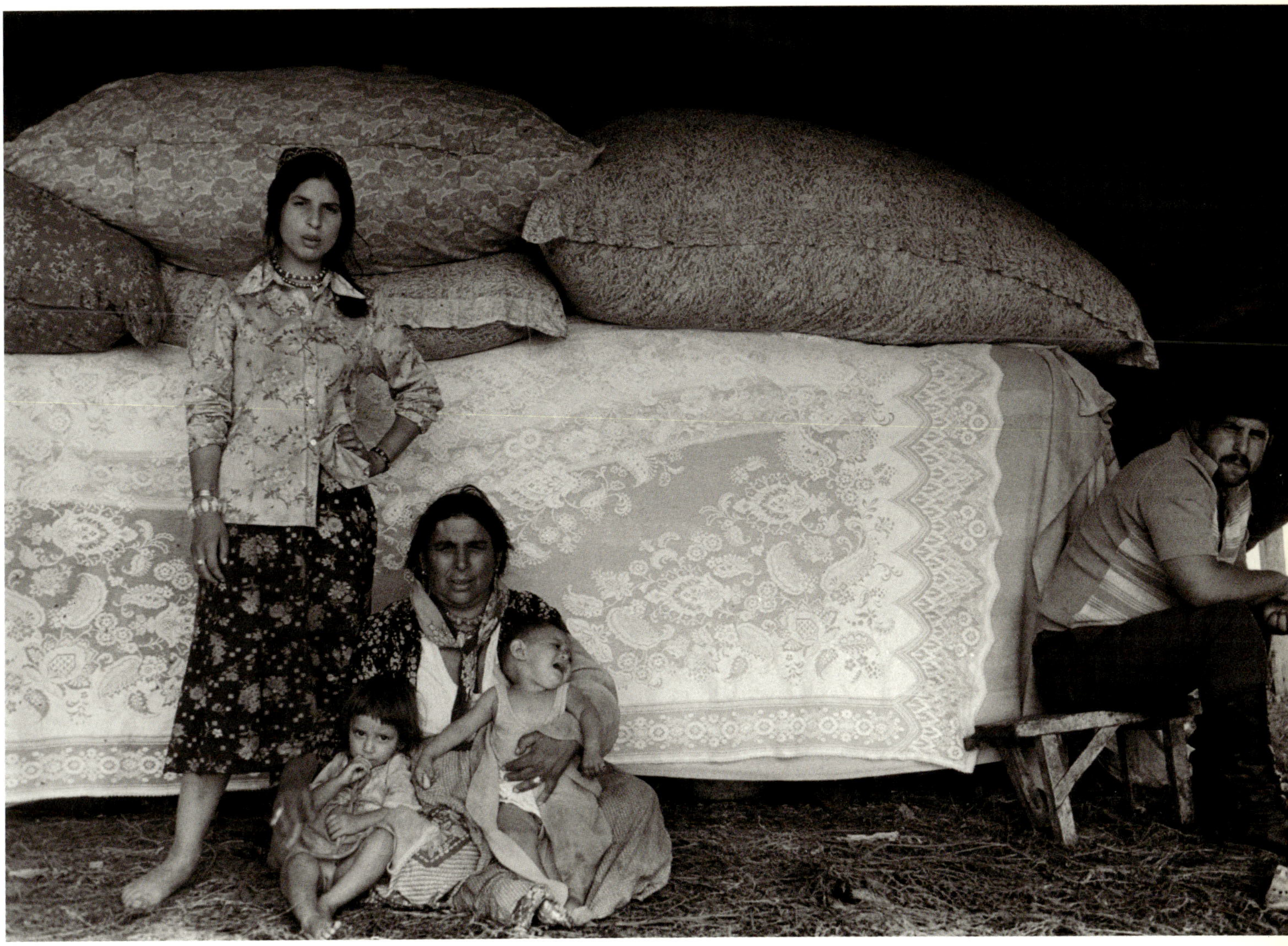

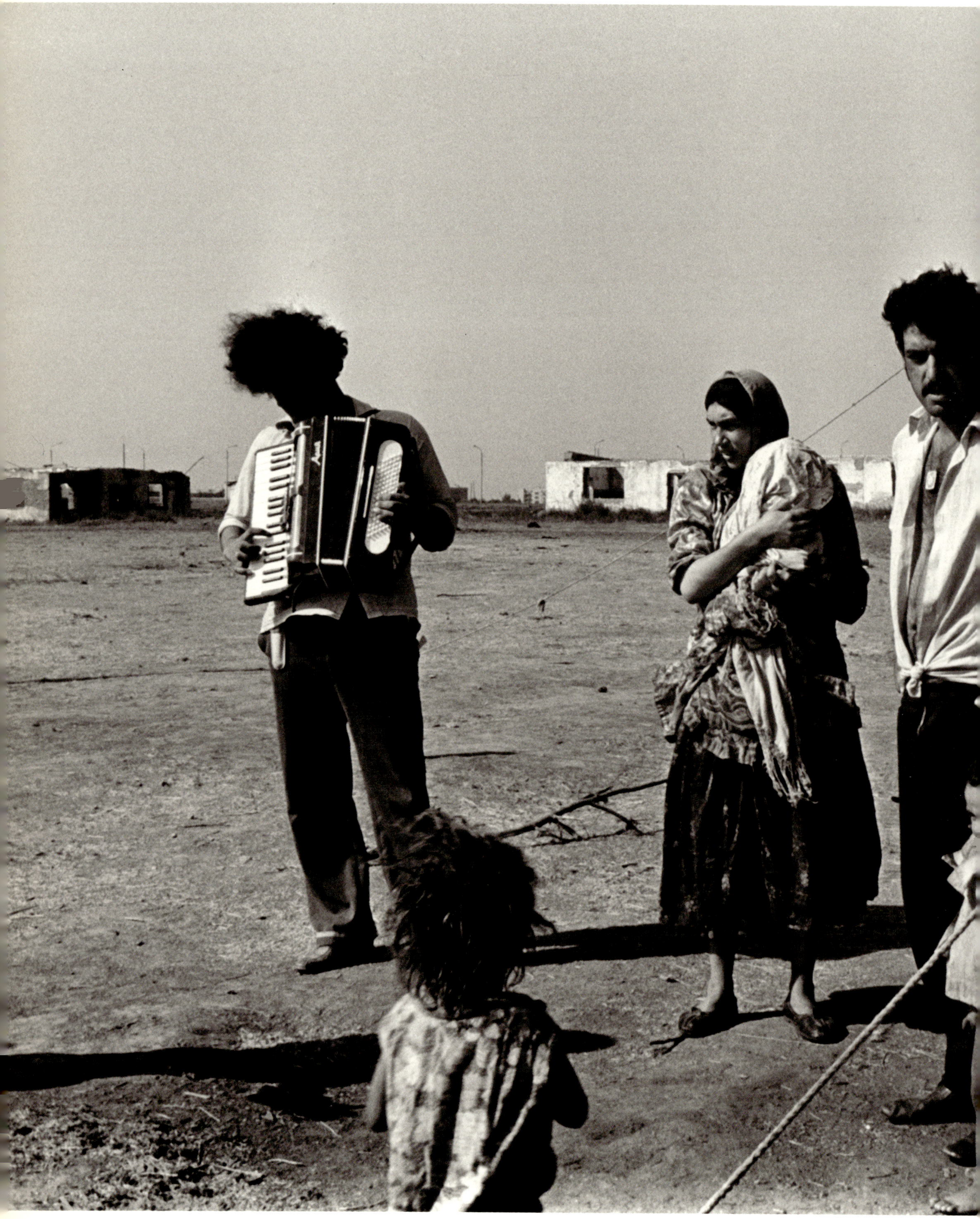

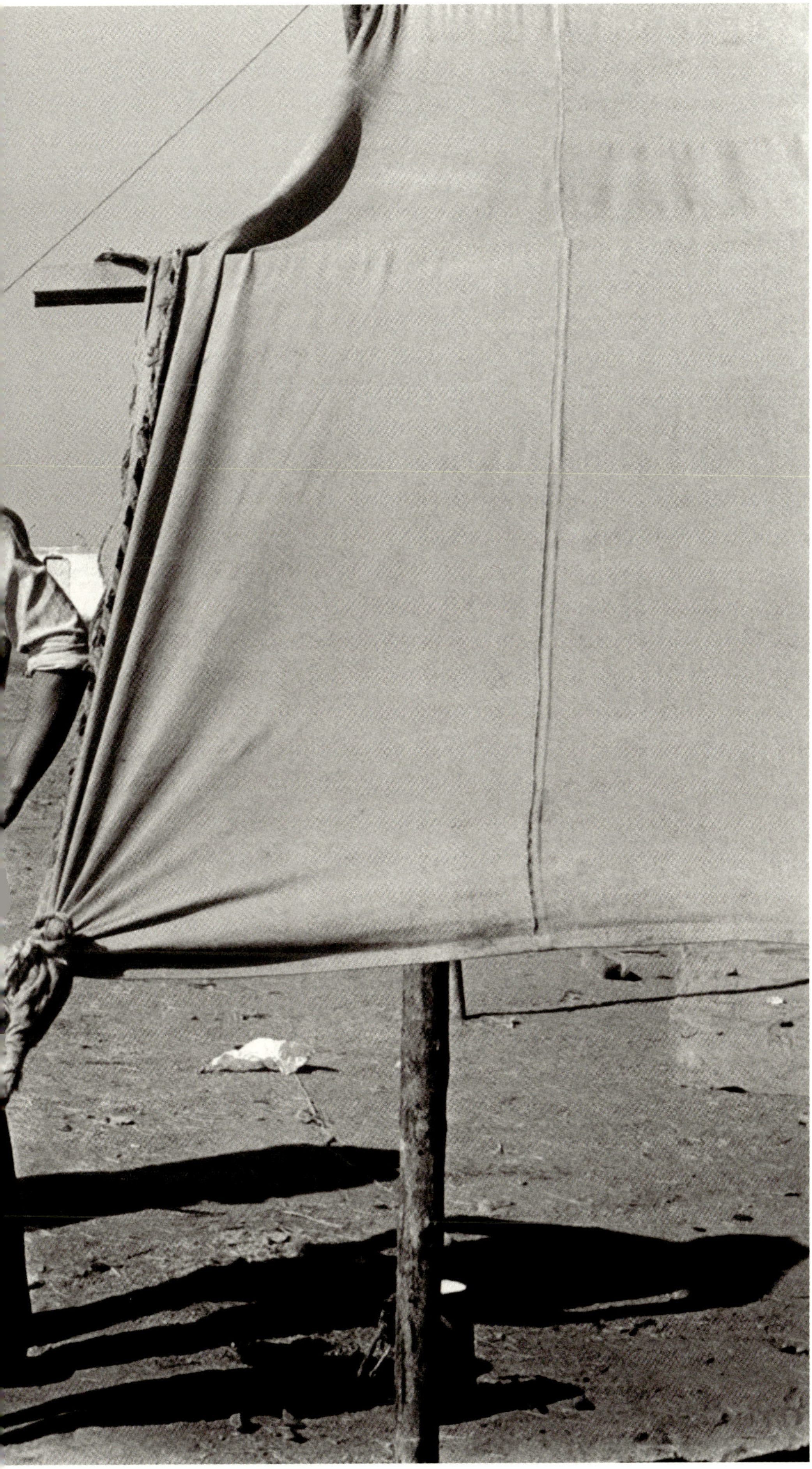

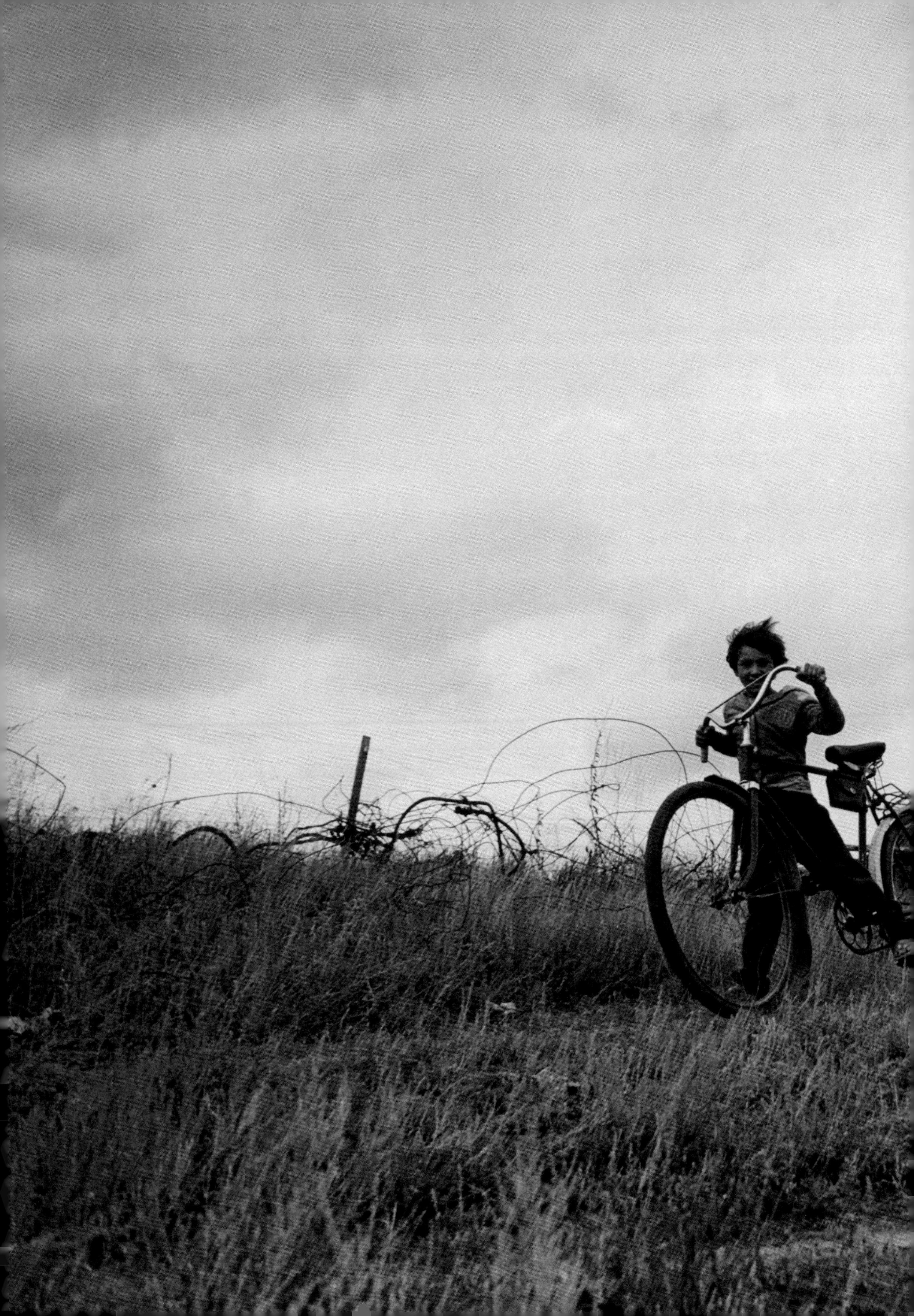

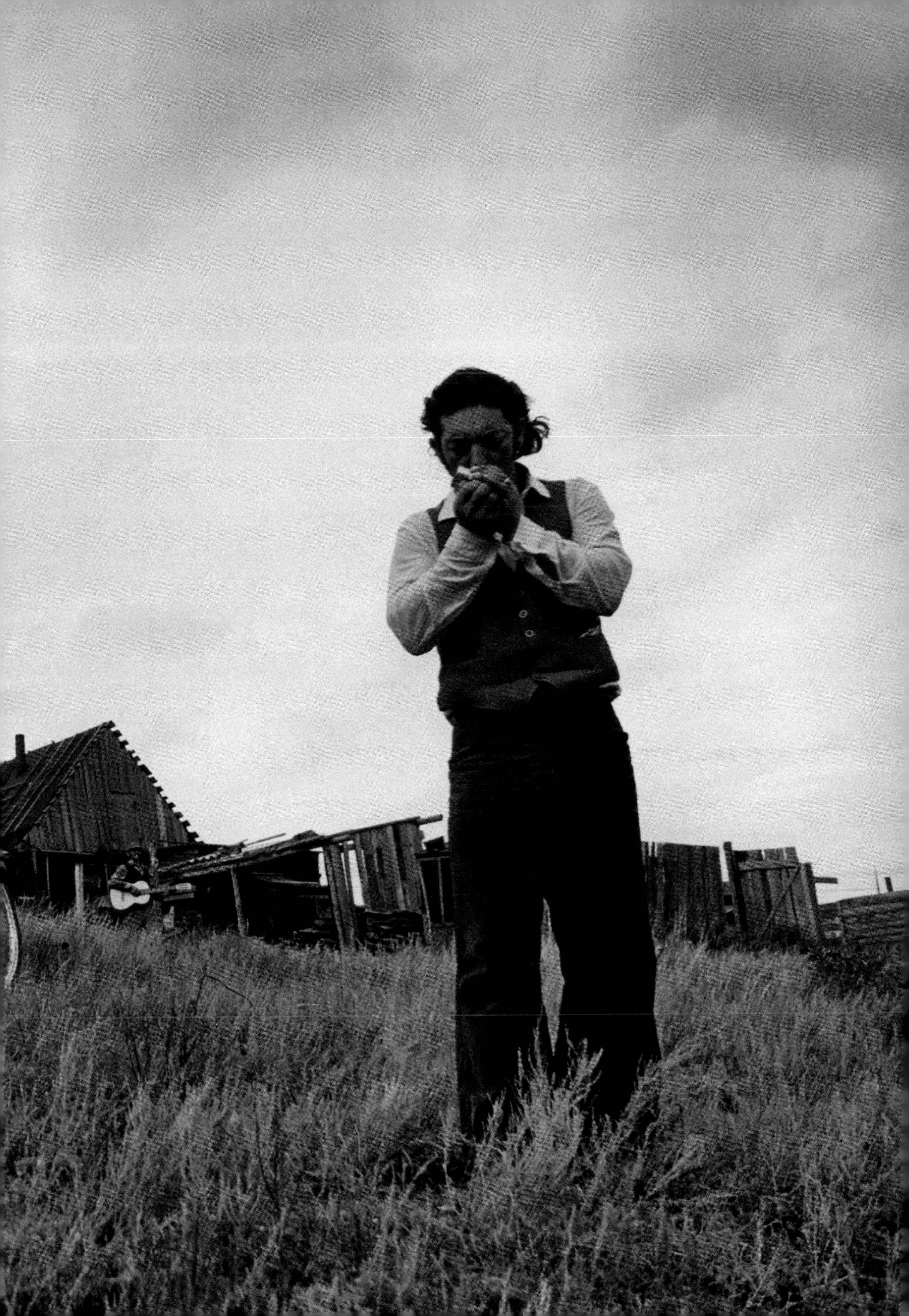

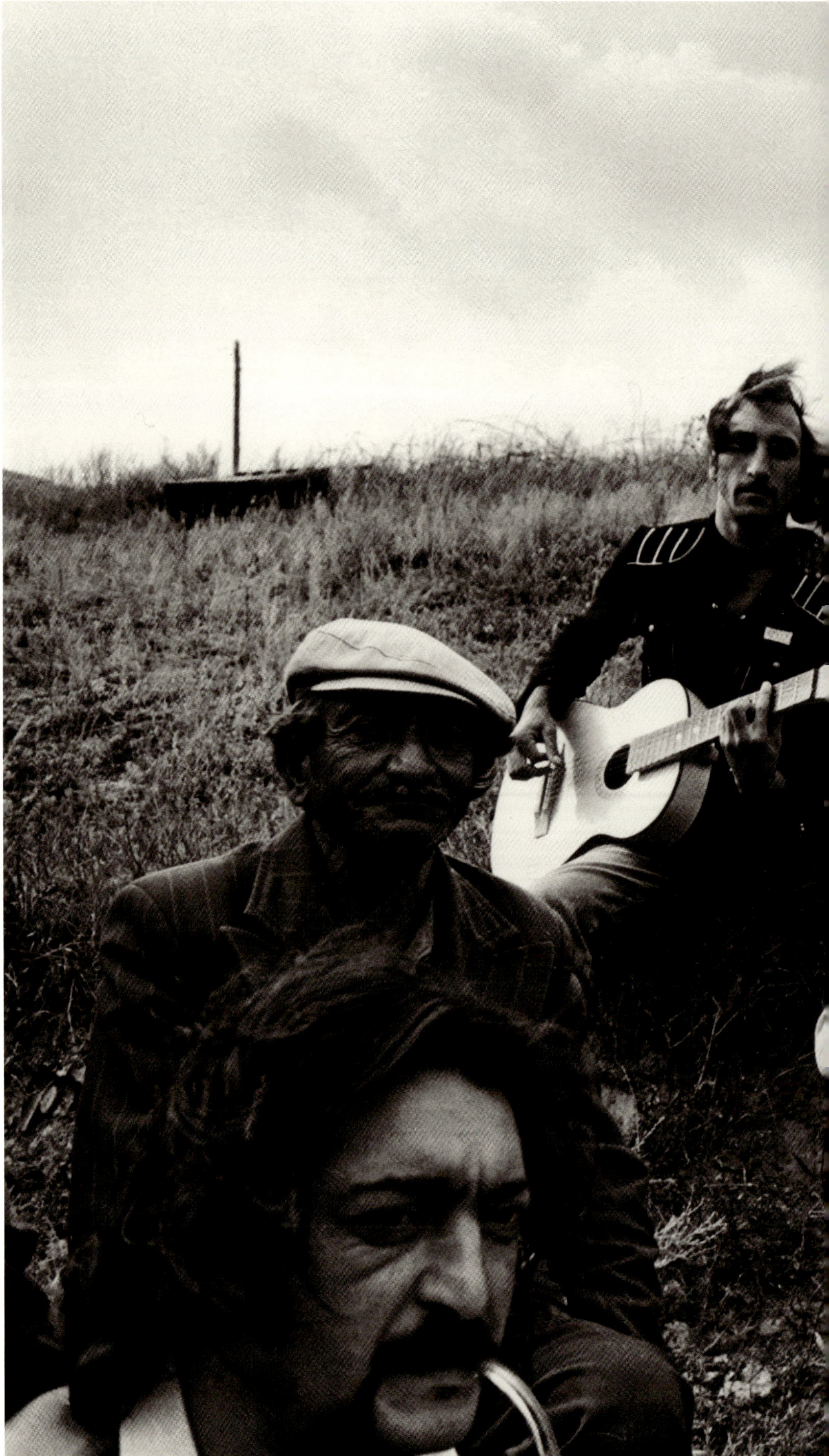

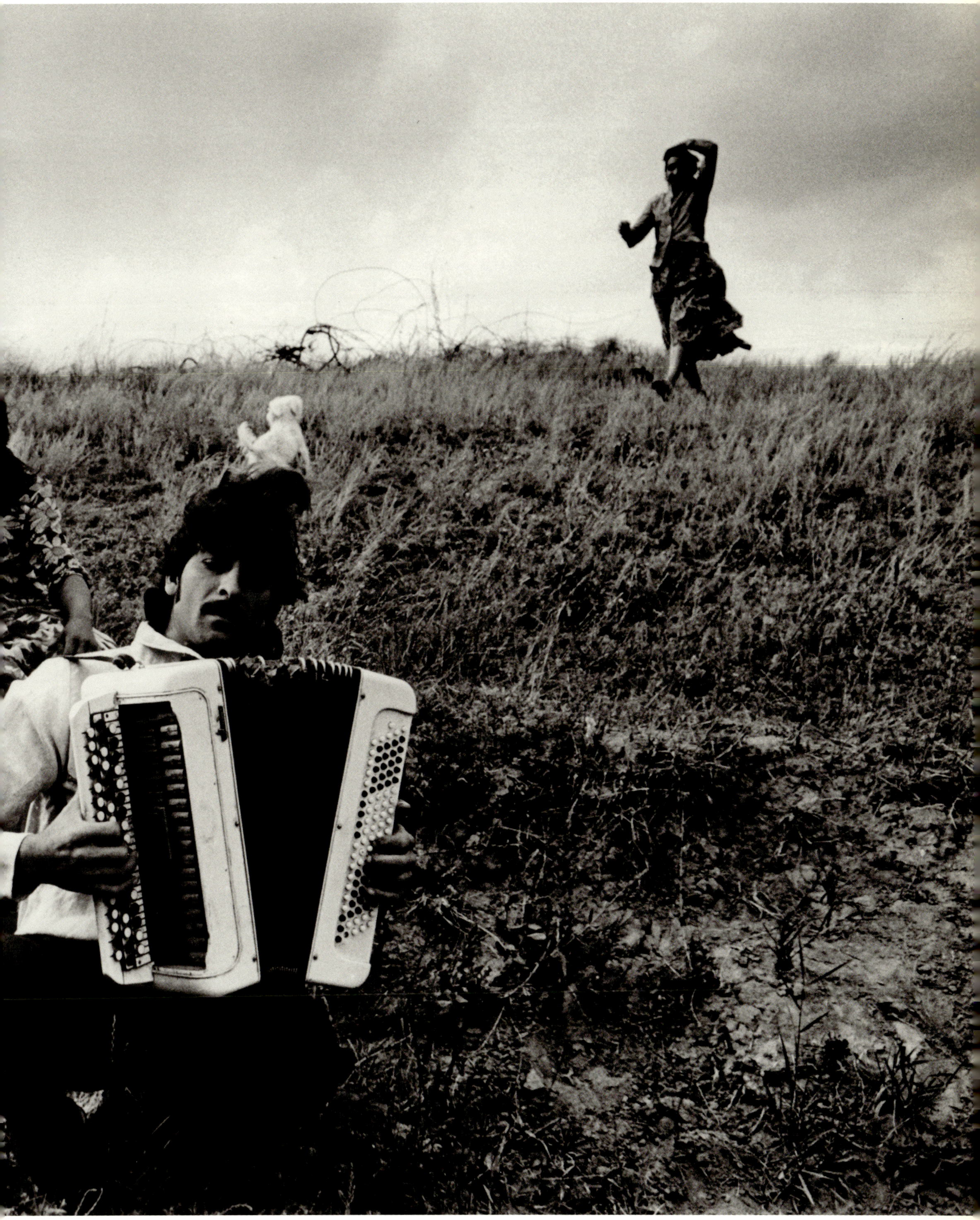

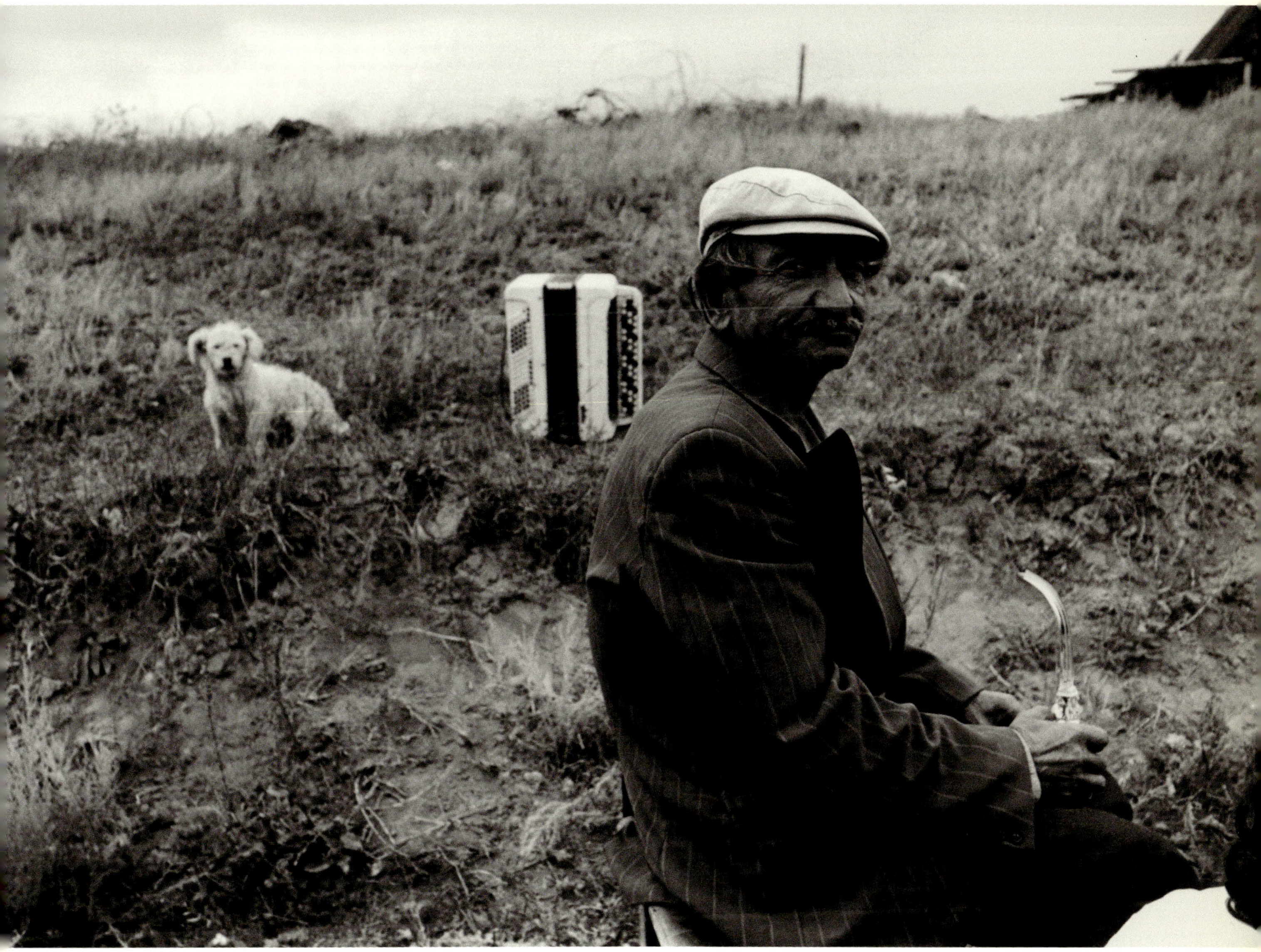

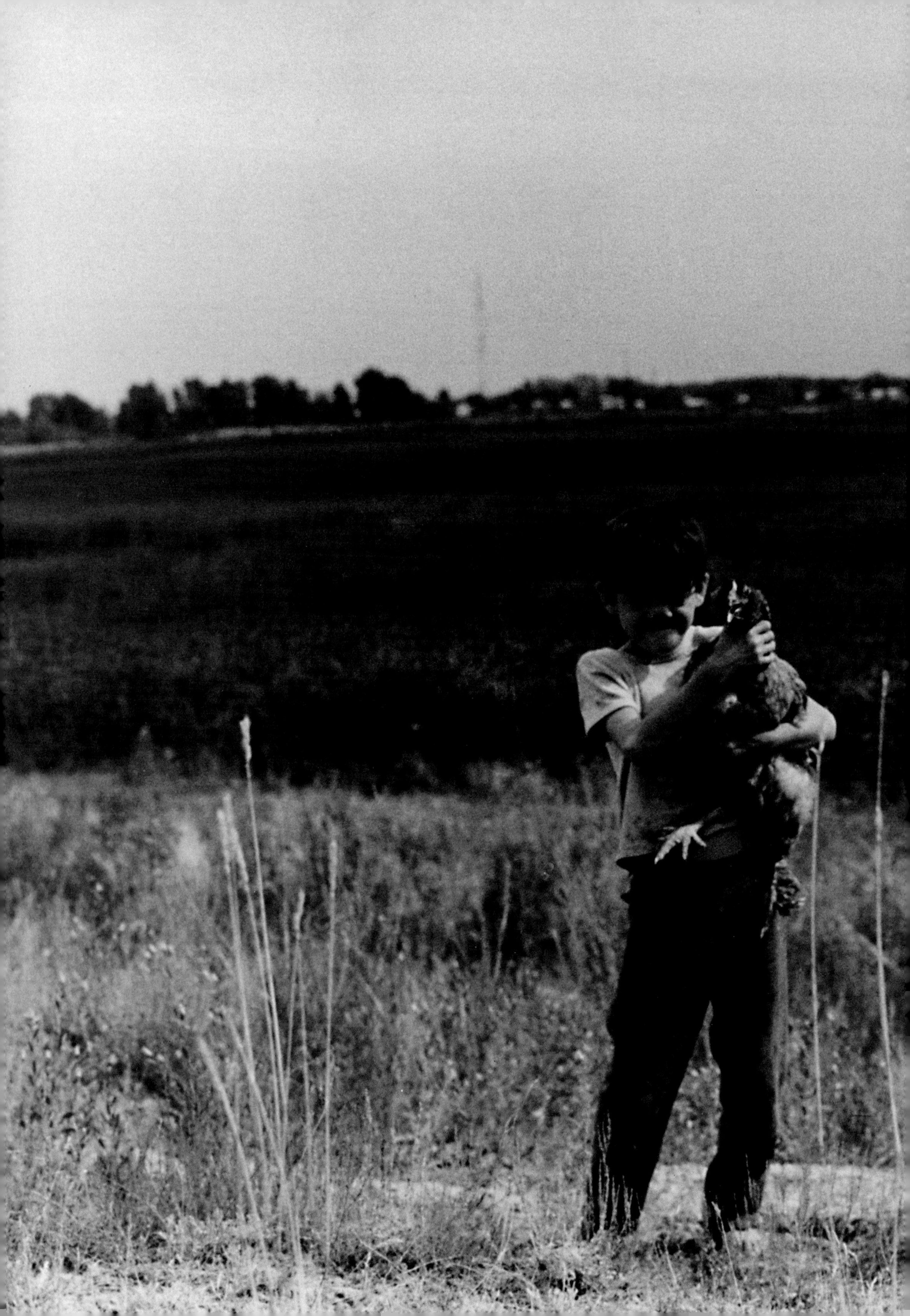

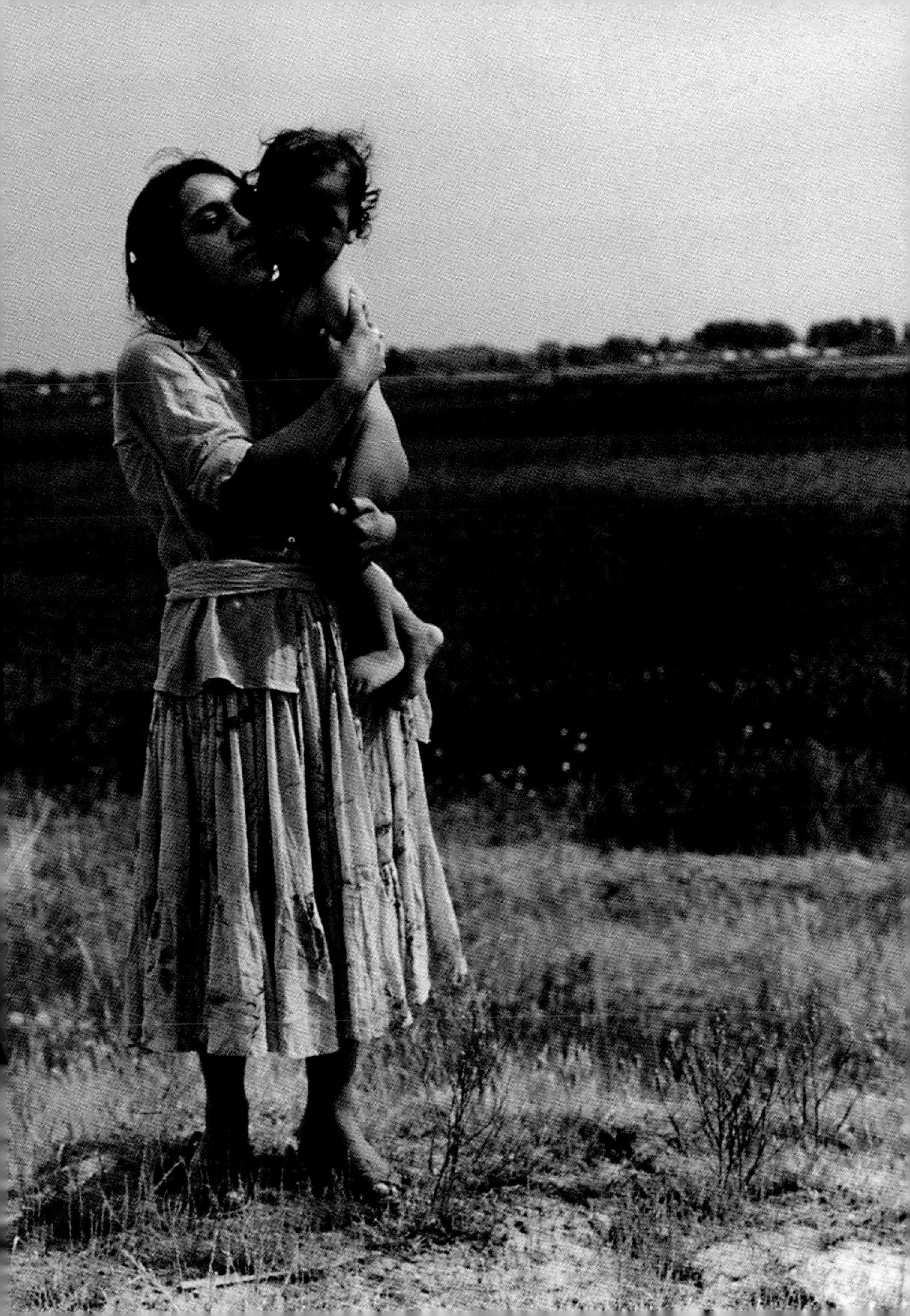

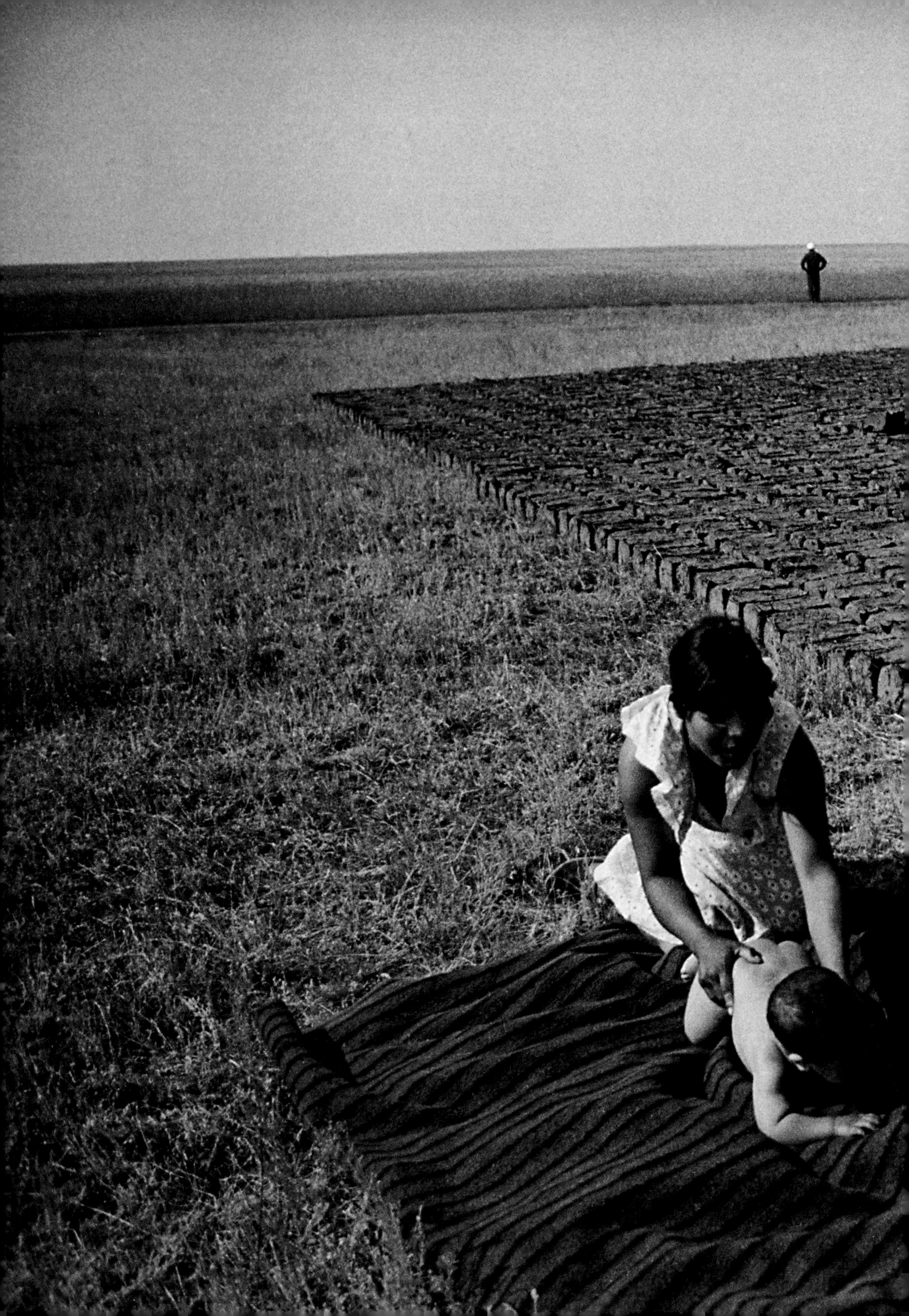

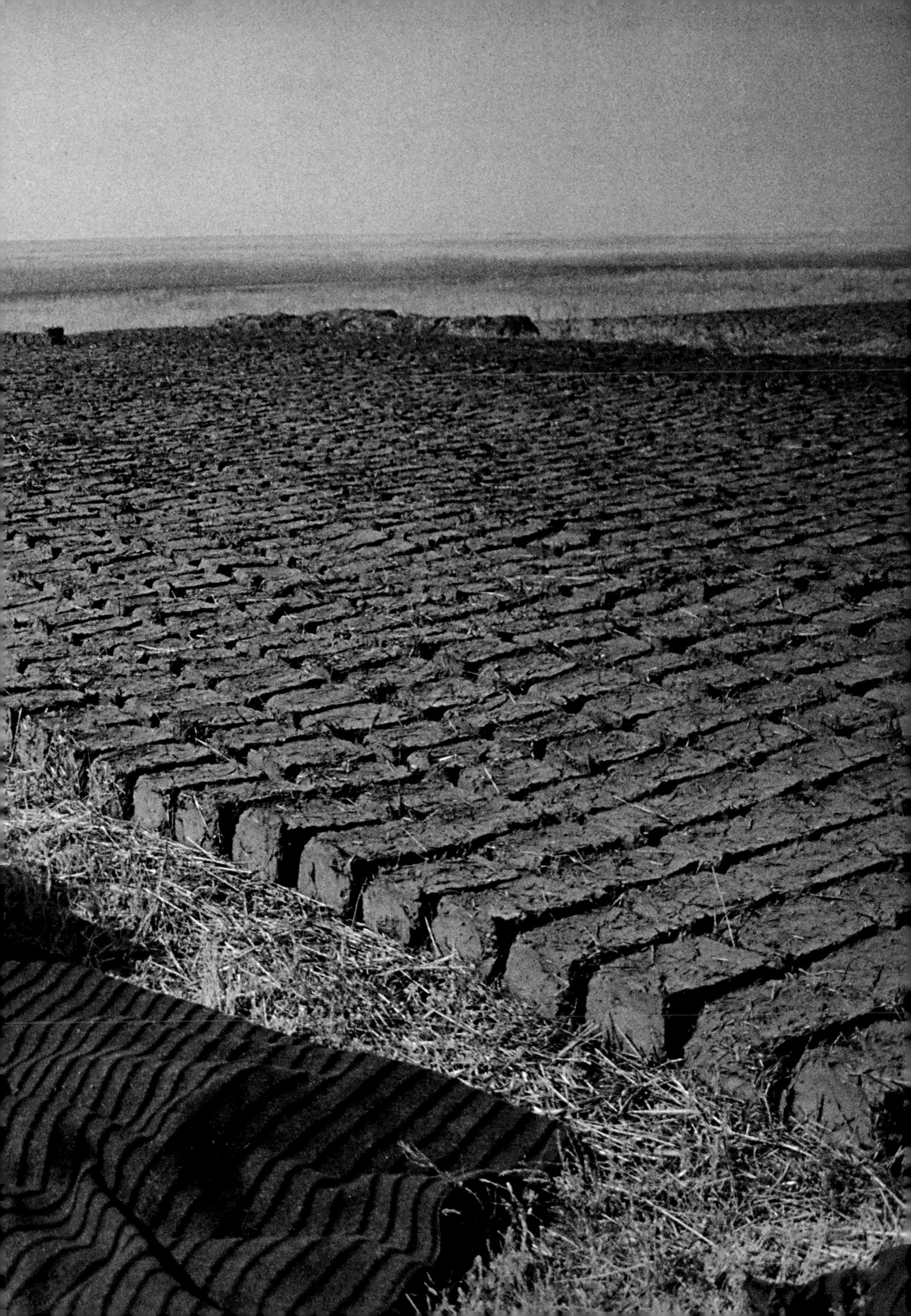

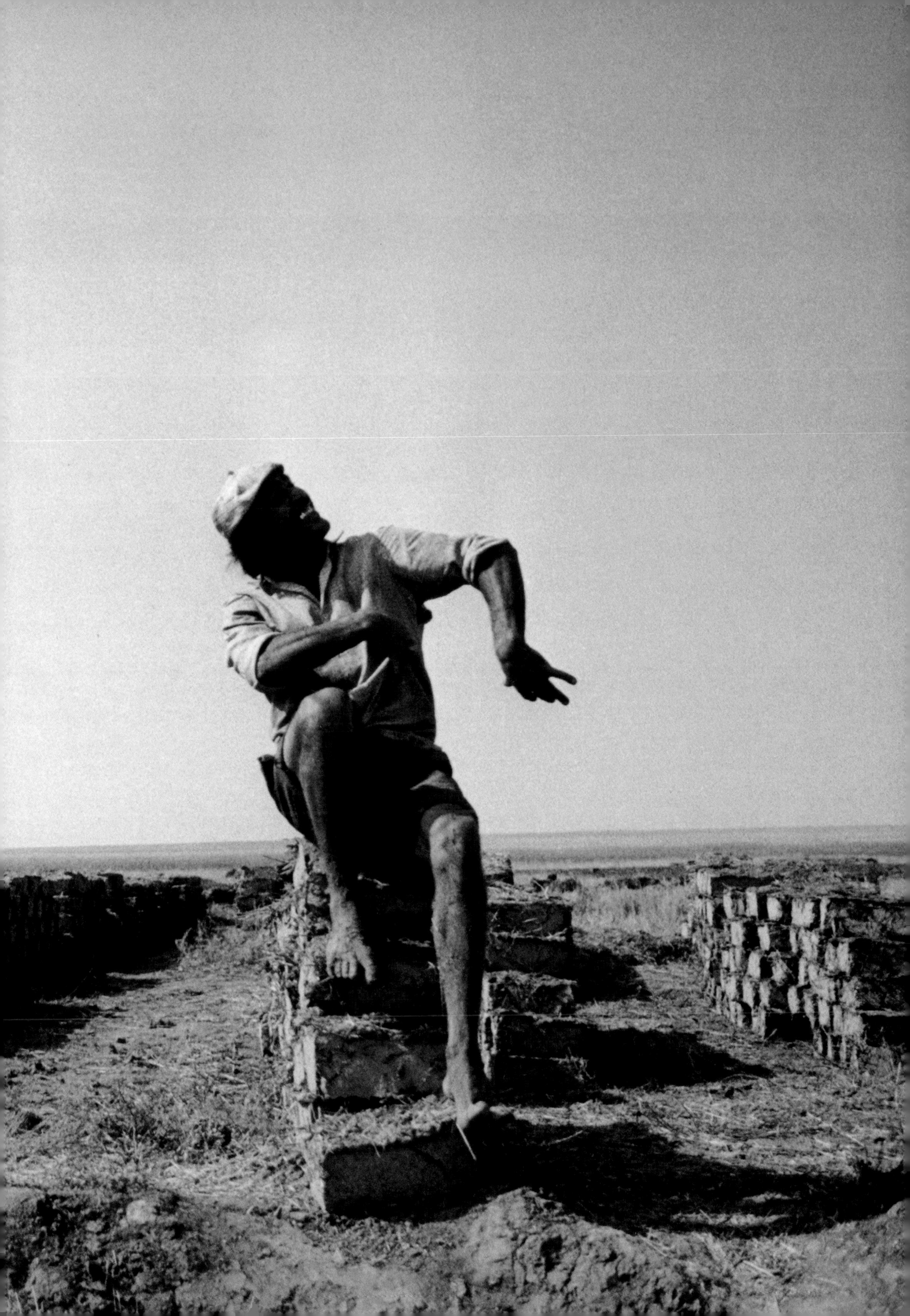

ОДЕССА

Odessa Odessa Odessa

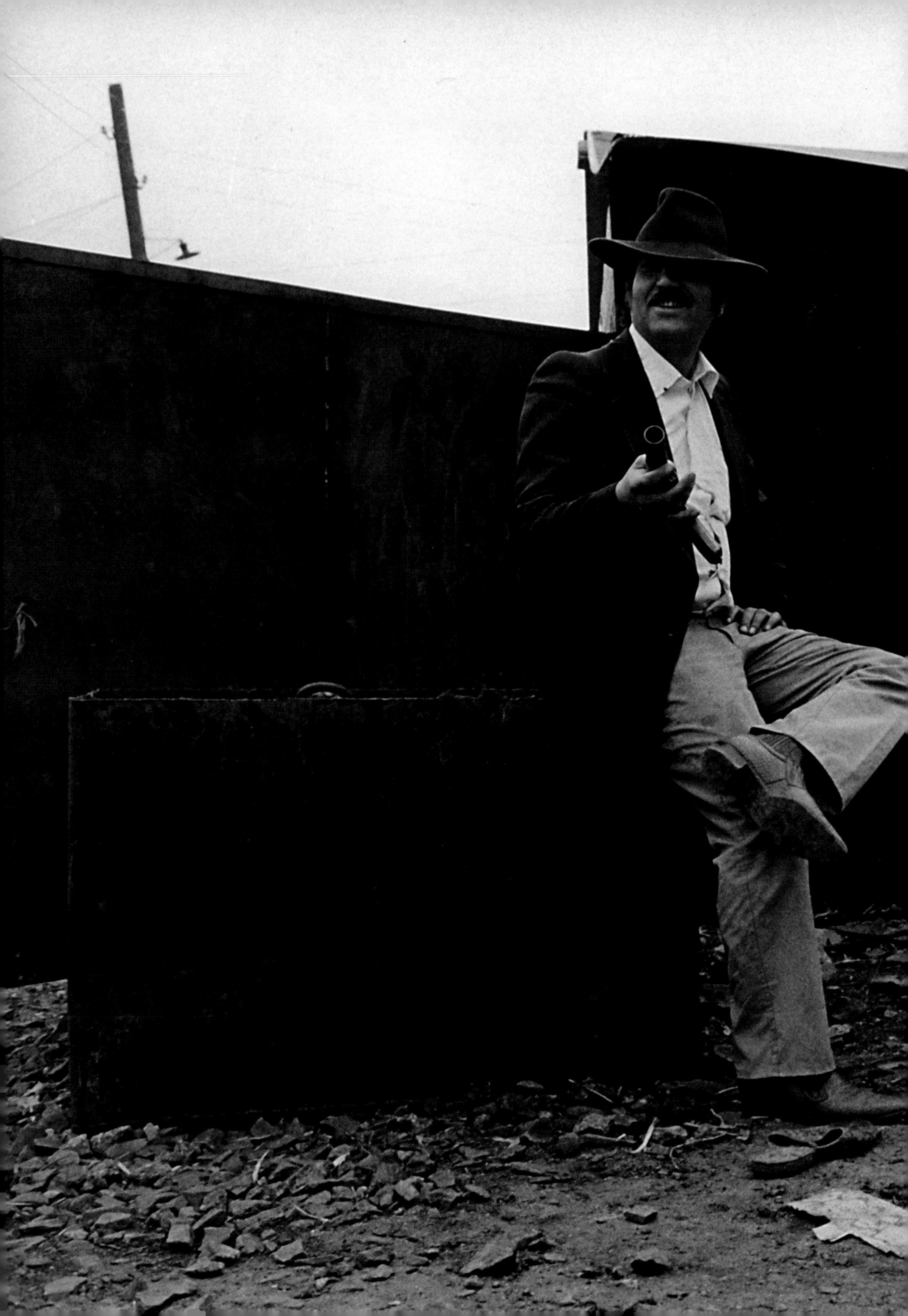

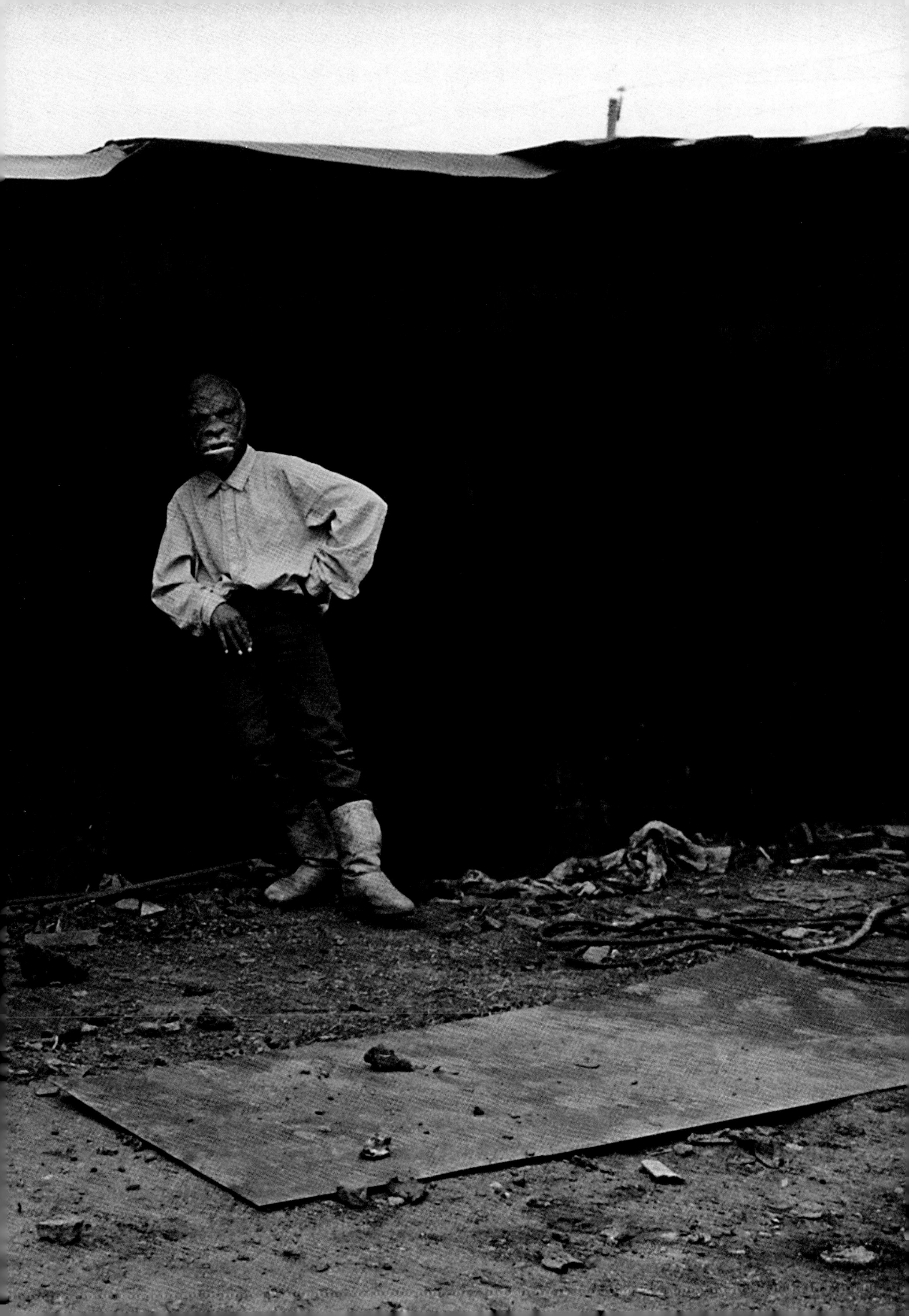

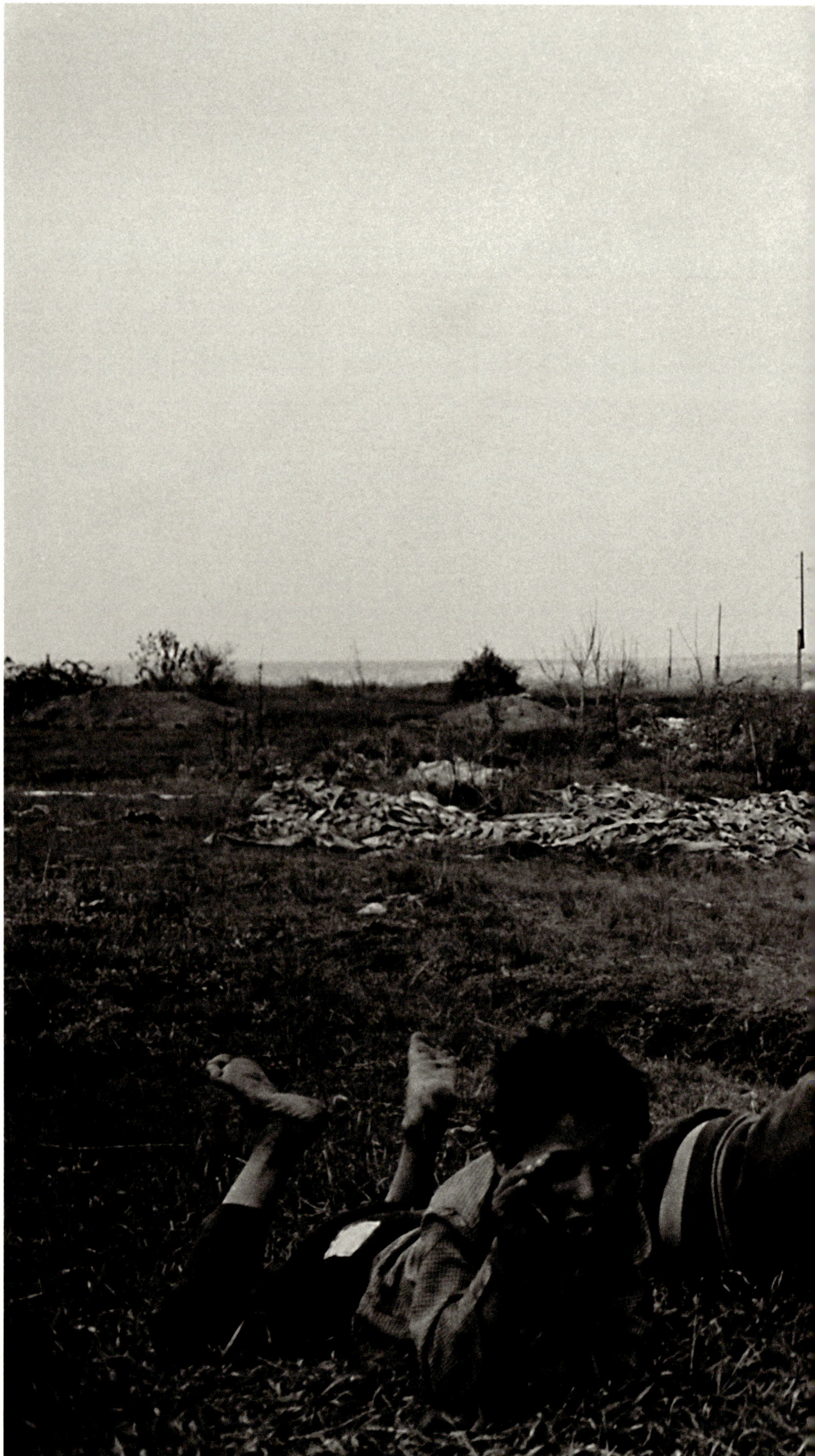

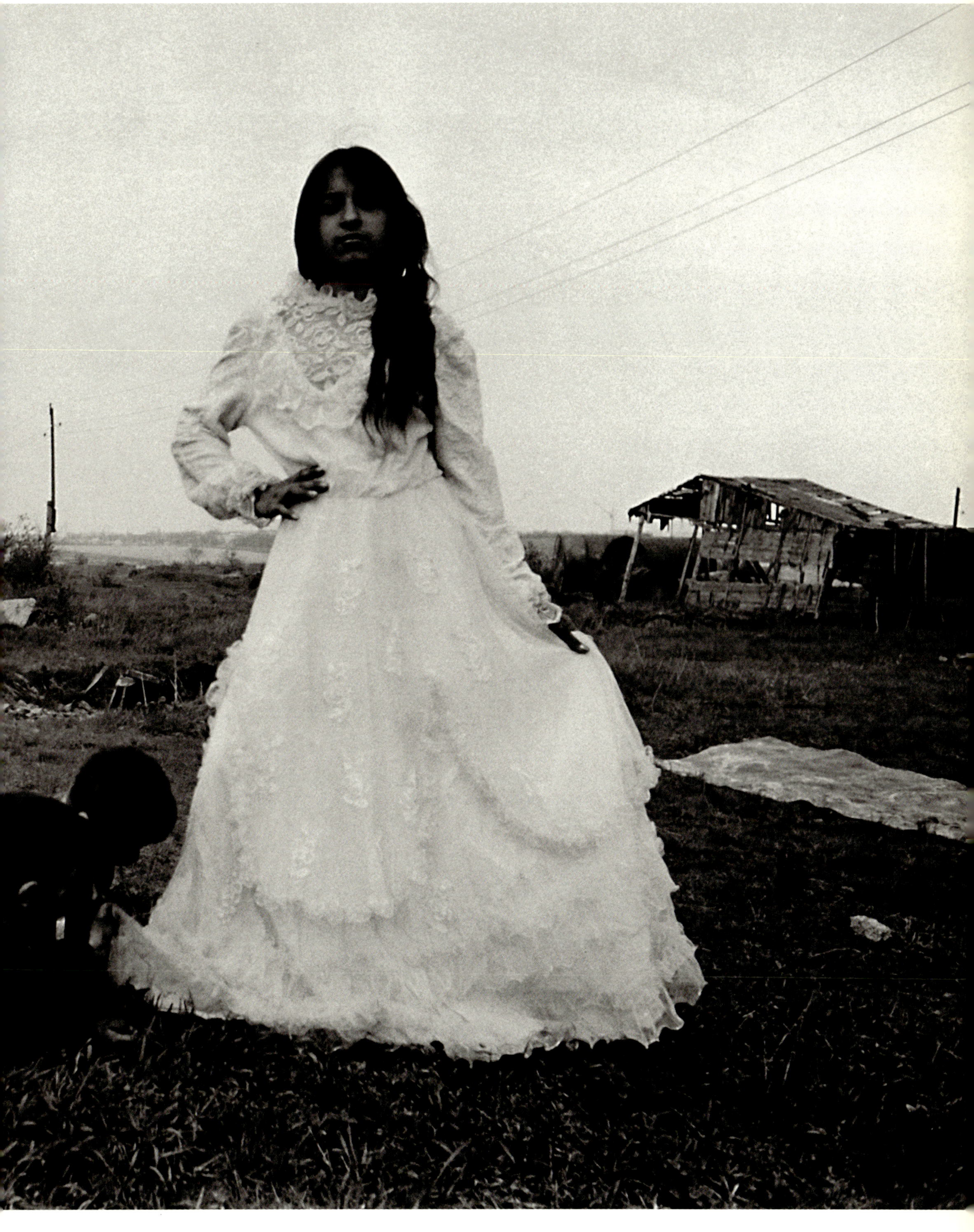

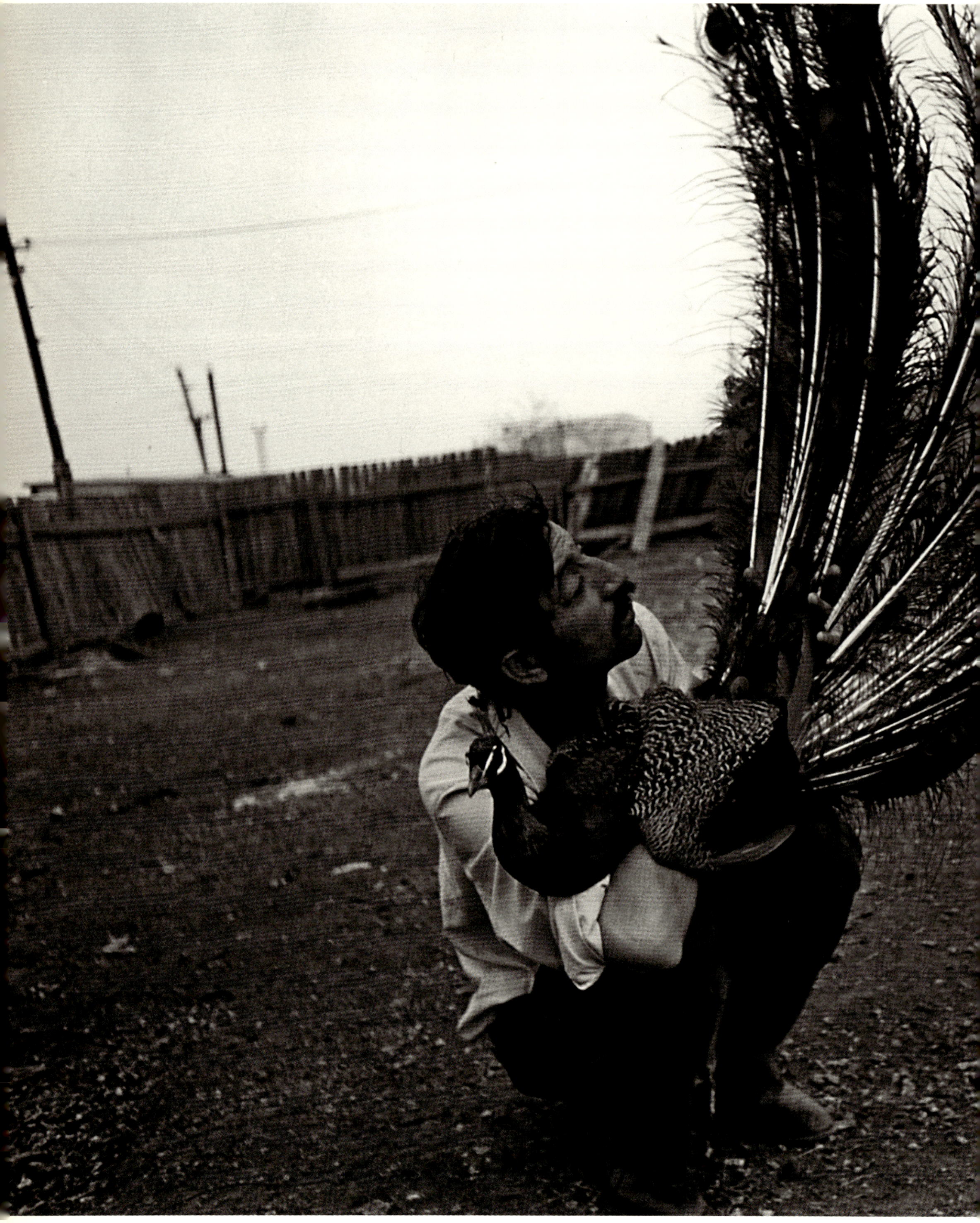

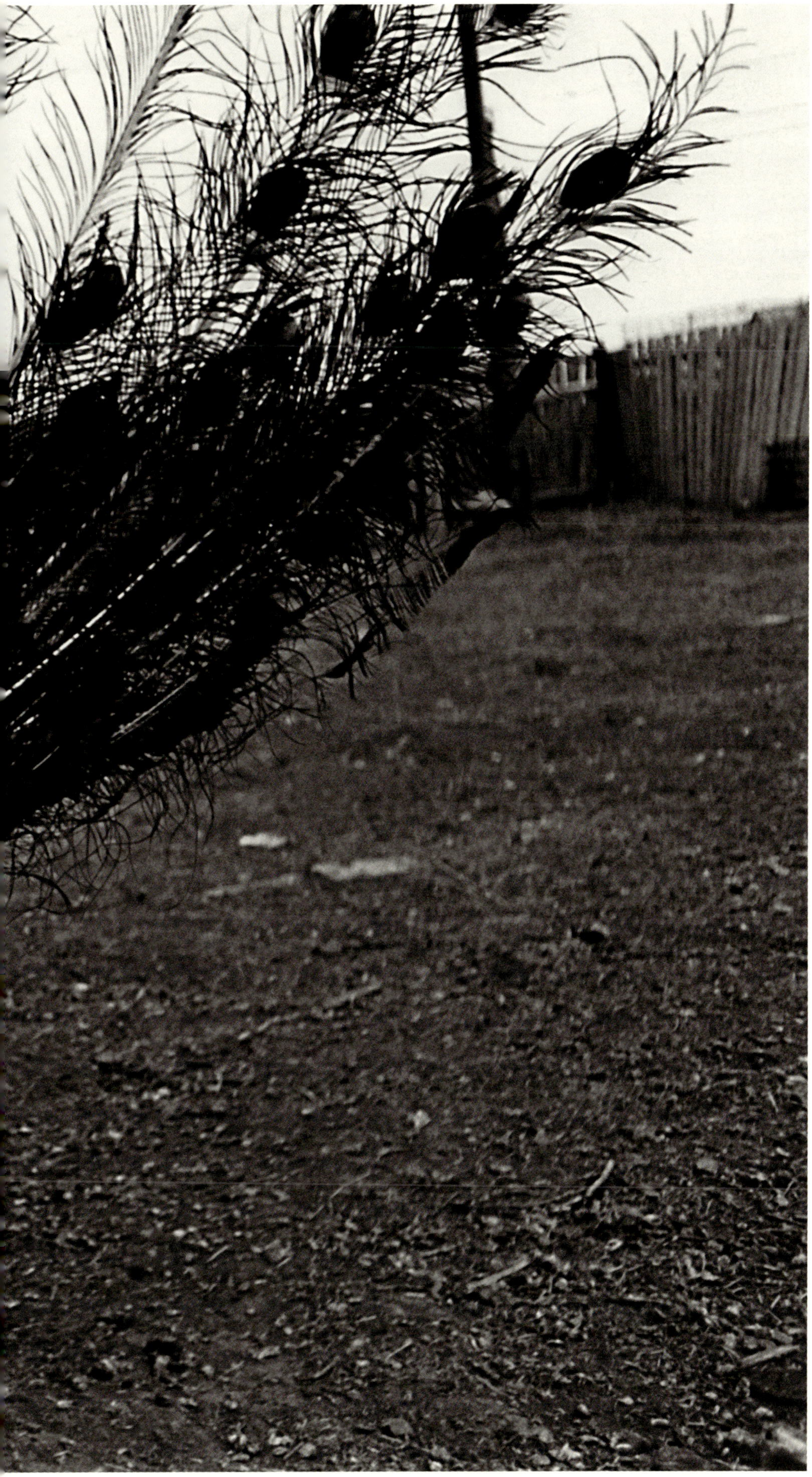

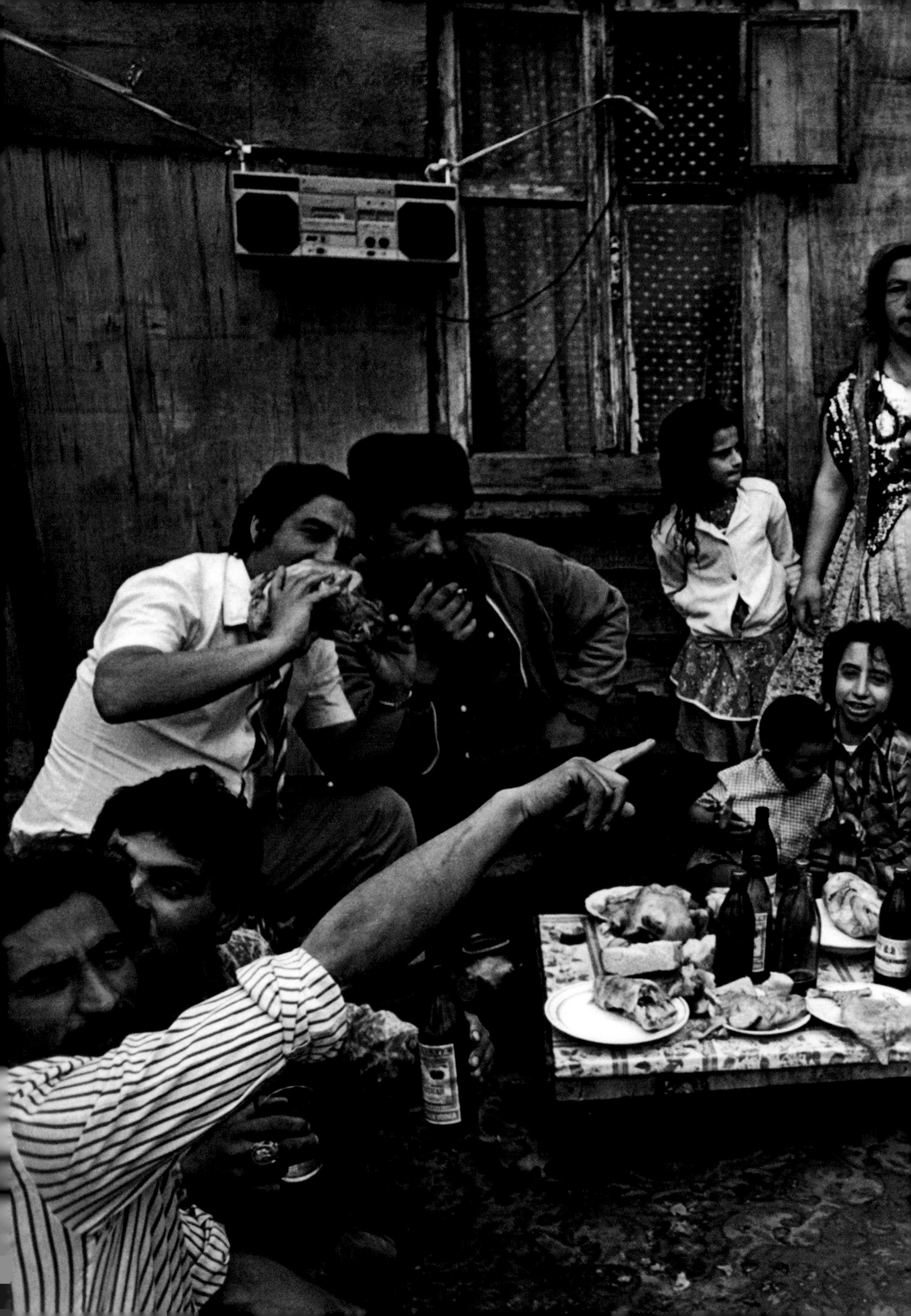

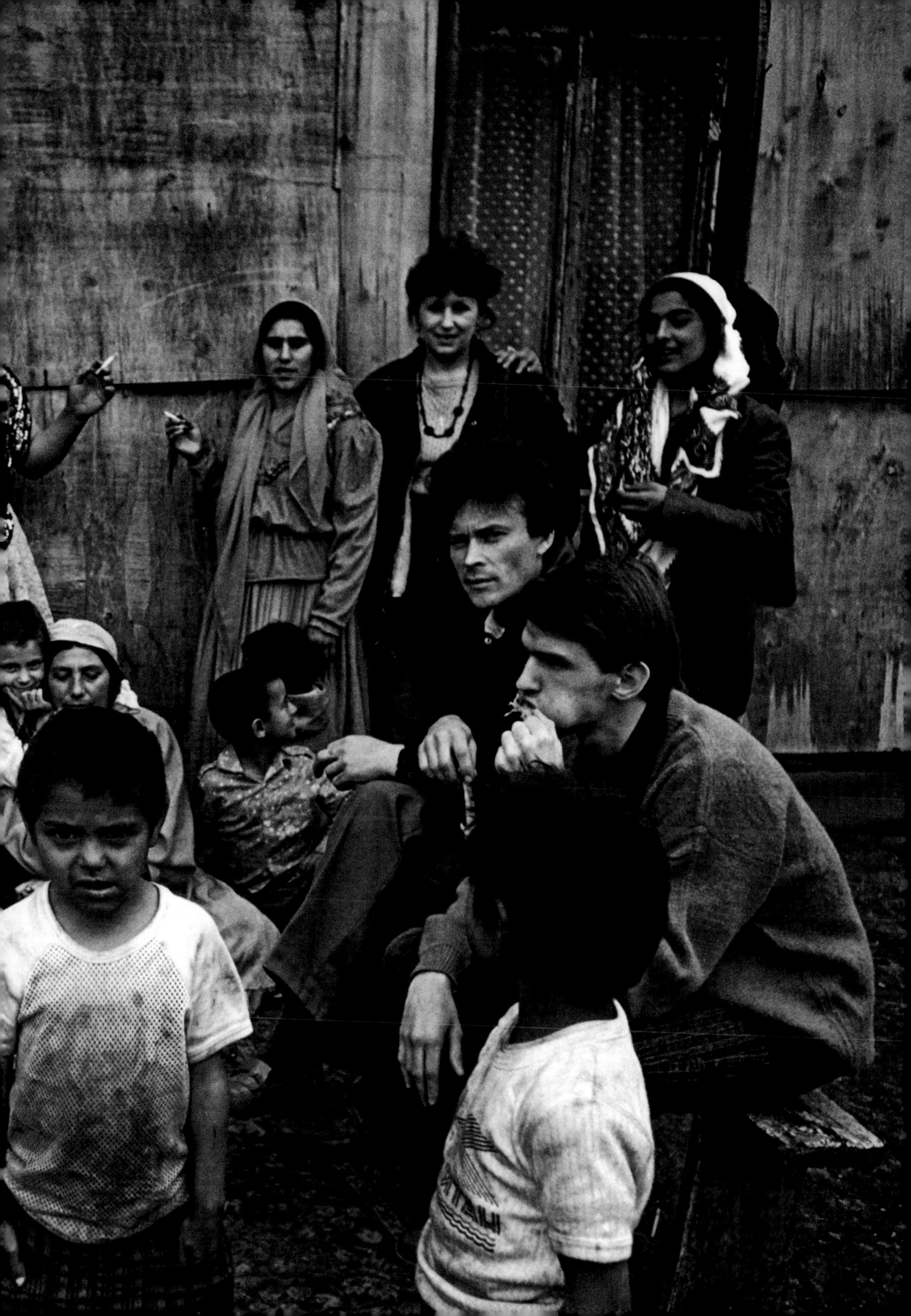

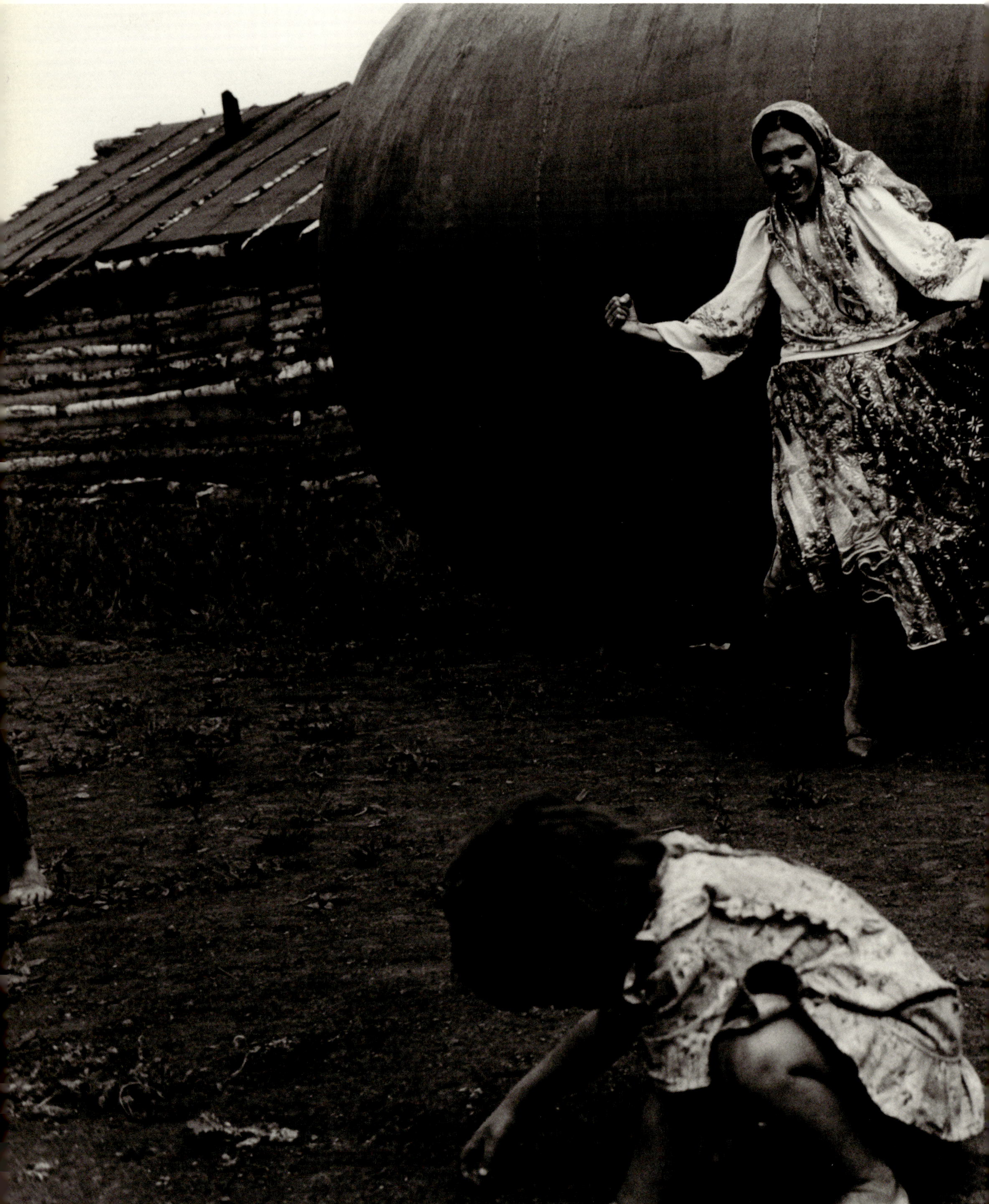

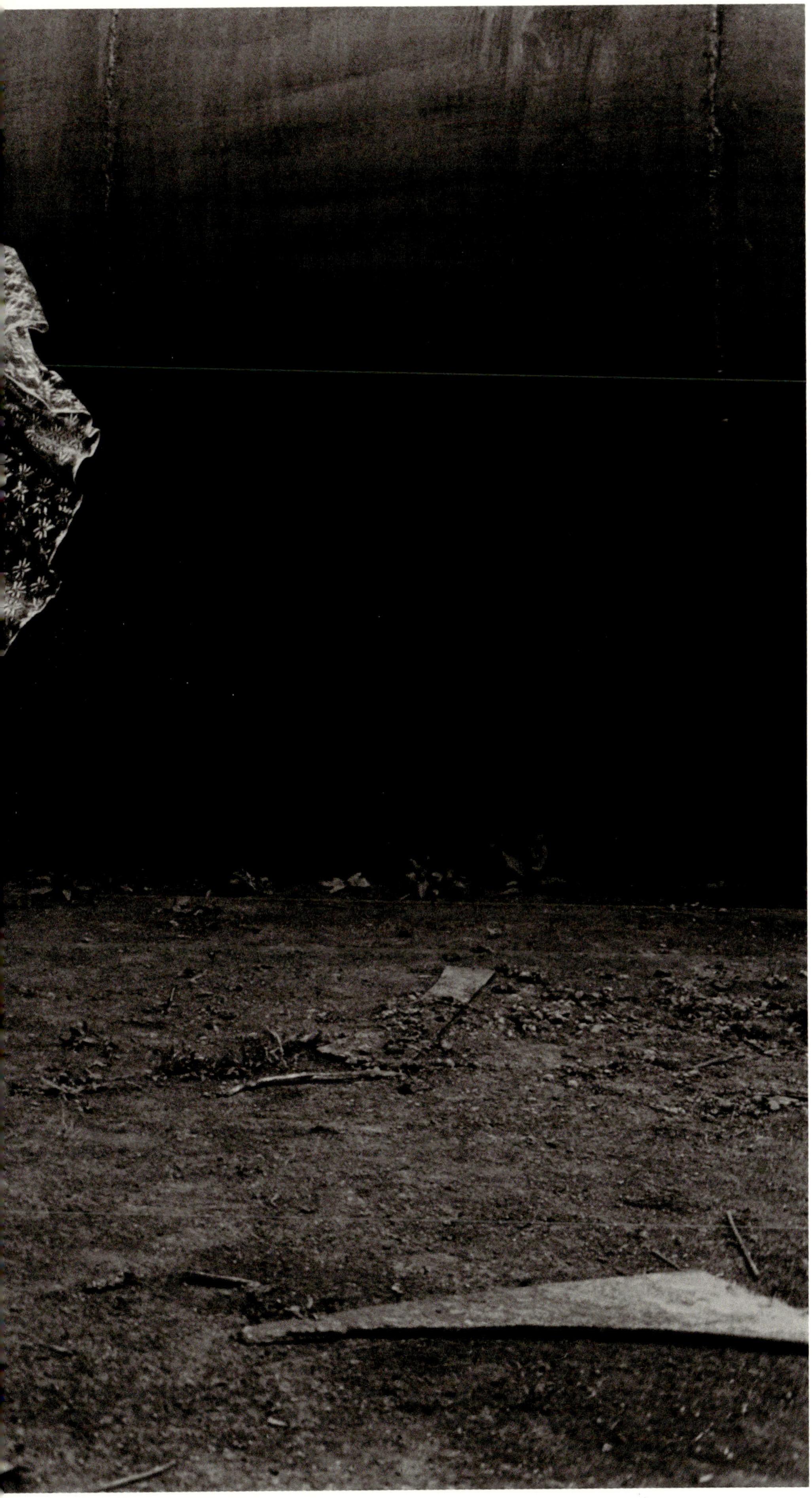

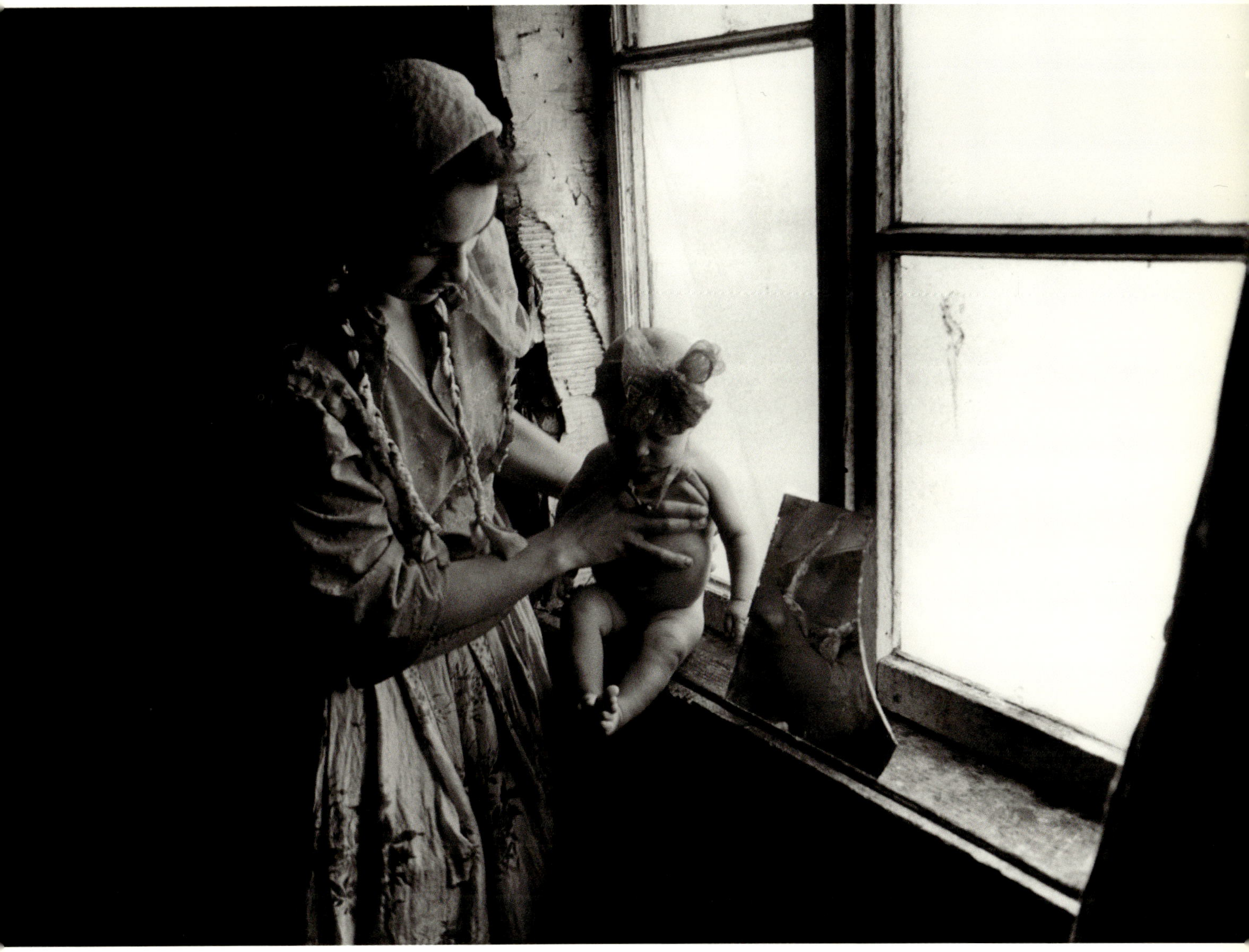

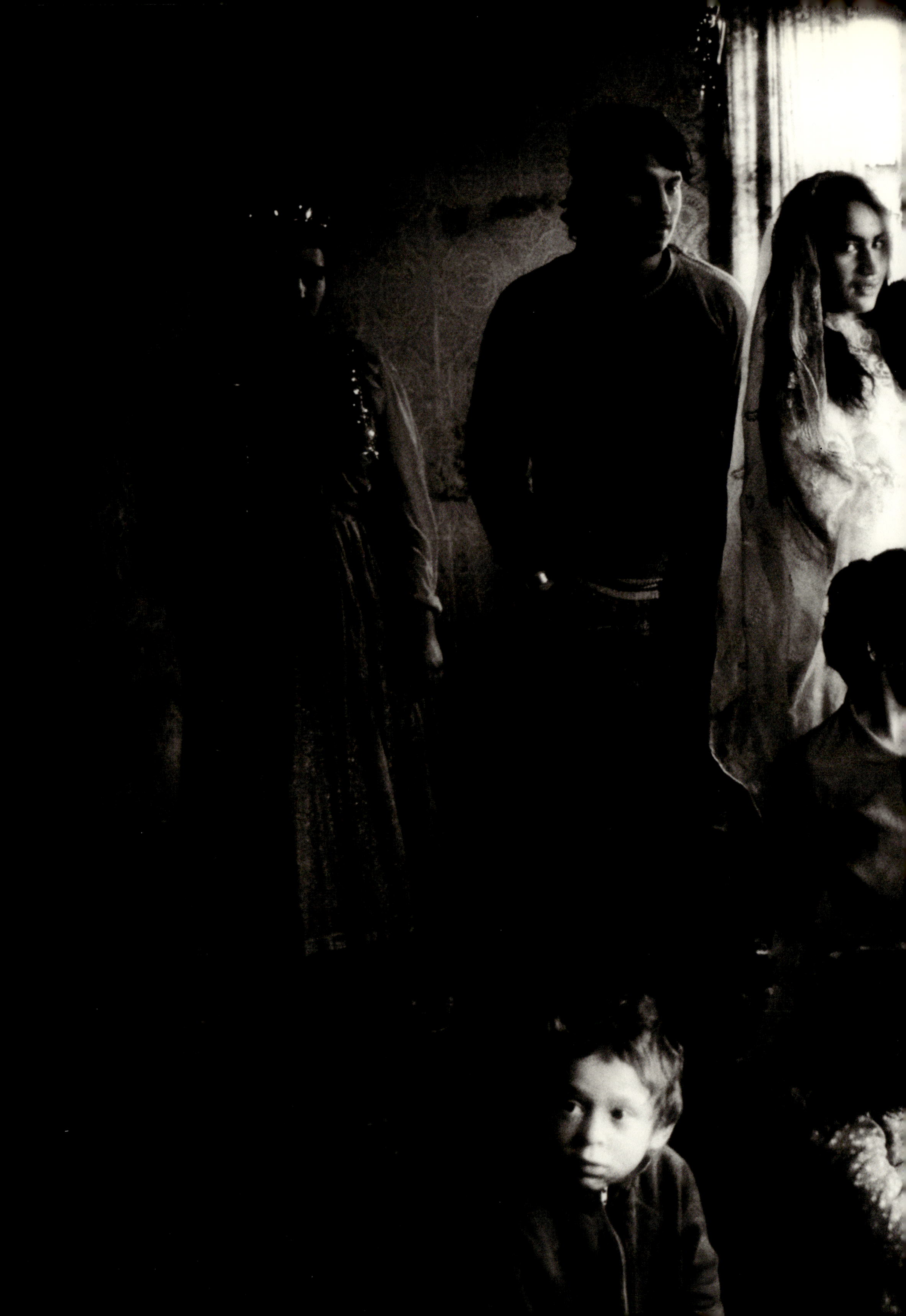

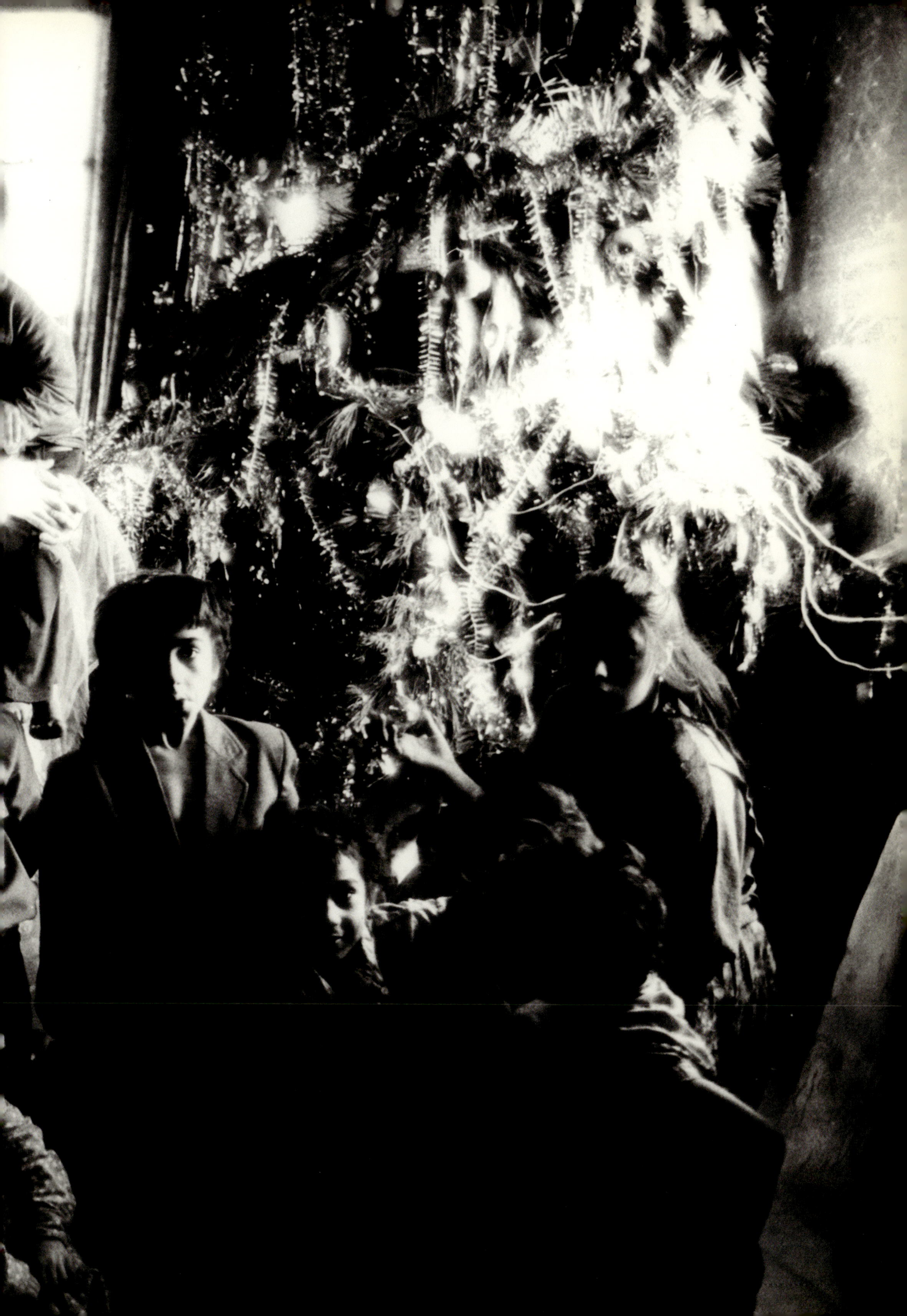

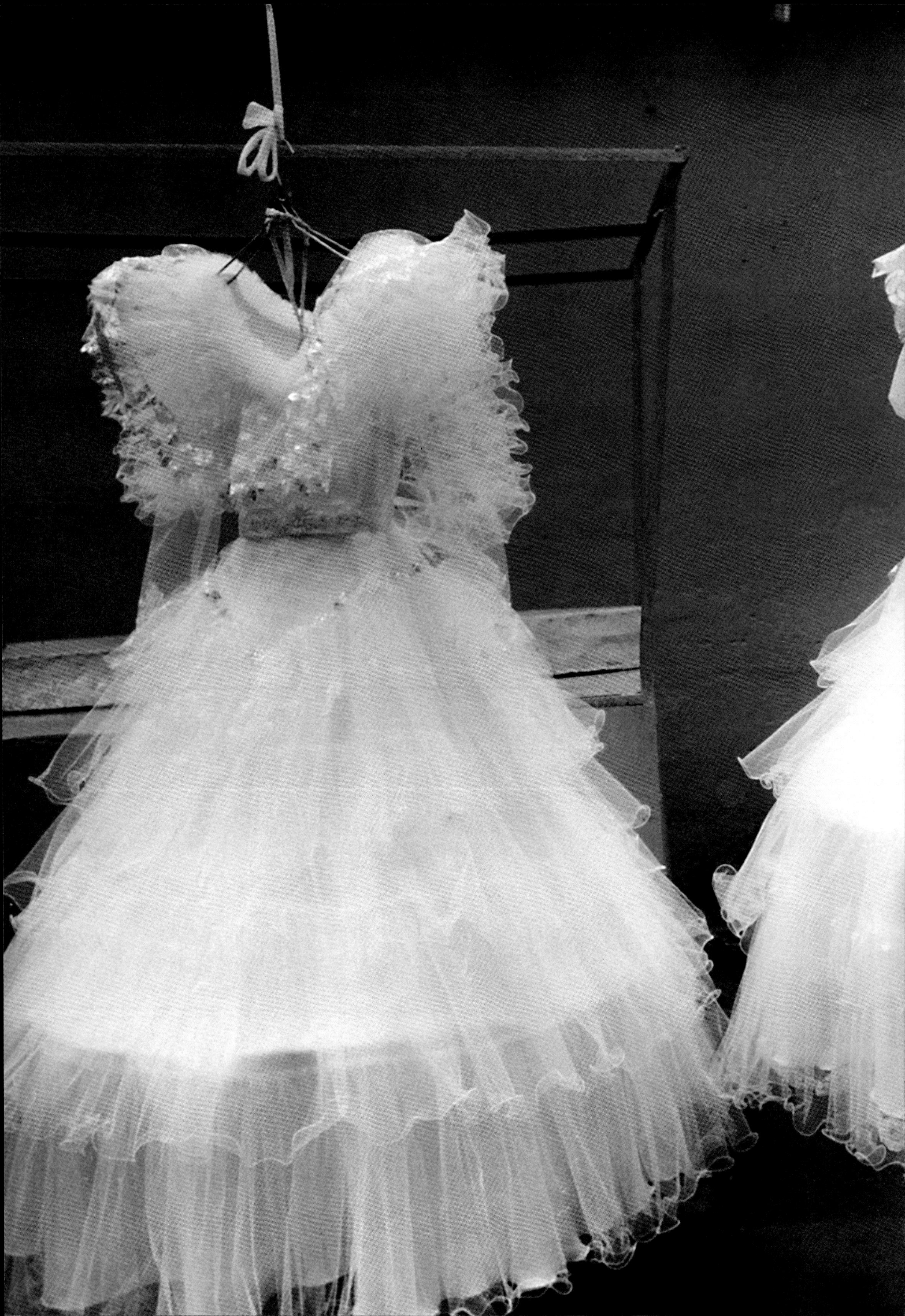

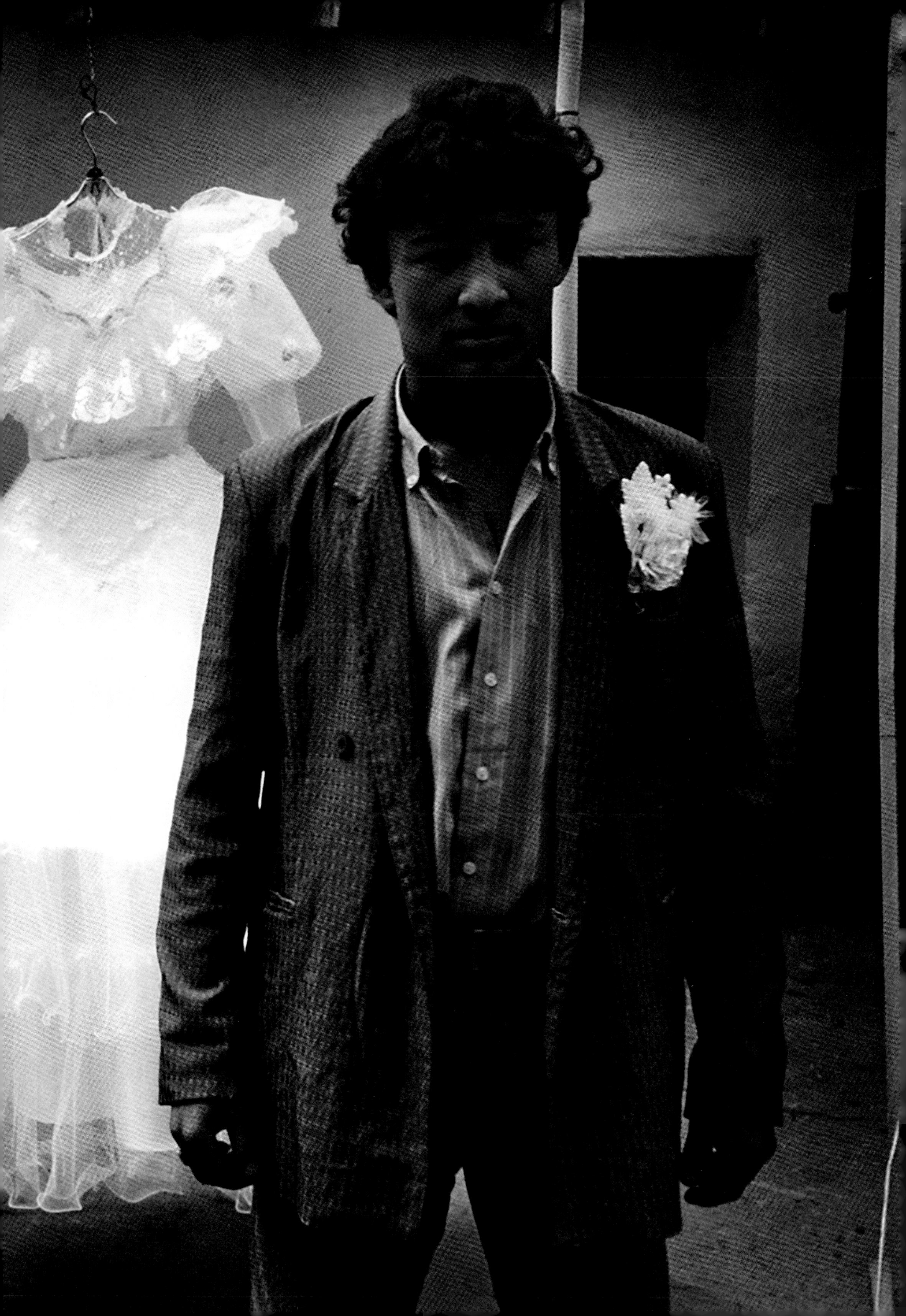

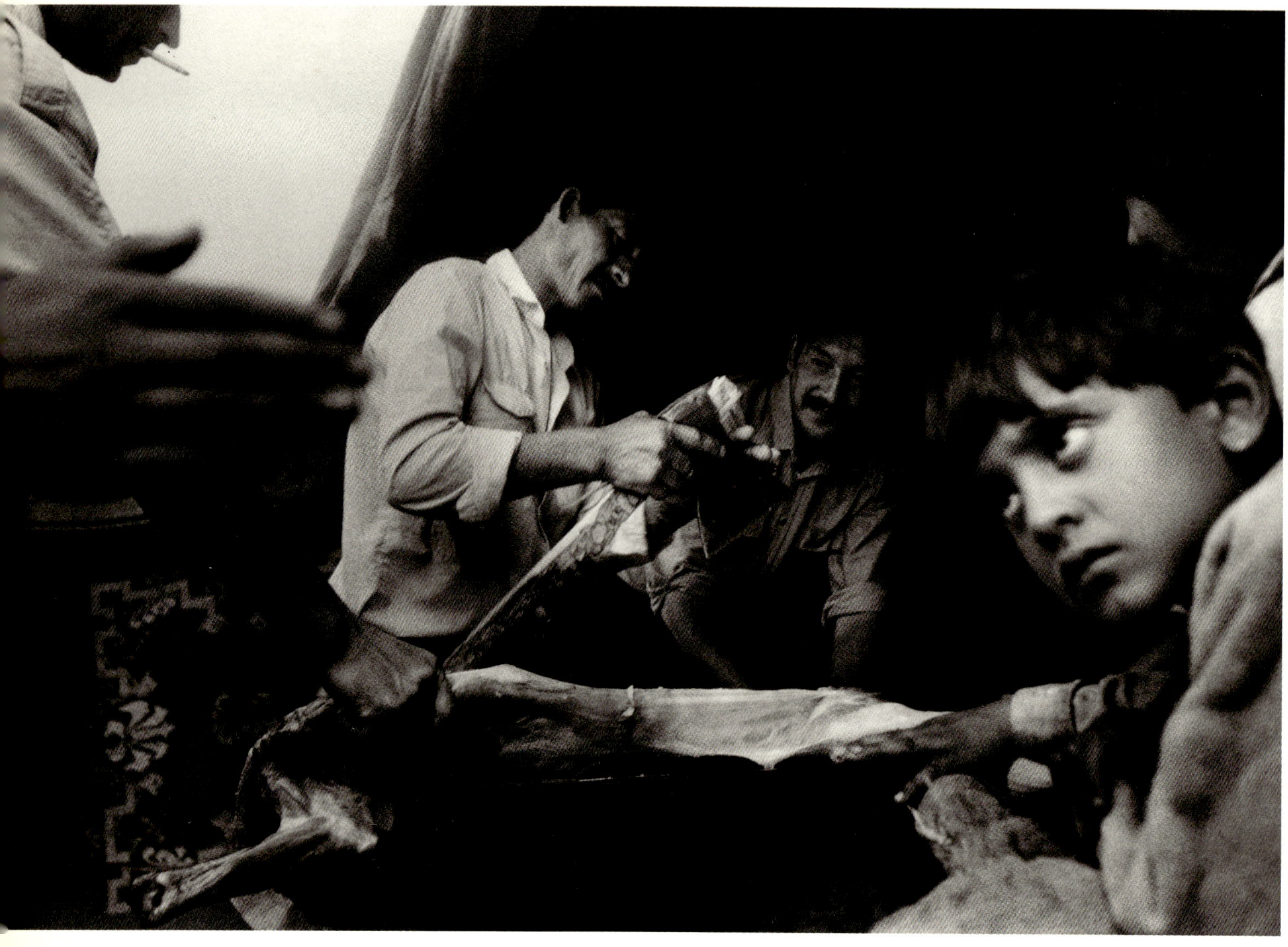

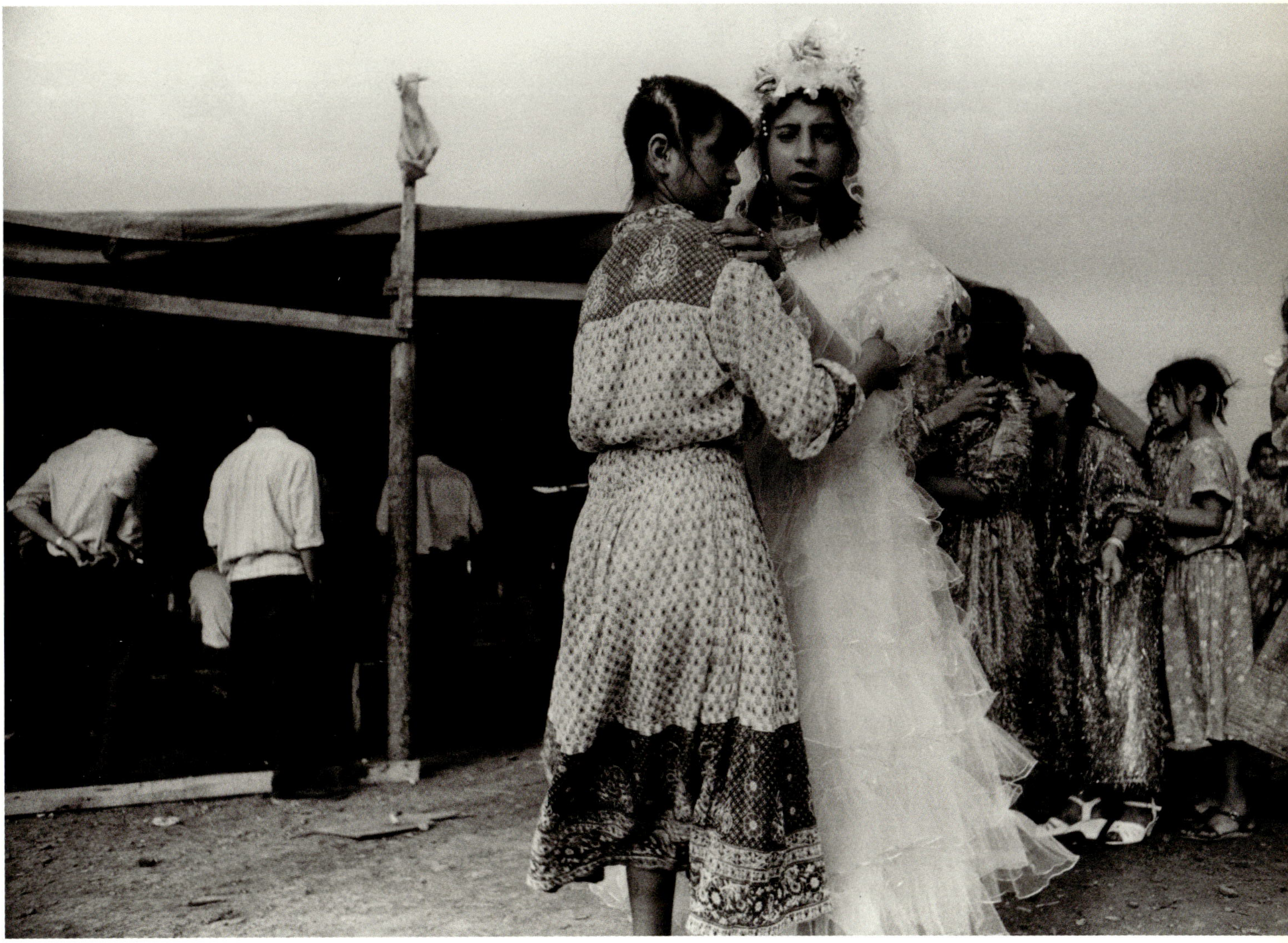

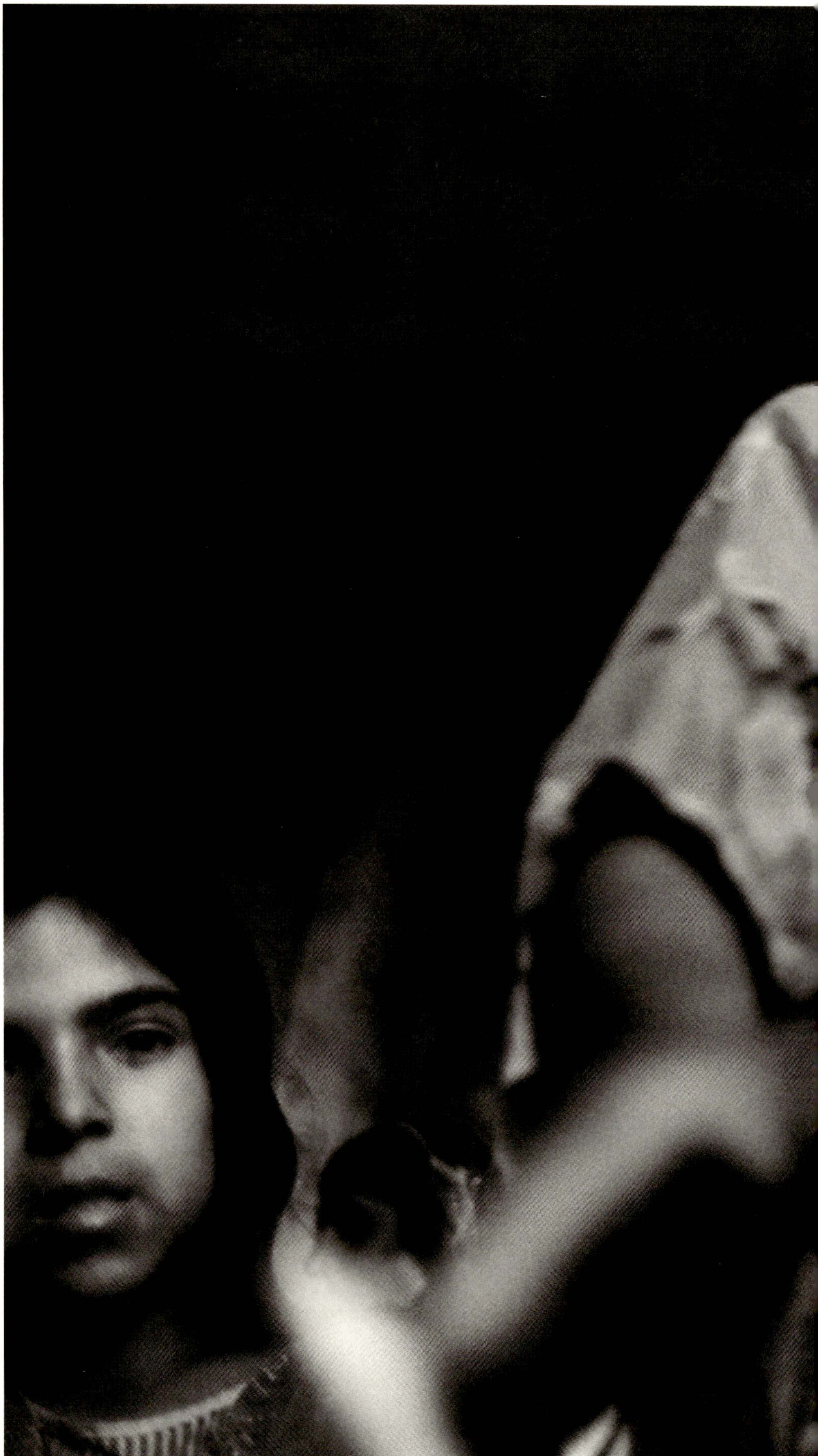

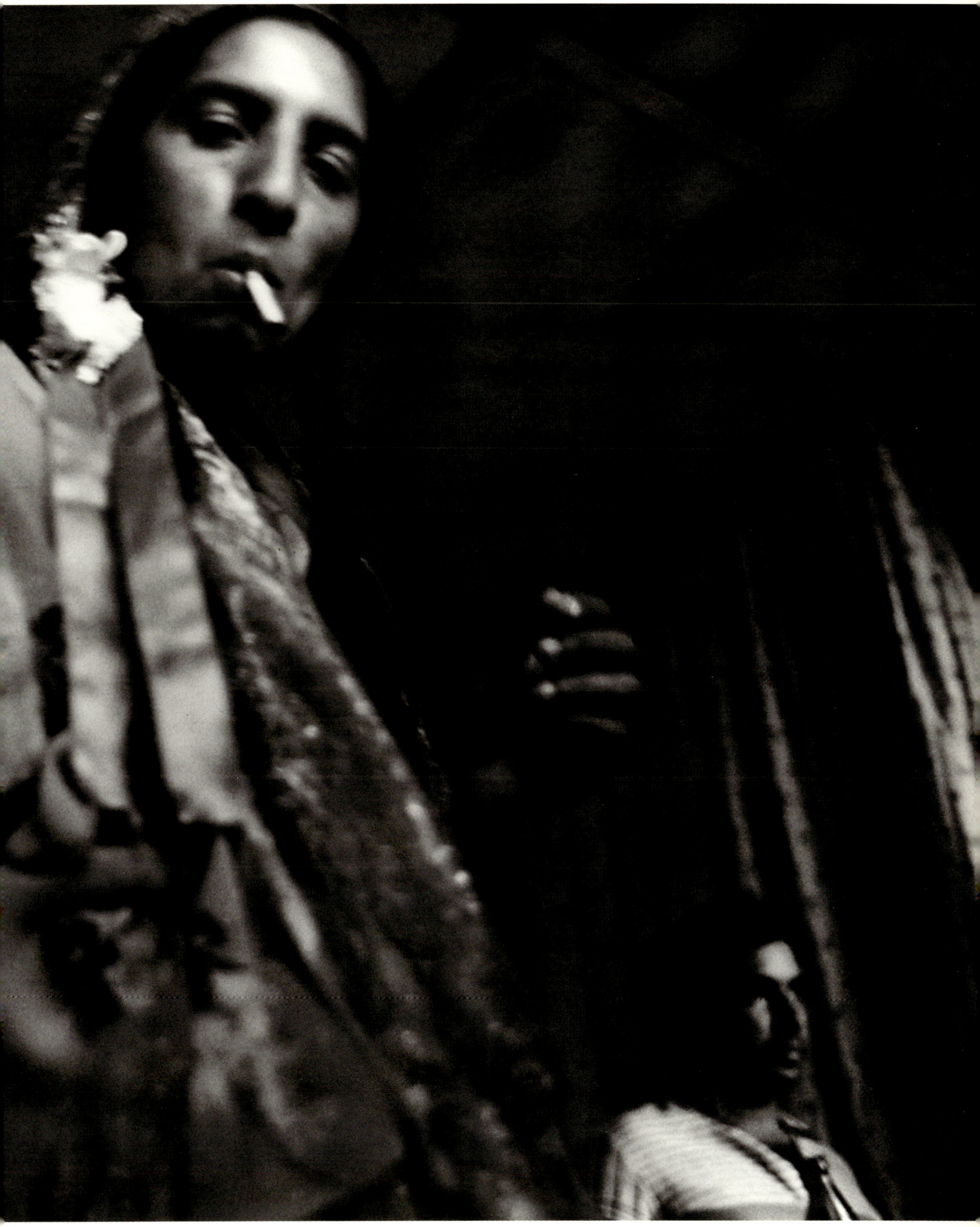

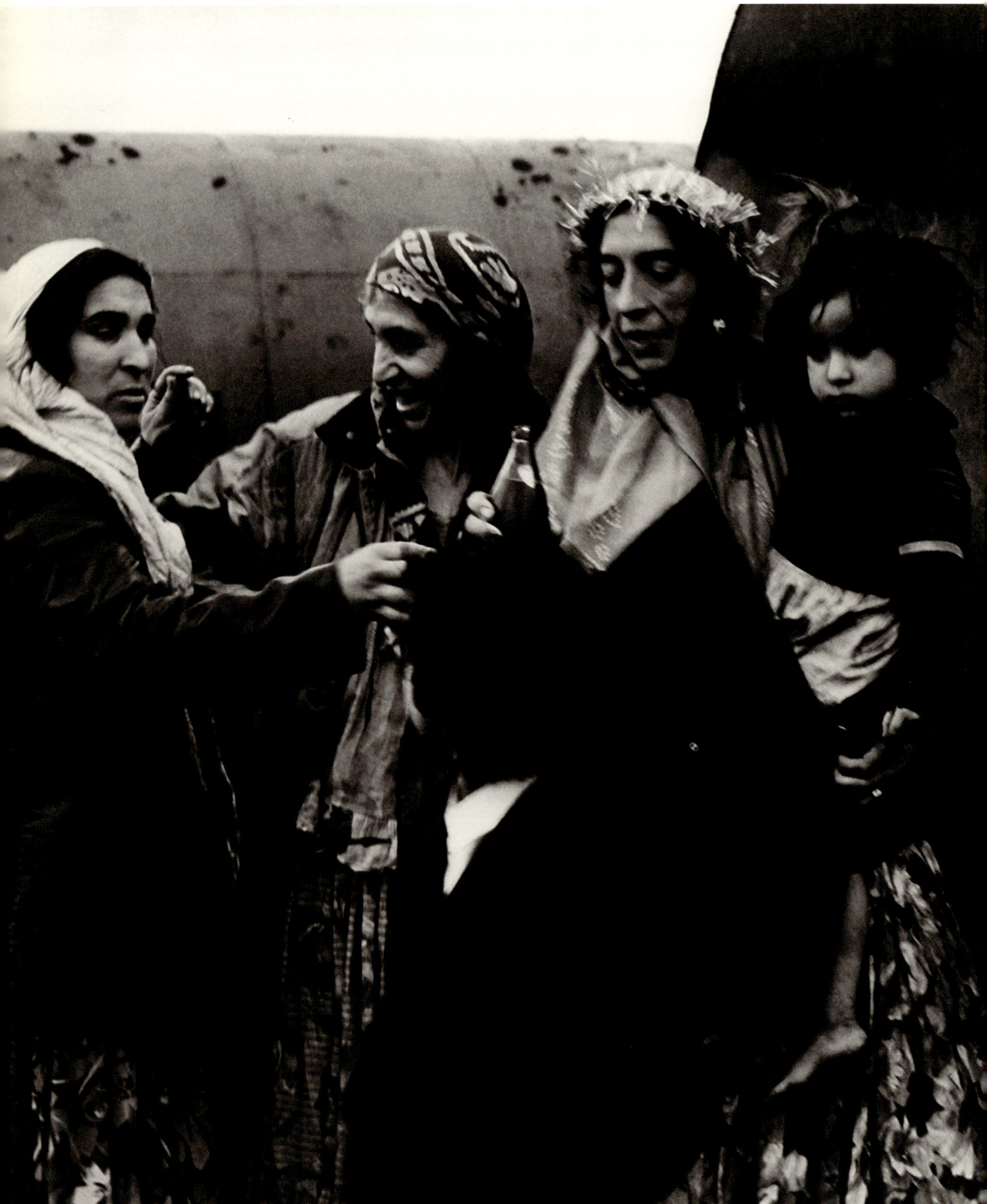

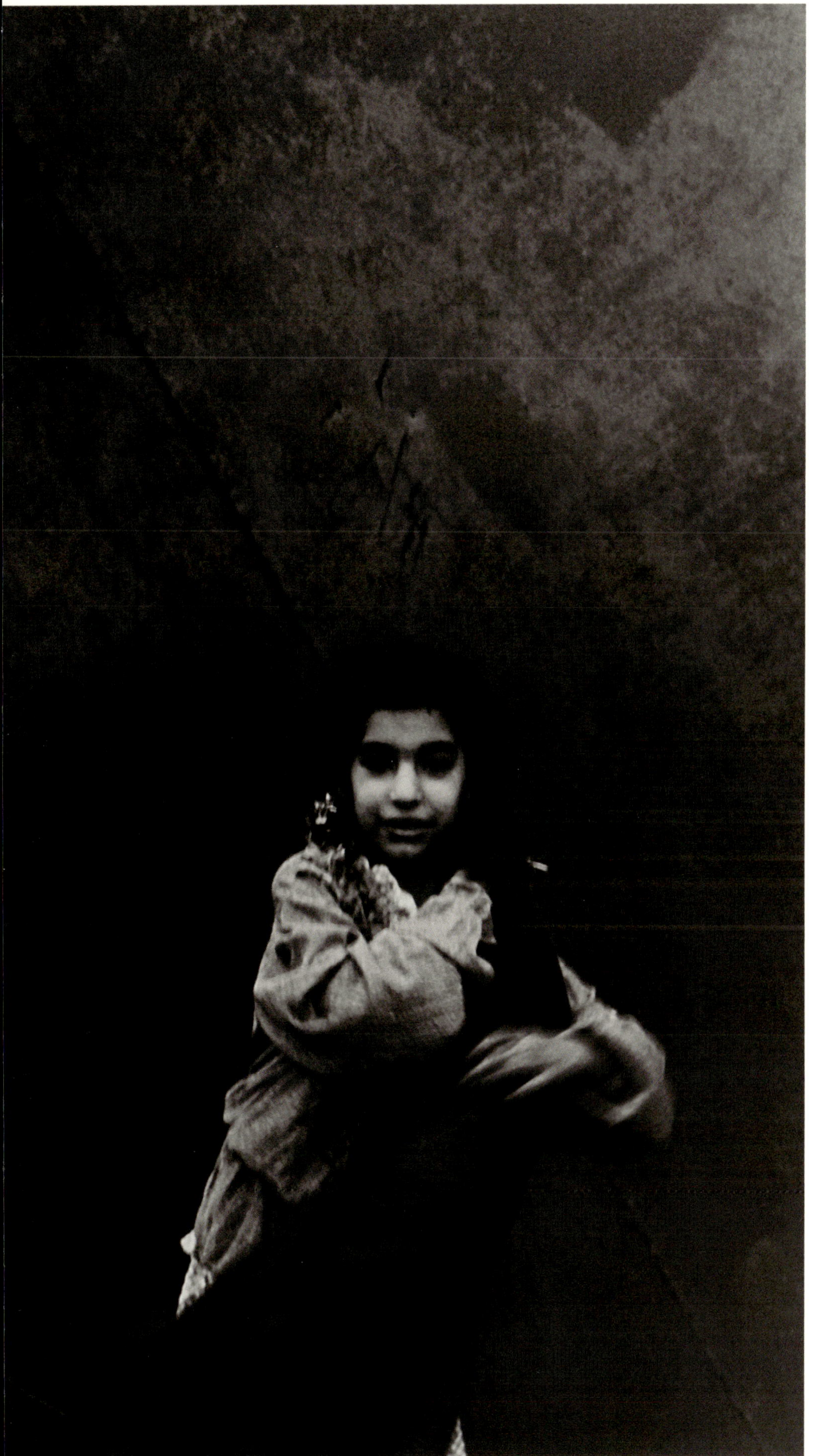

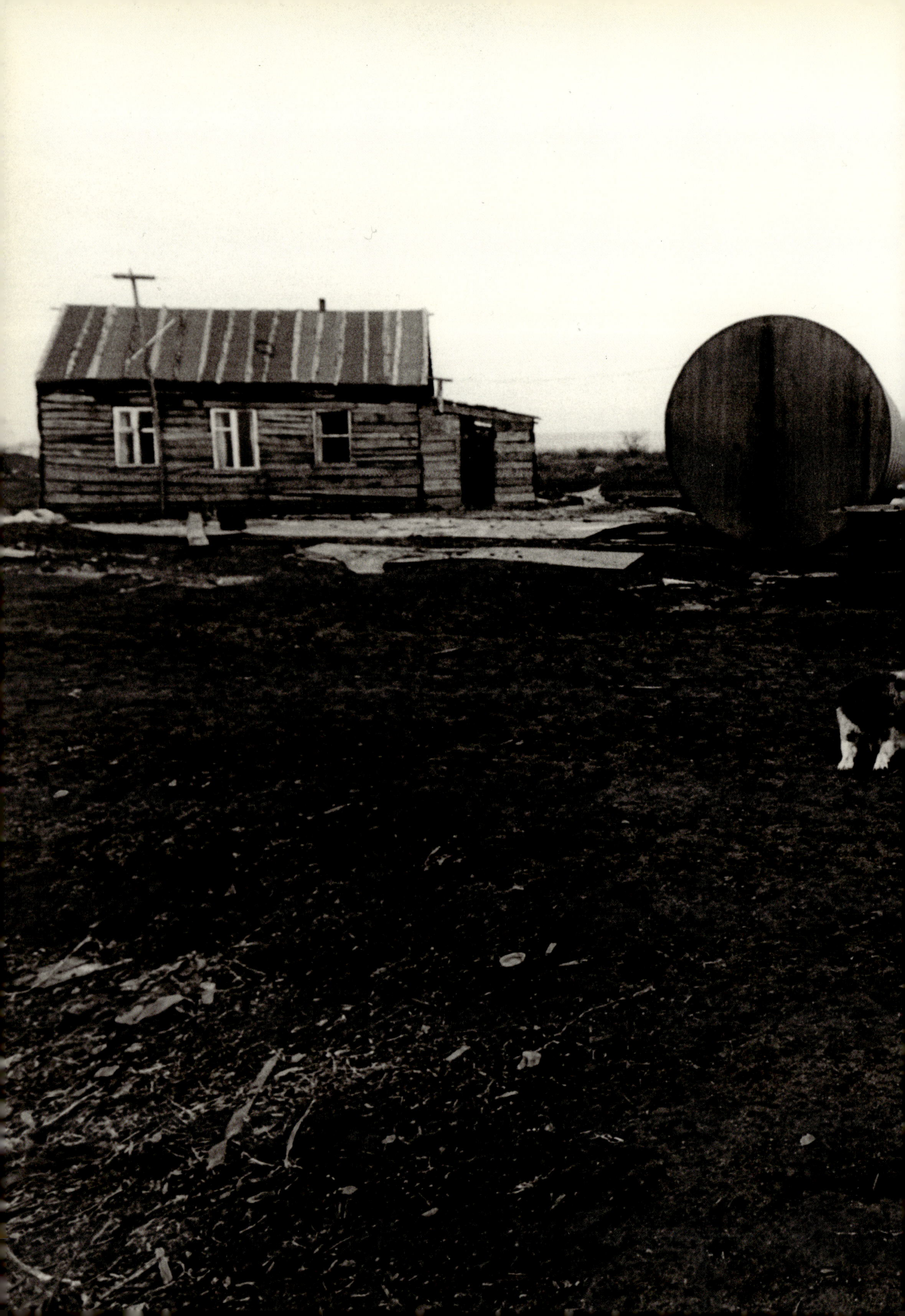

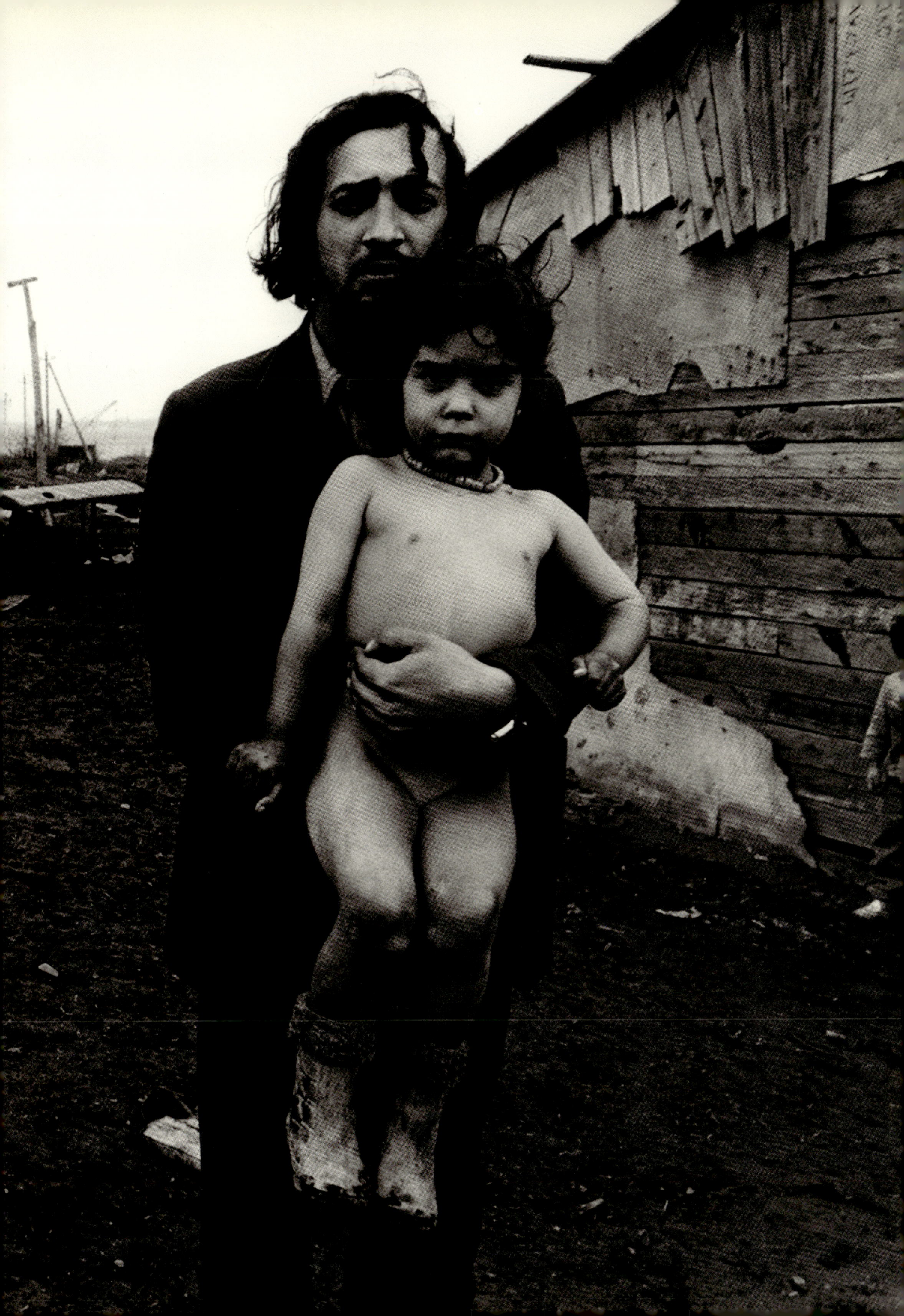

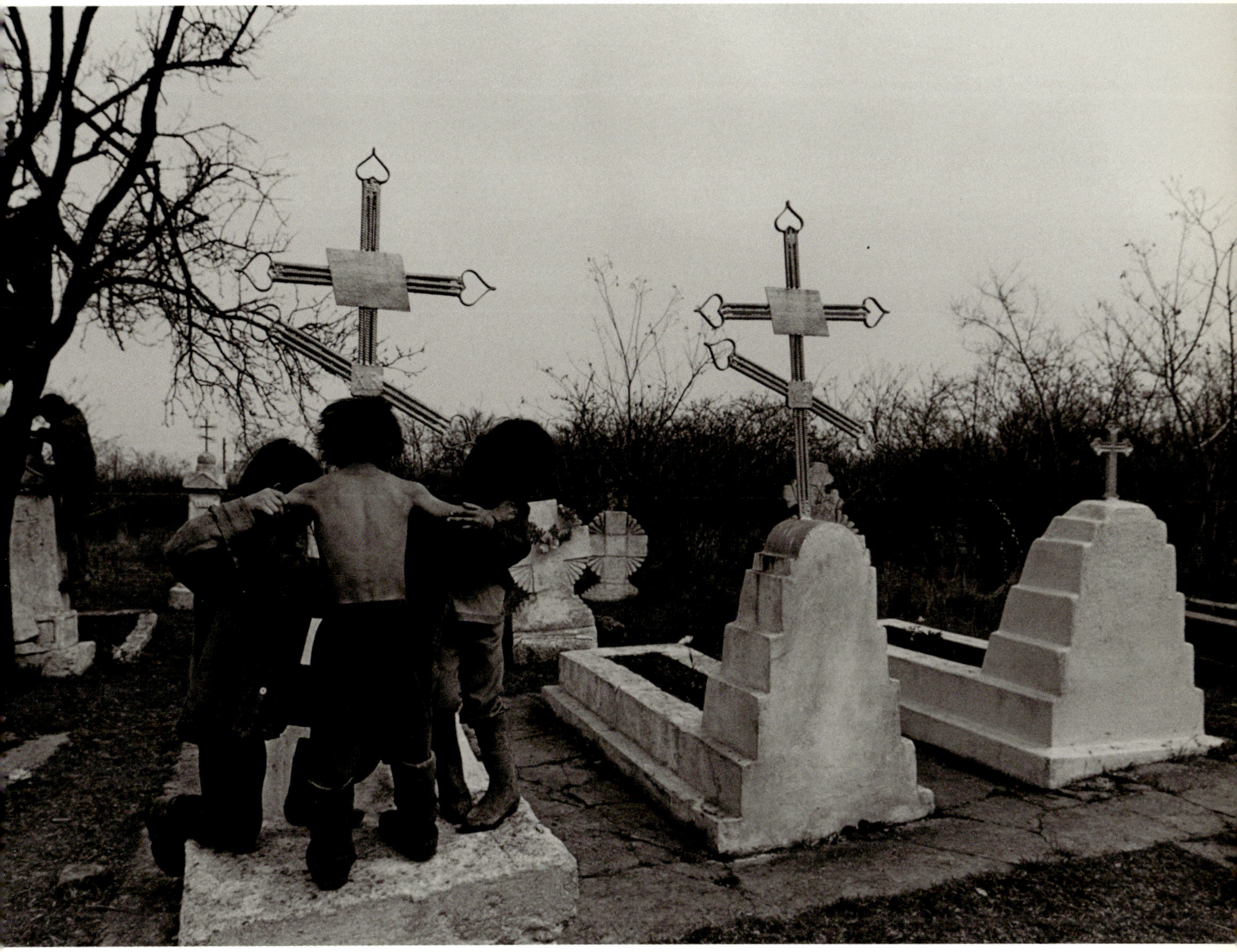

КАЗАНЬ

Kazan Kazan Kasan

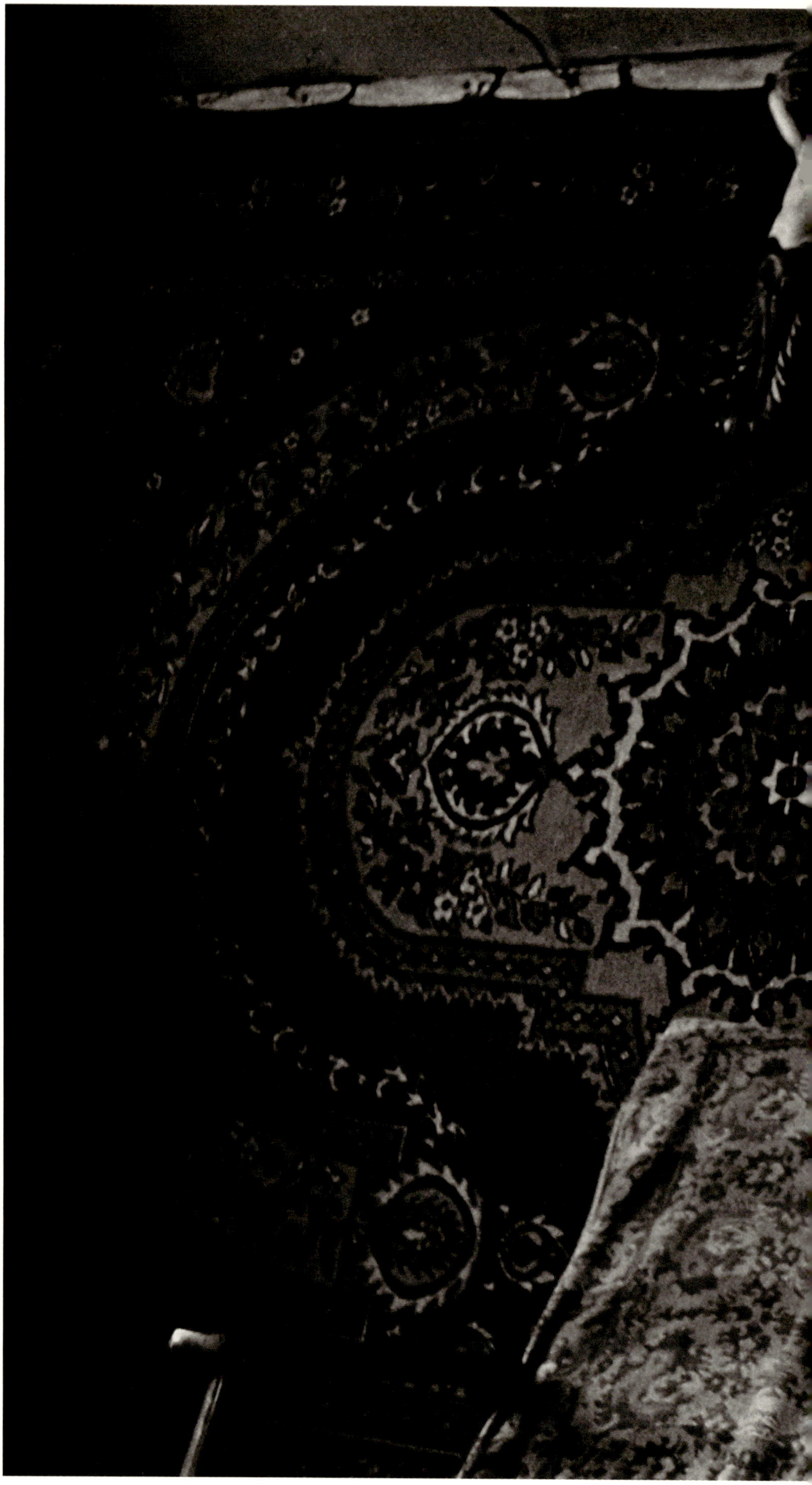

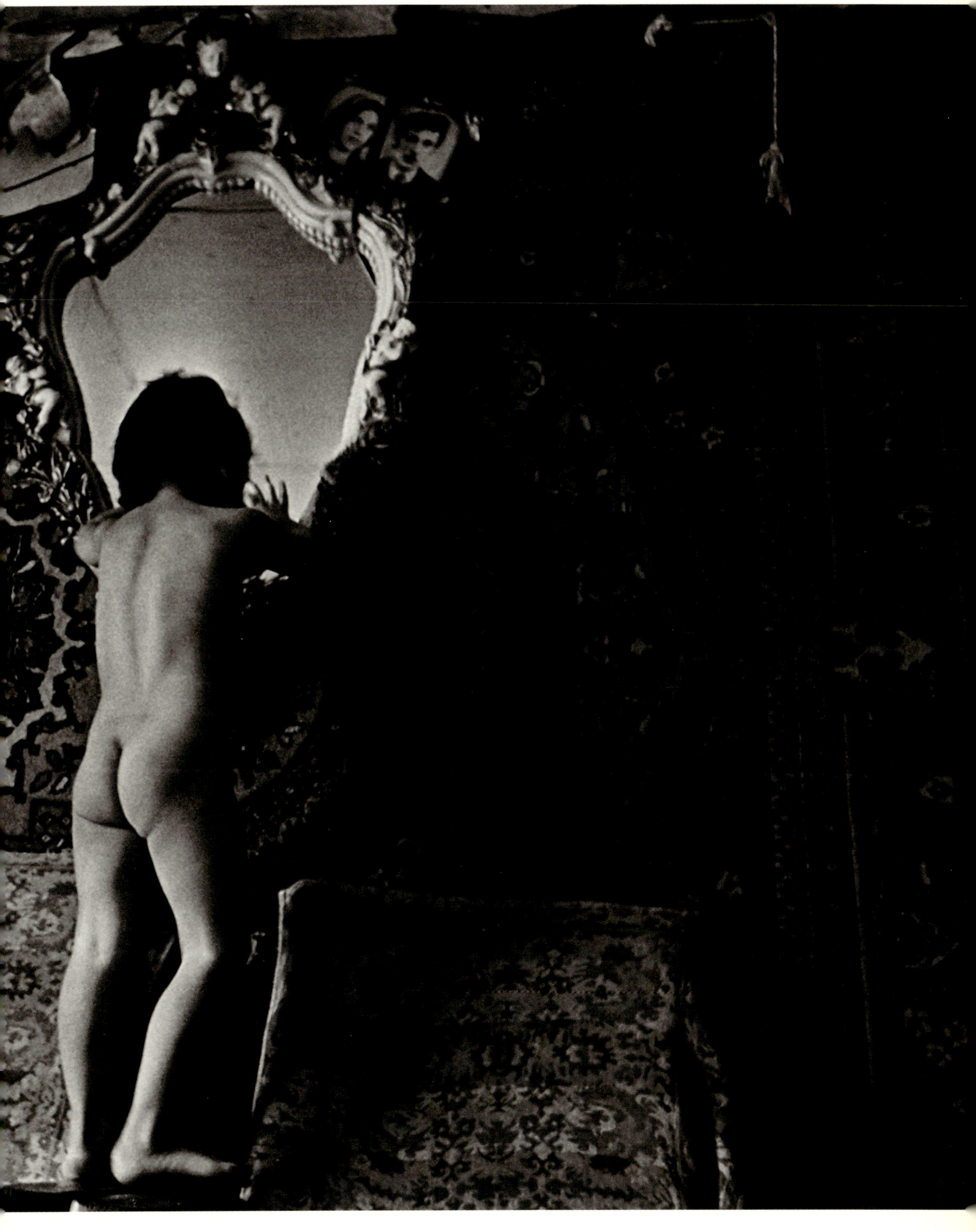

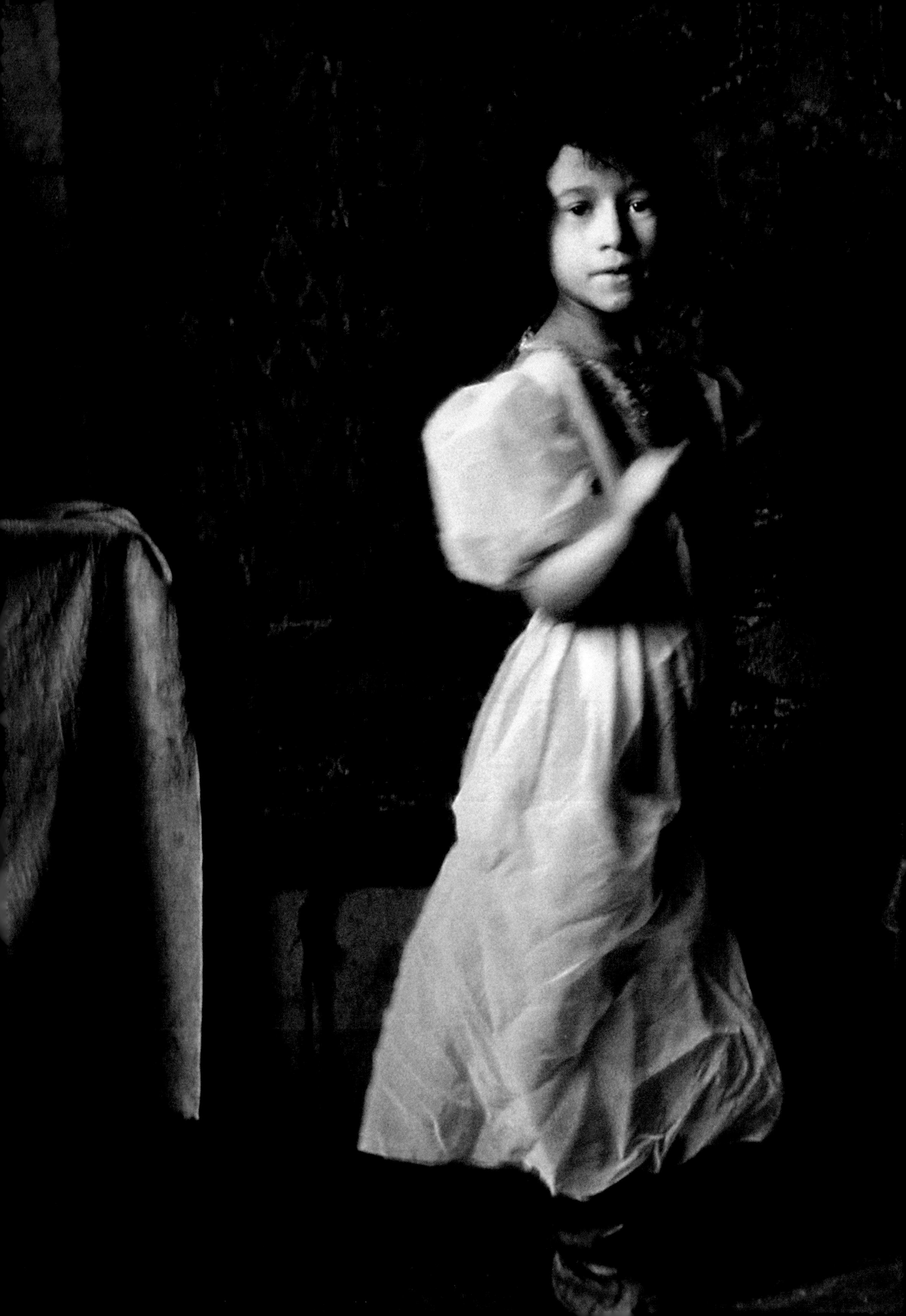

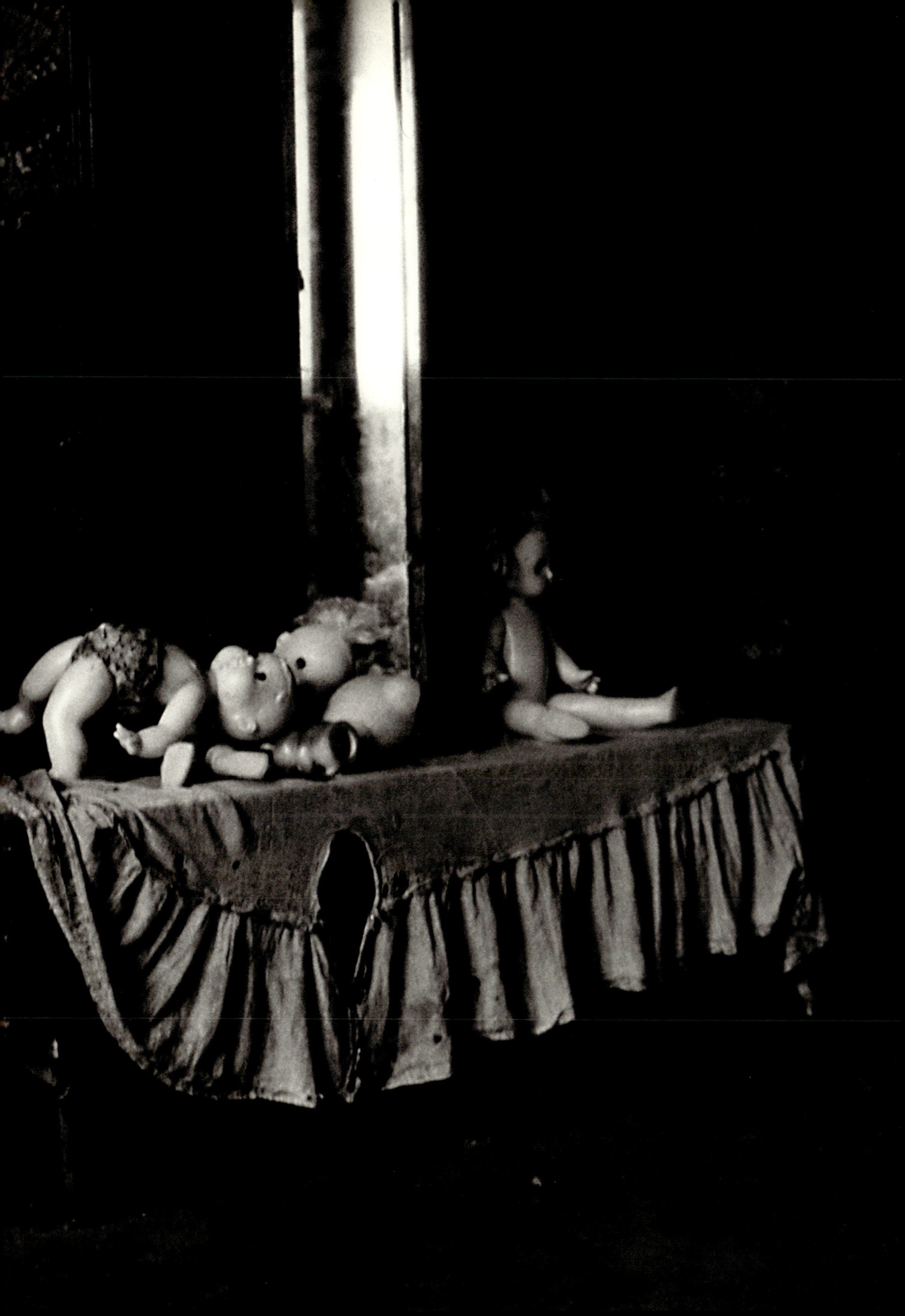

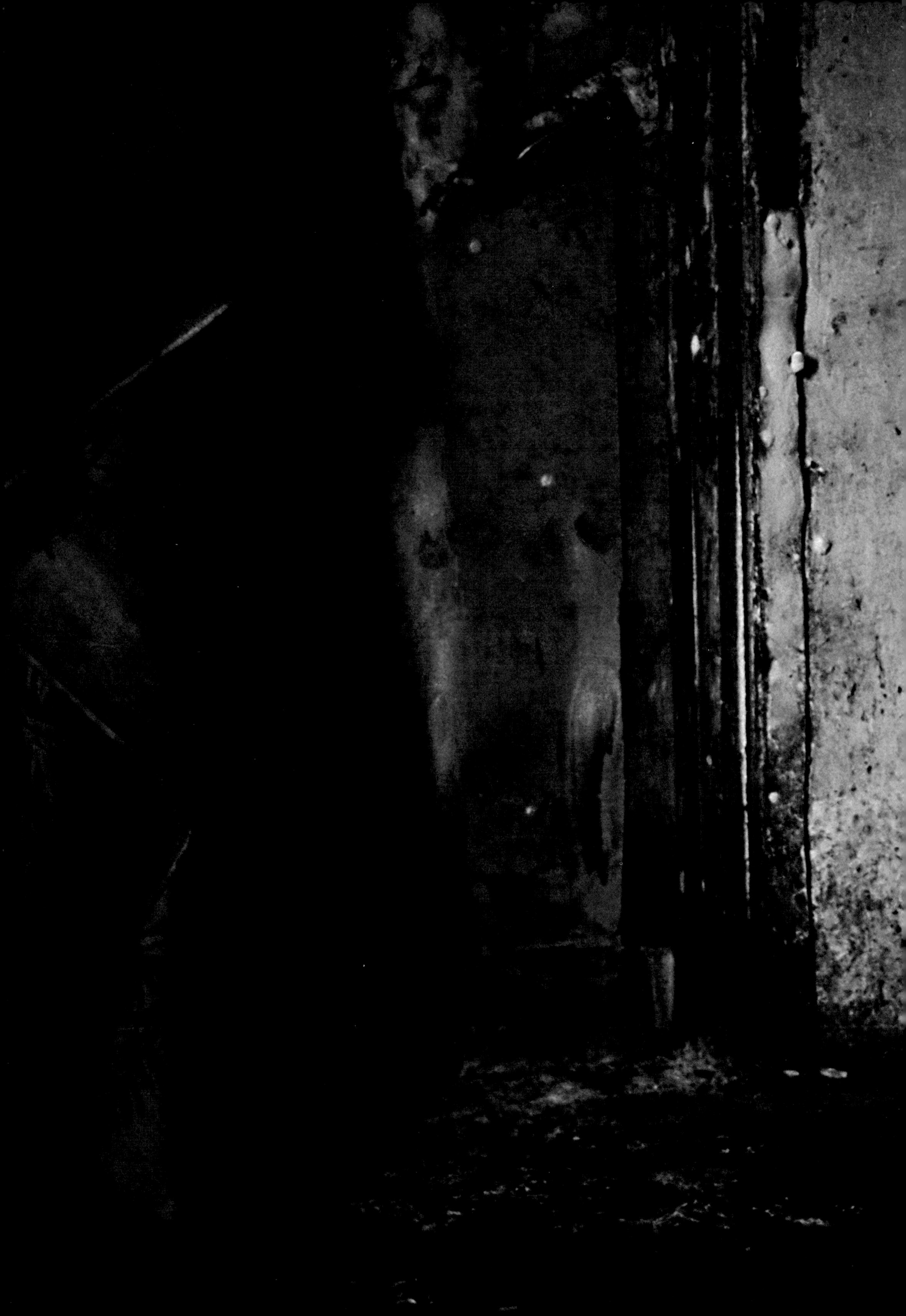

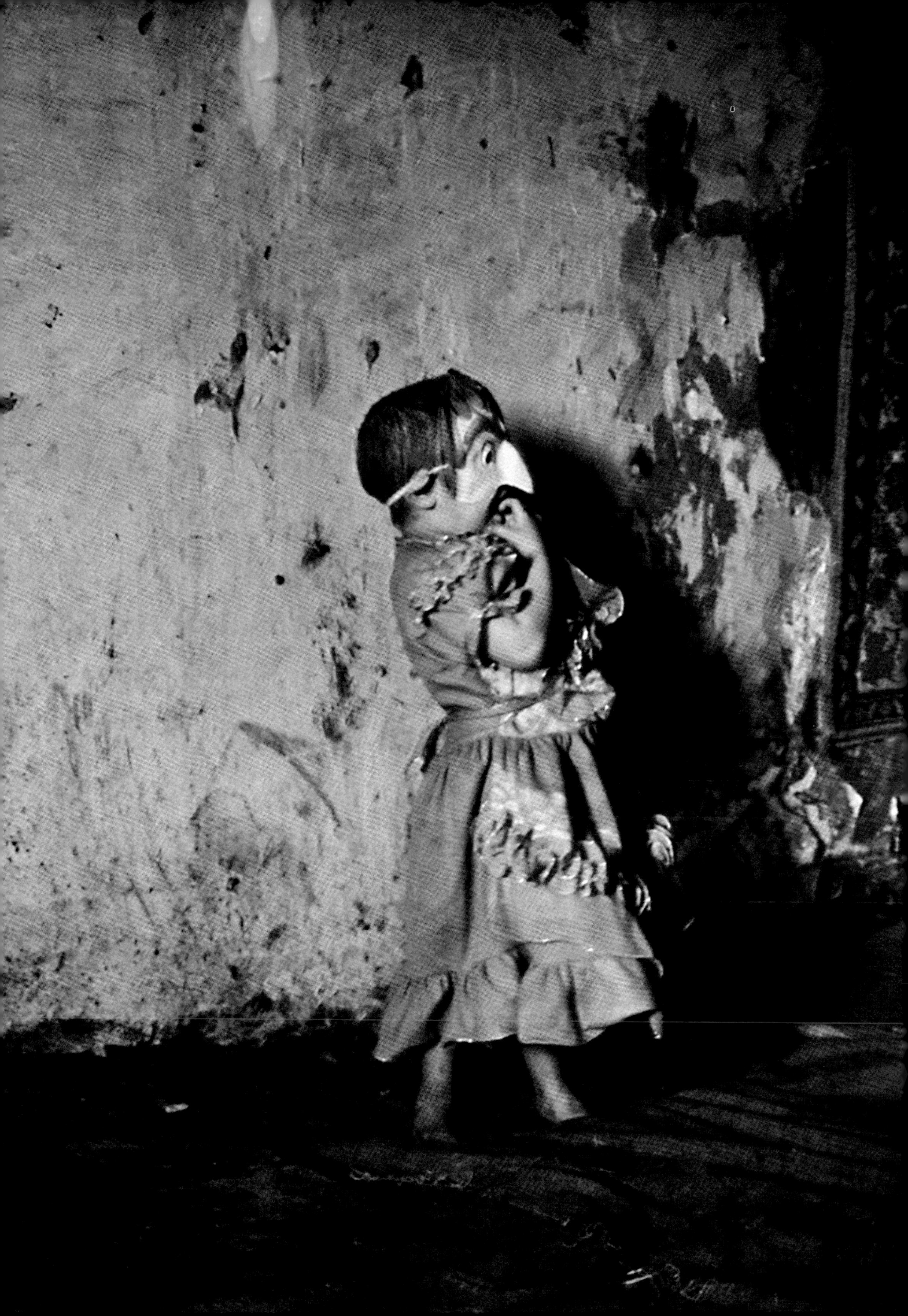

УЗБЕКИСТАН

Uzbekistan Ouzbékistan Usbekistan

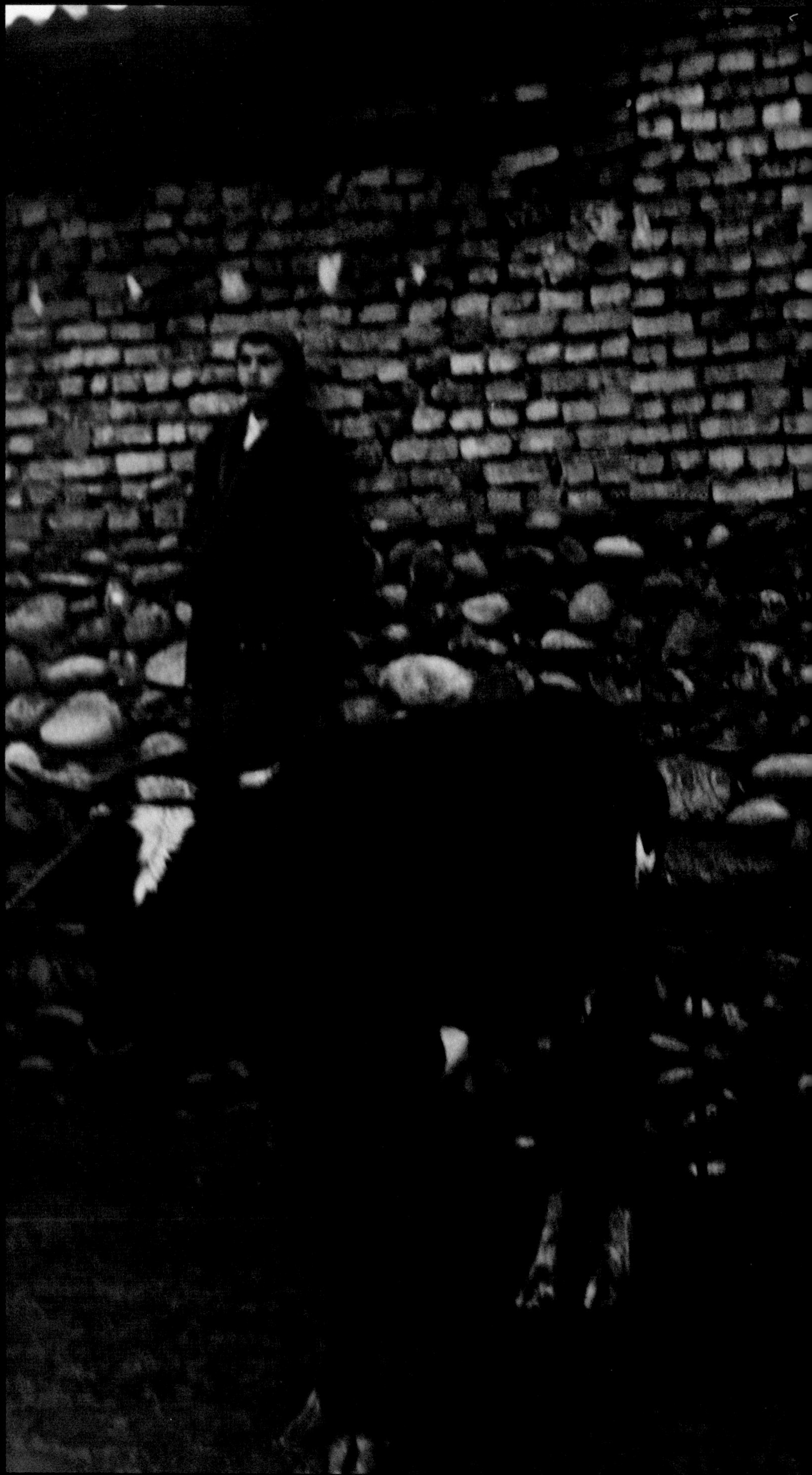

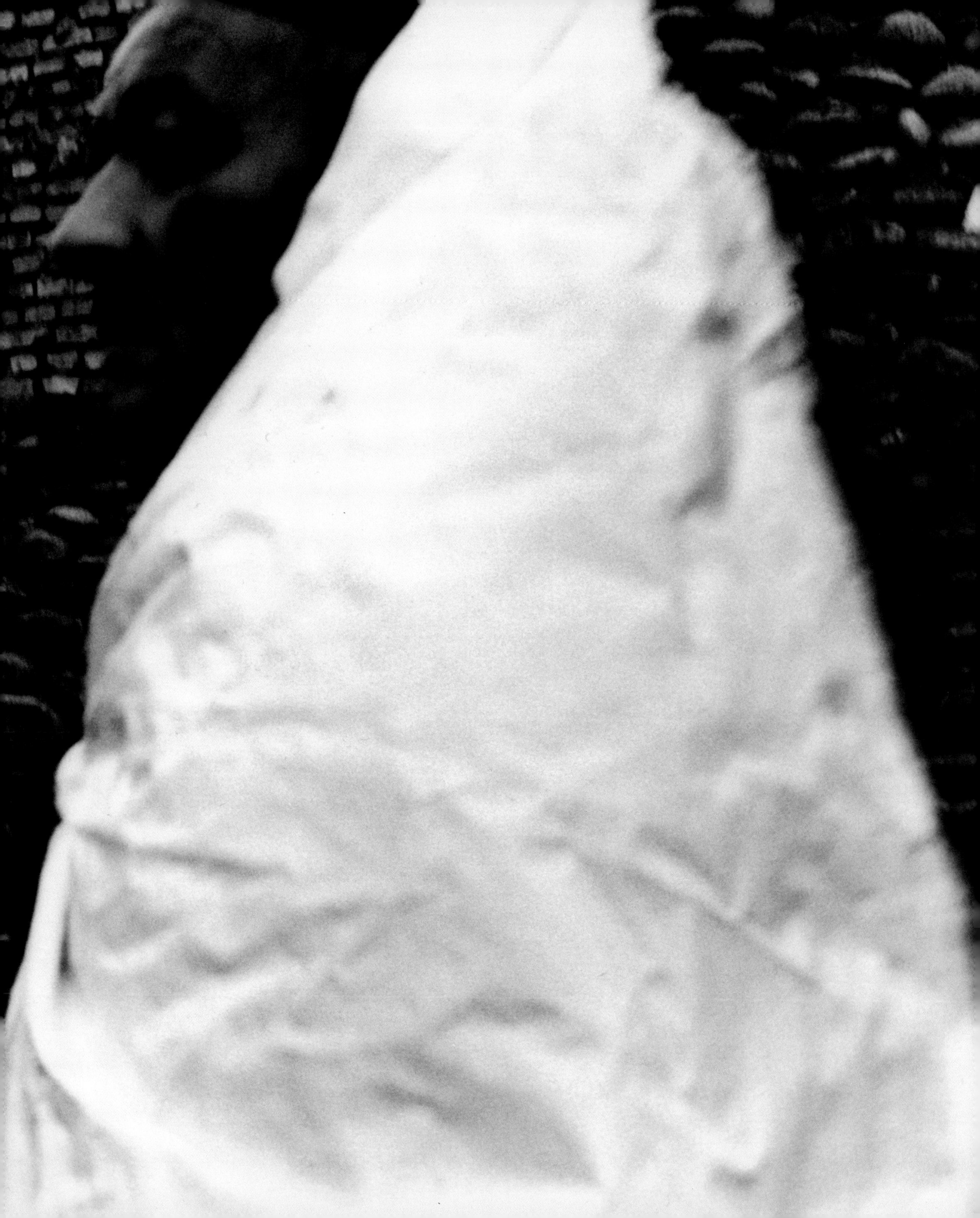

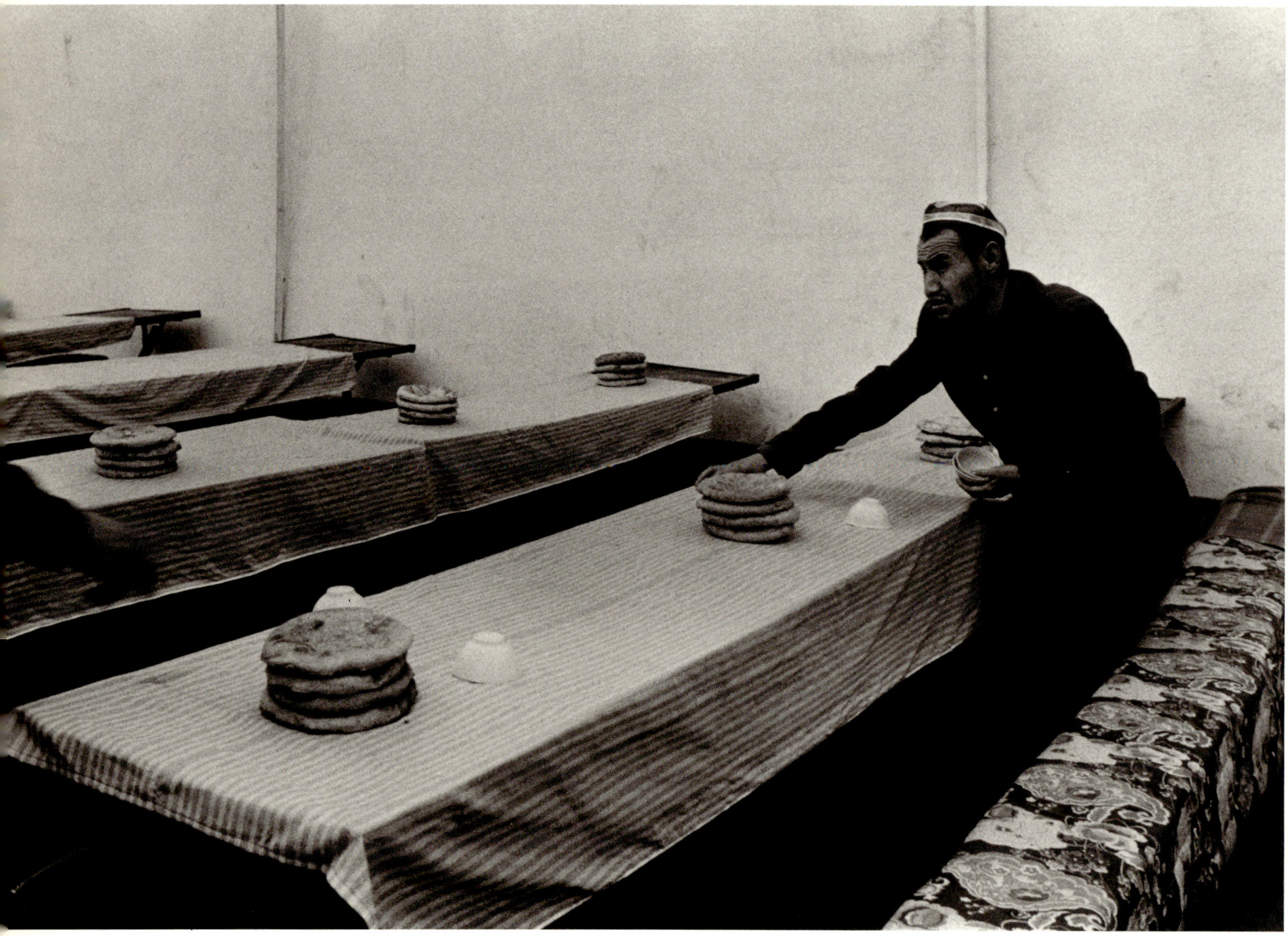

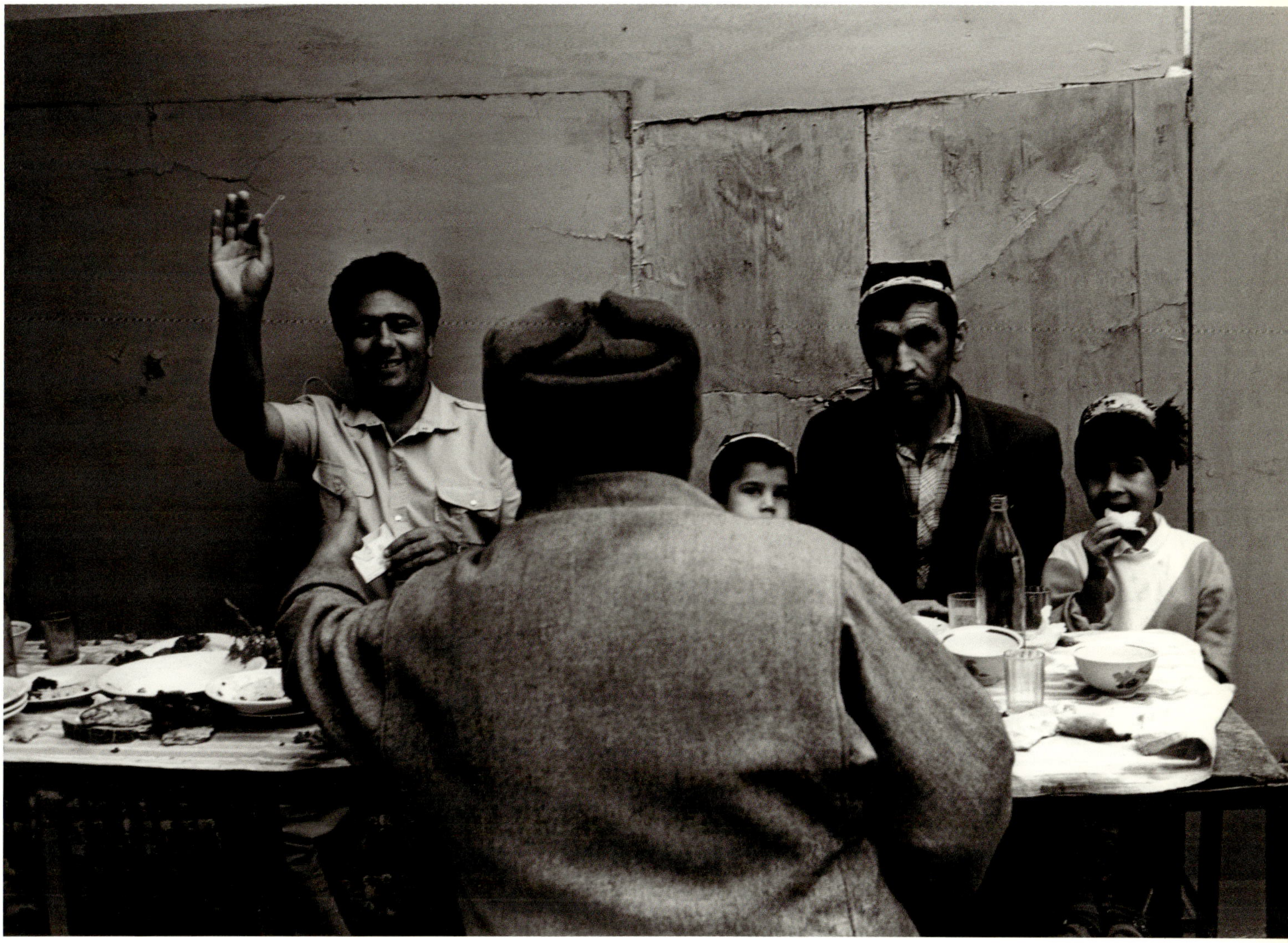

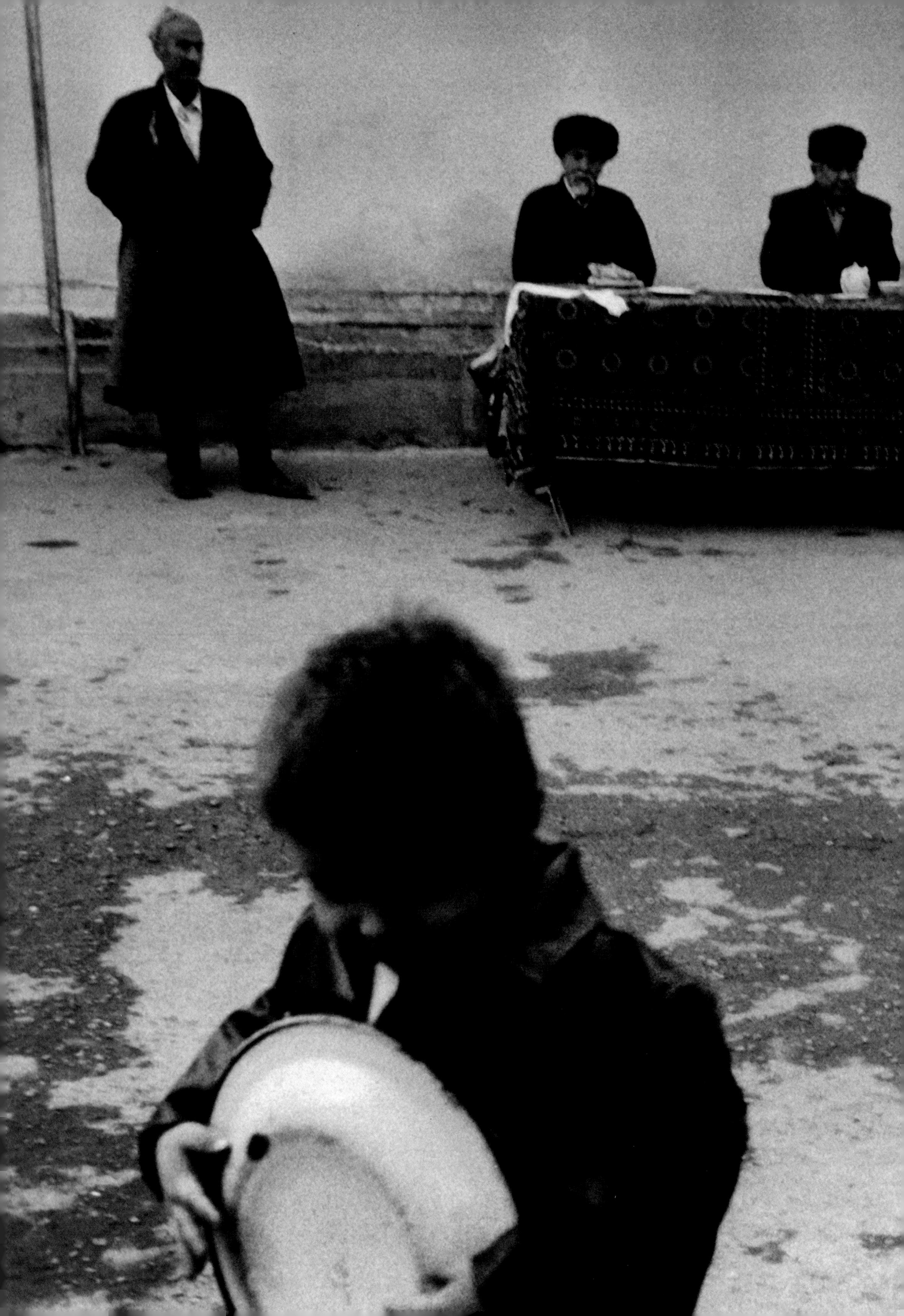

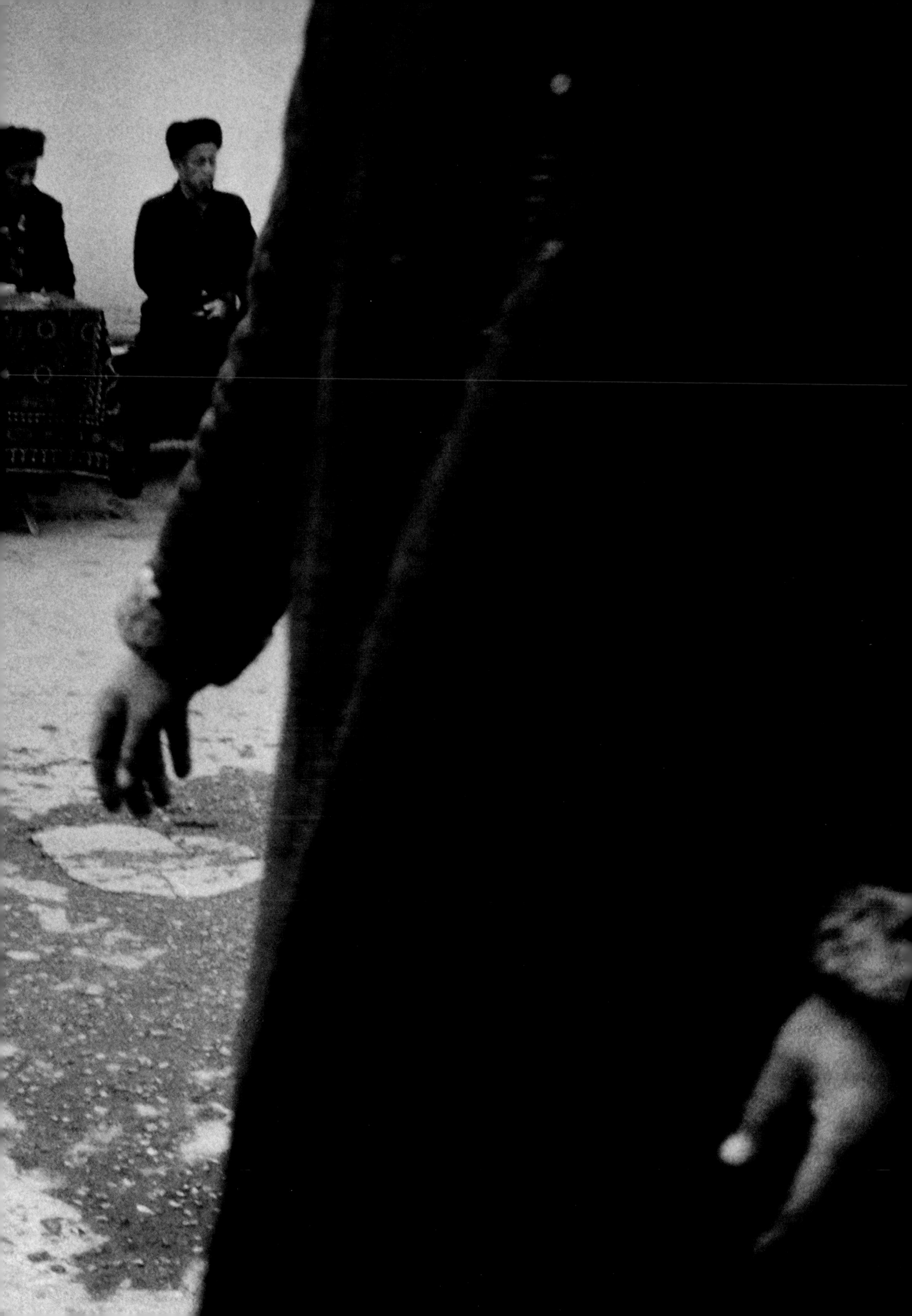

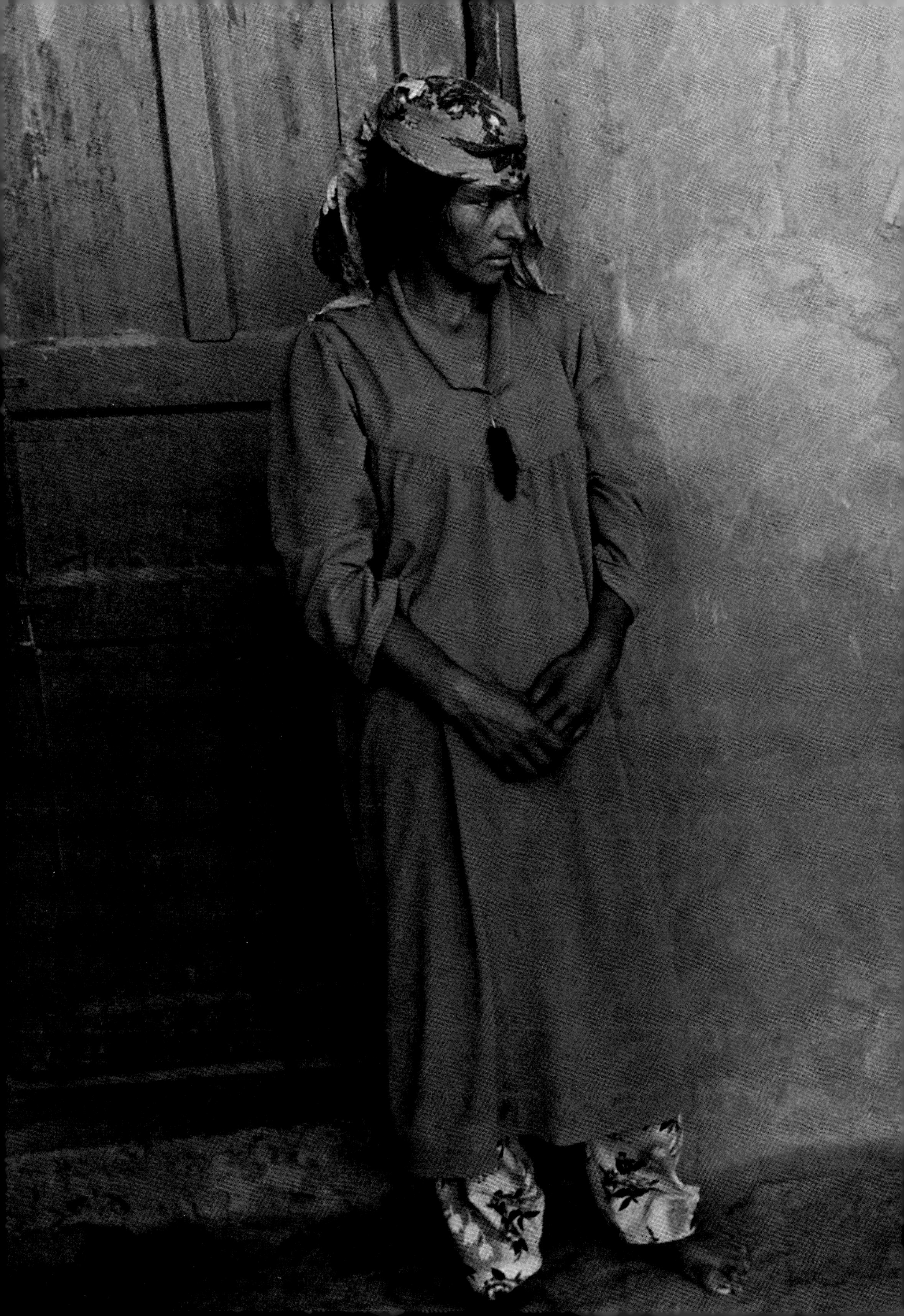

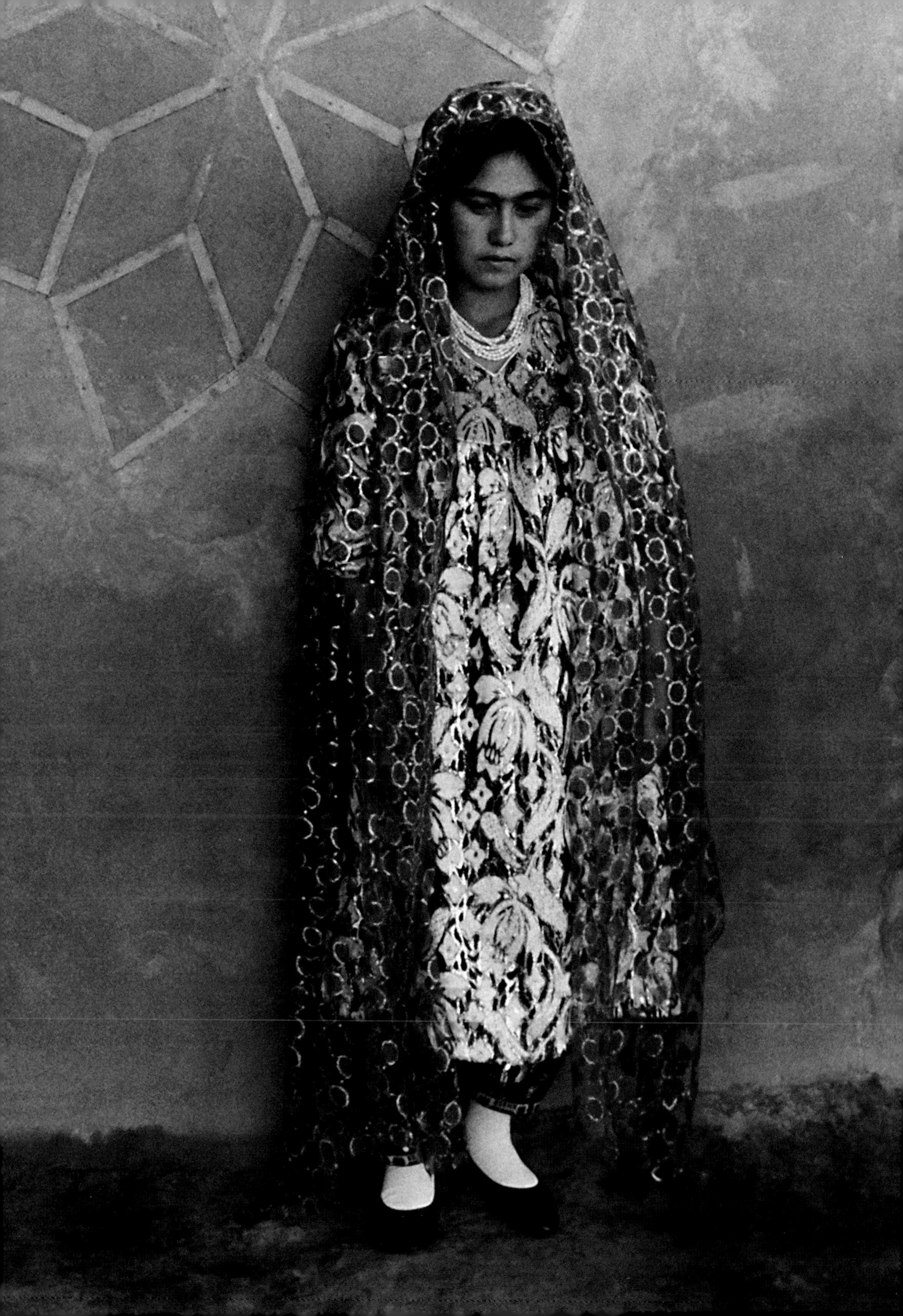

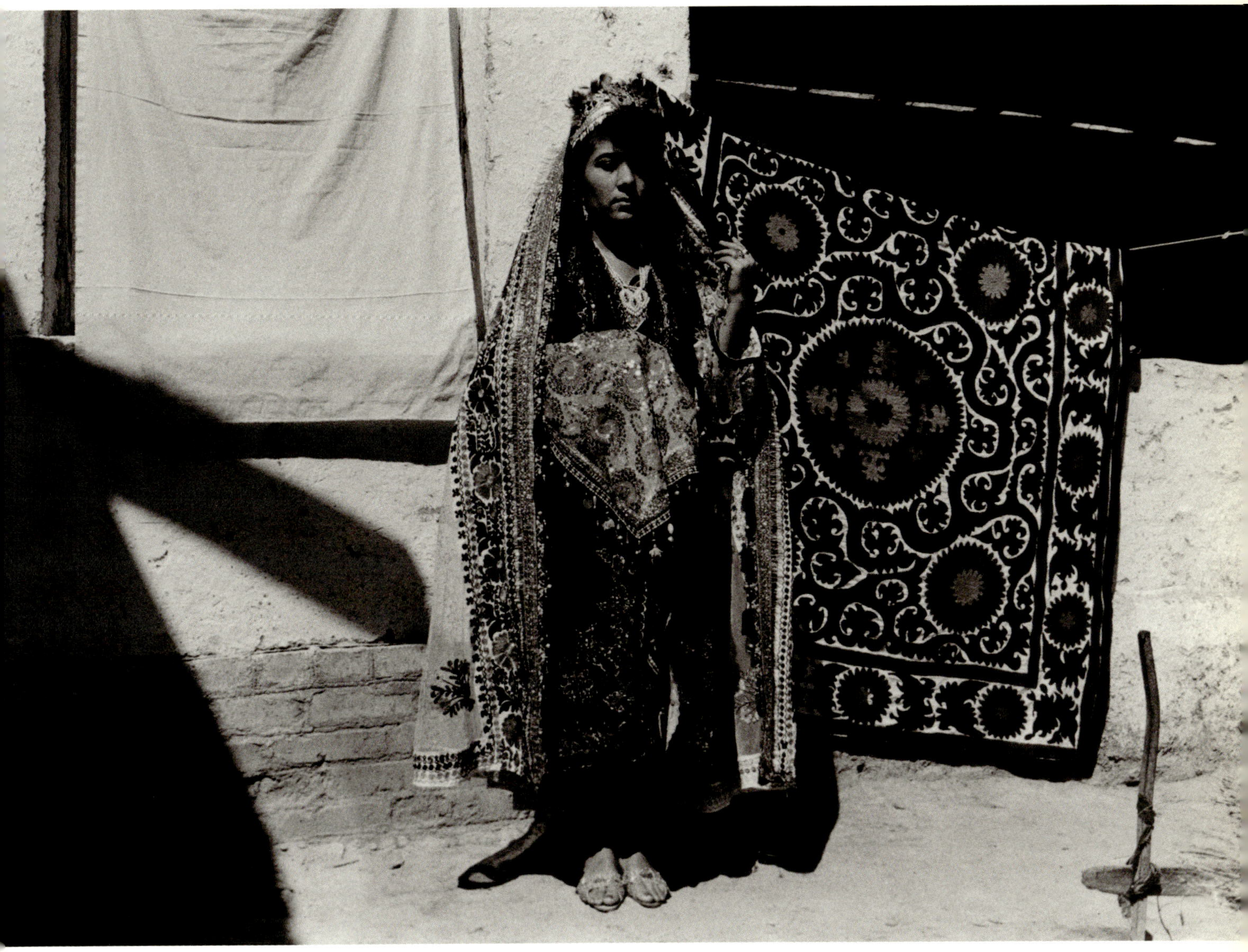

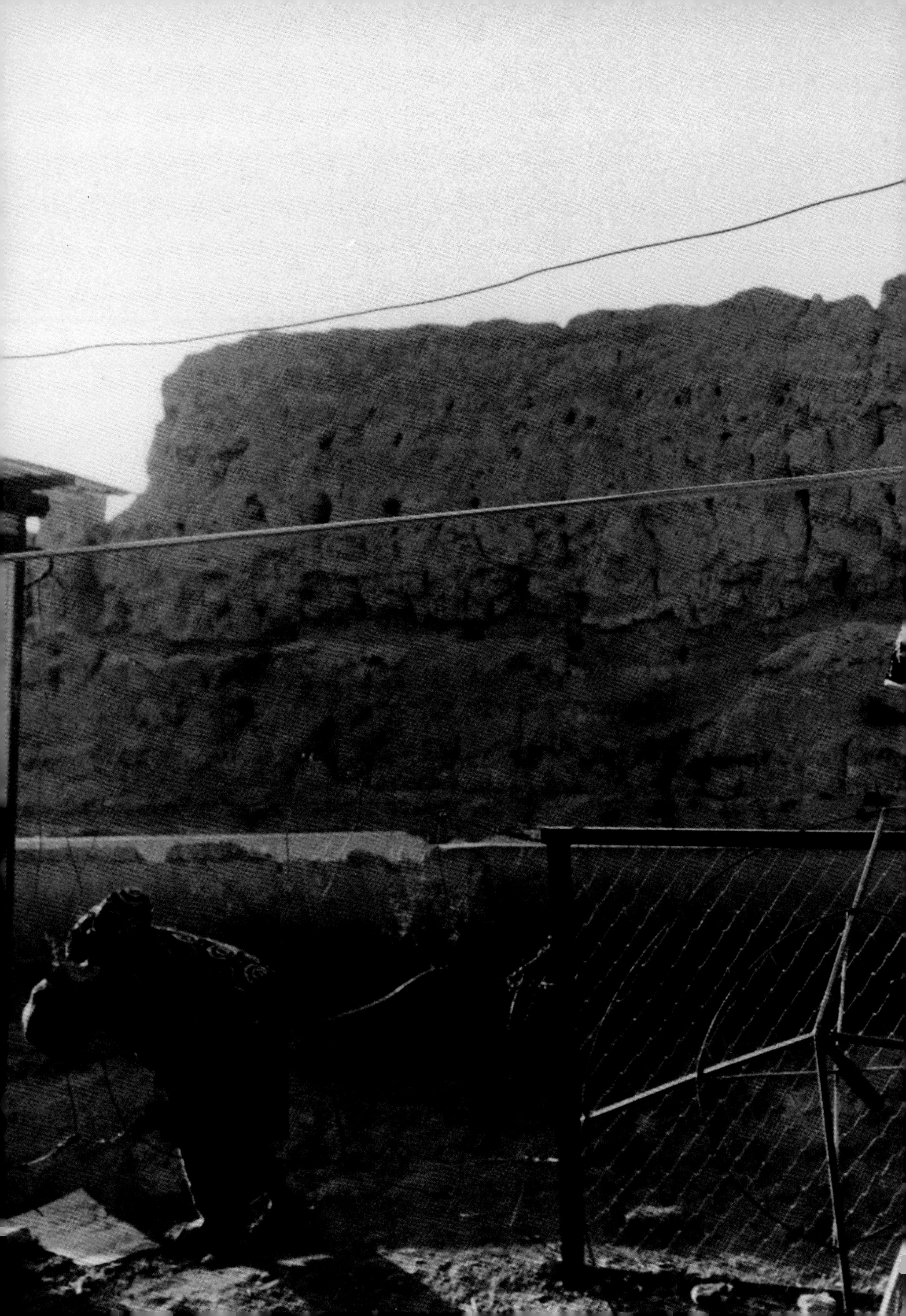

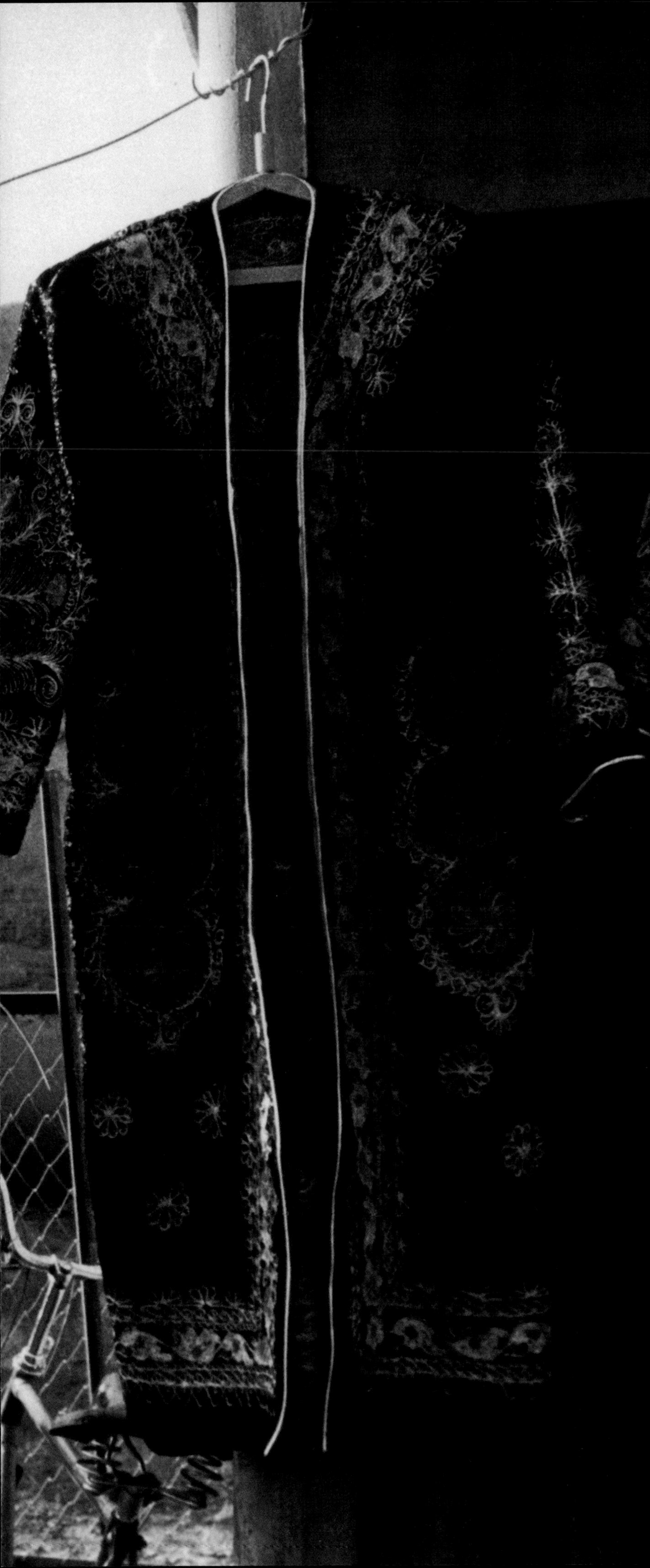

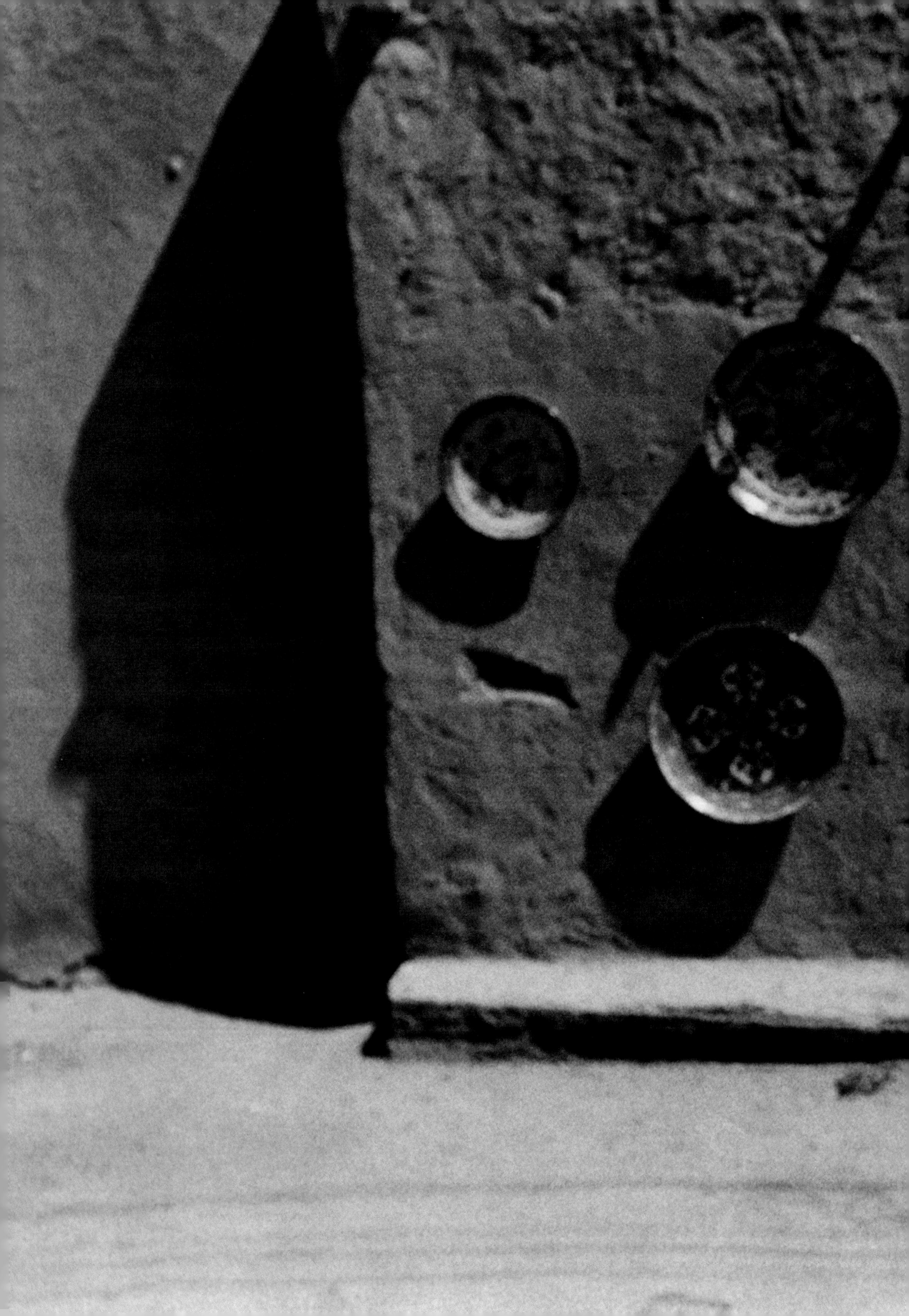

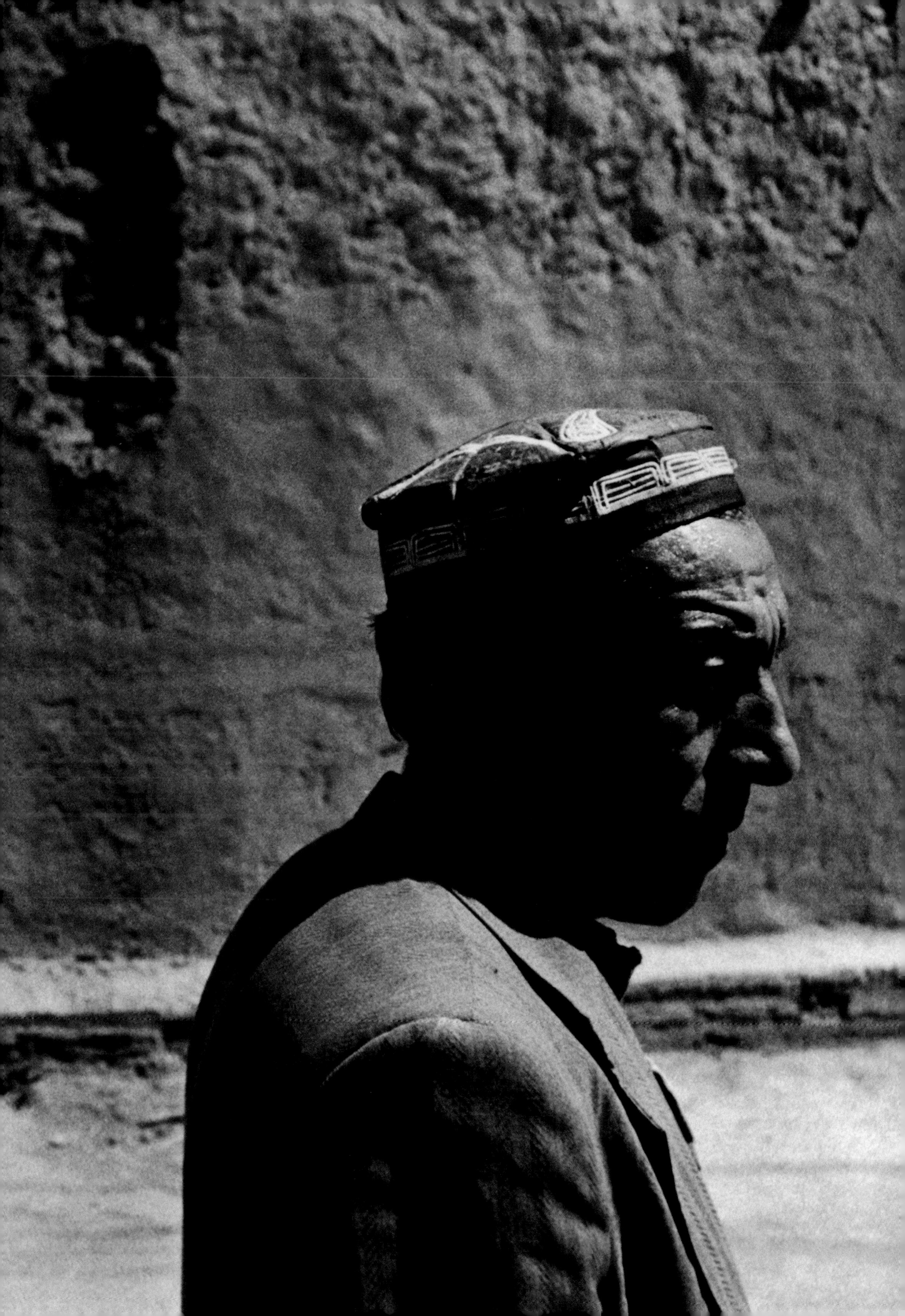

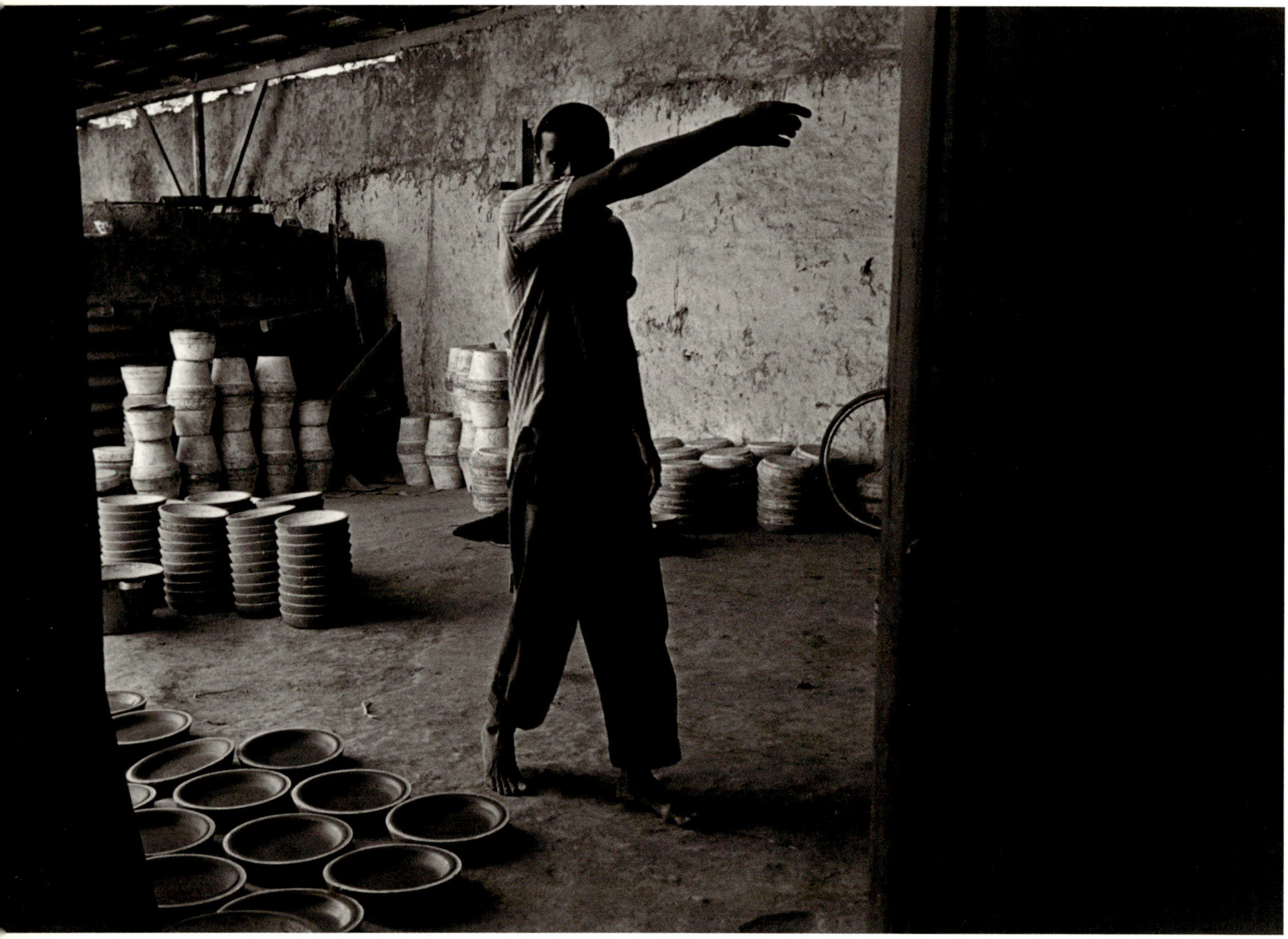

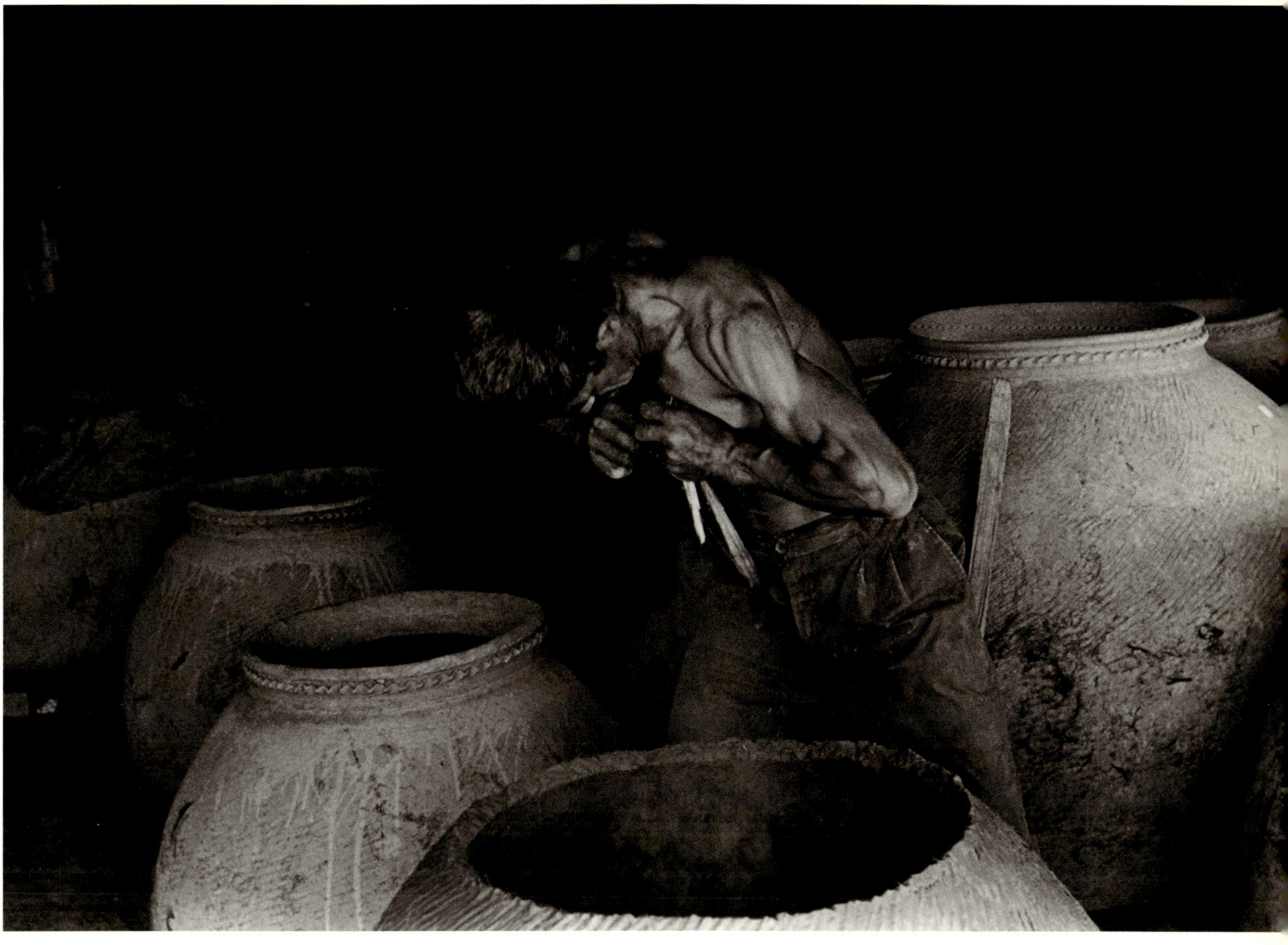

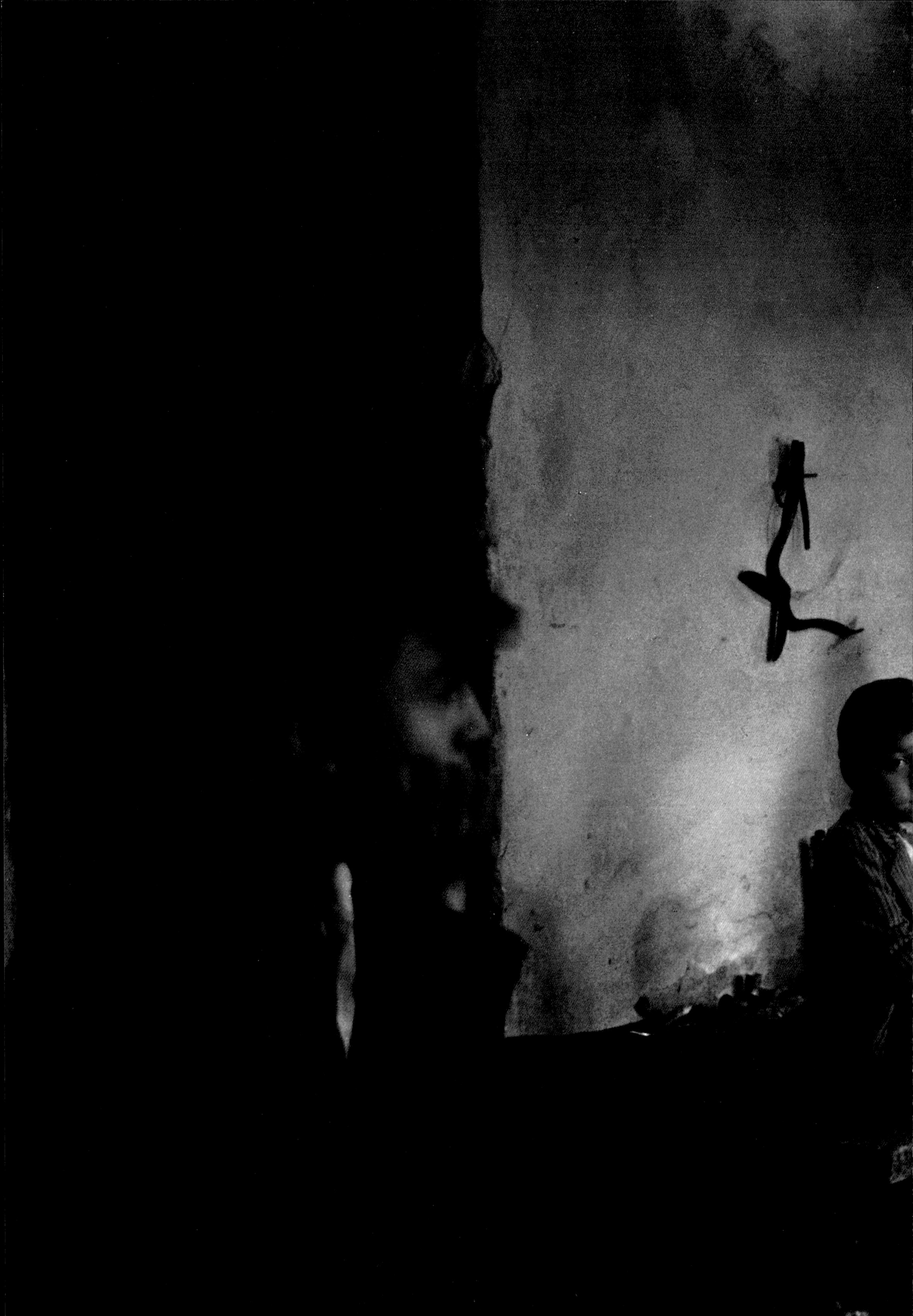

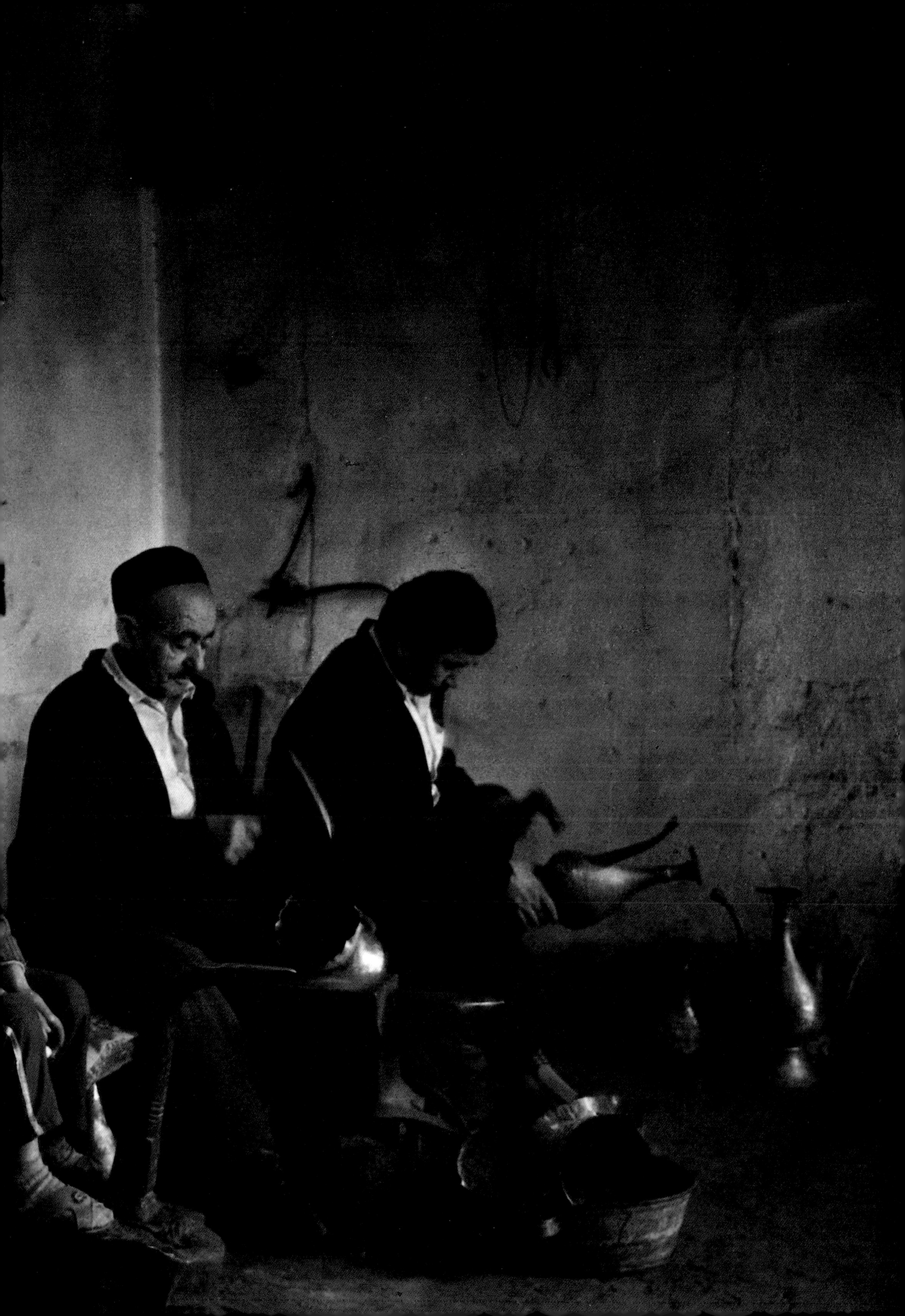

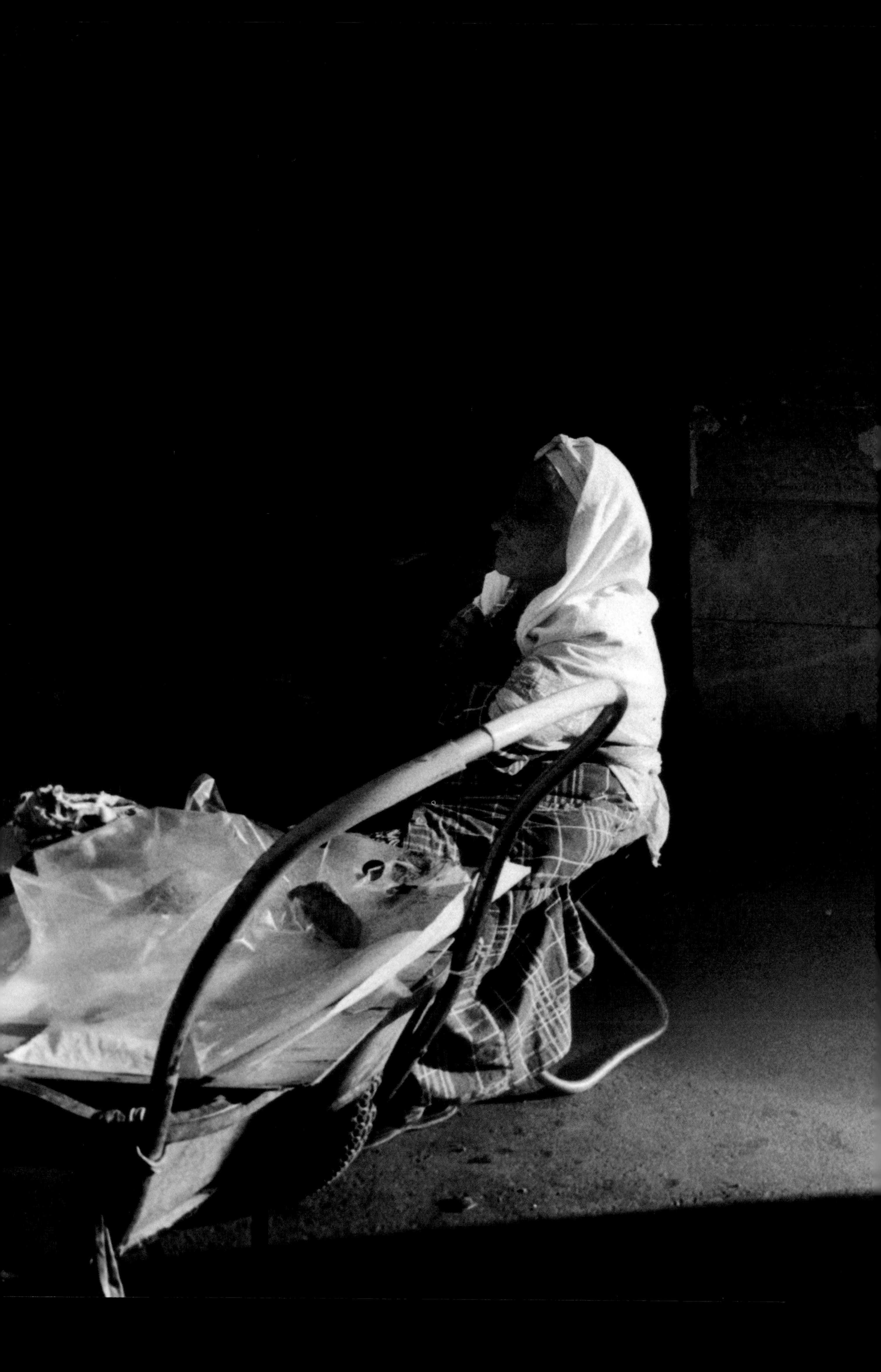

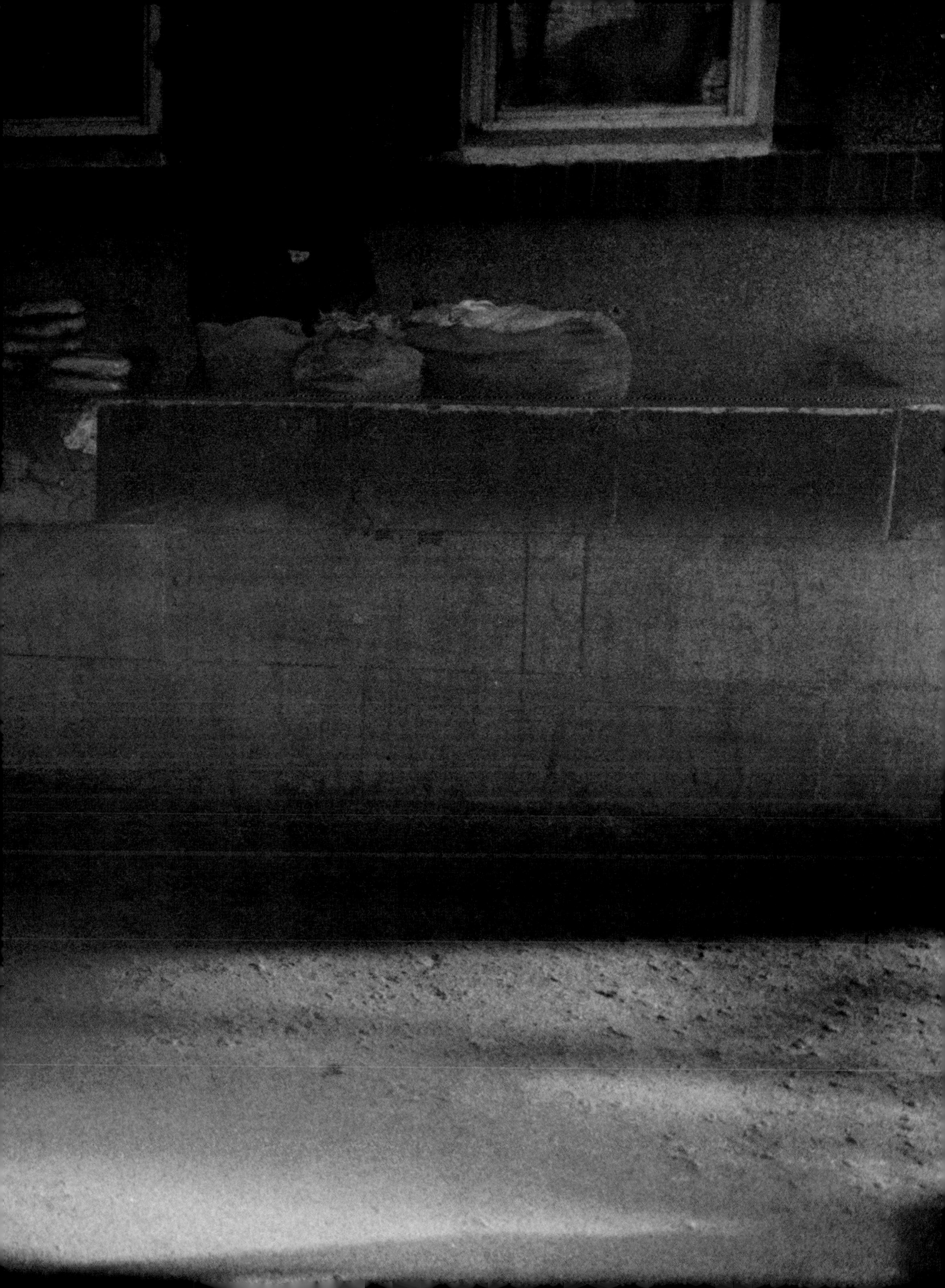

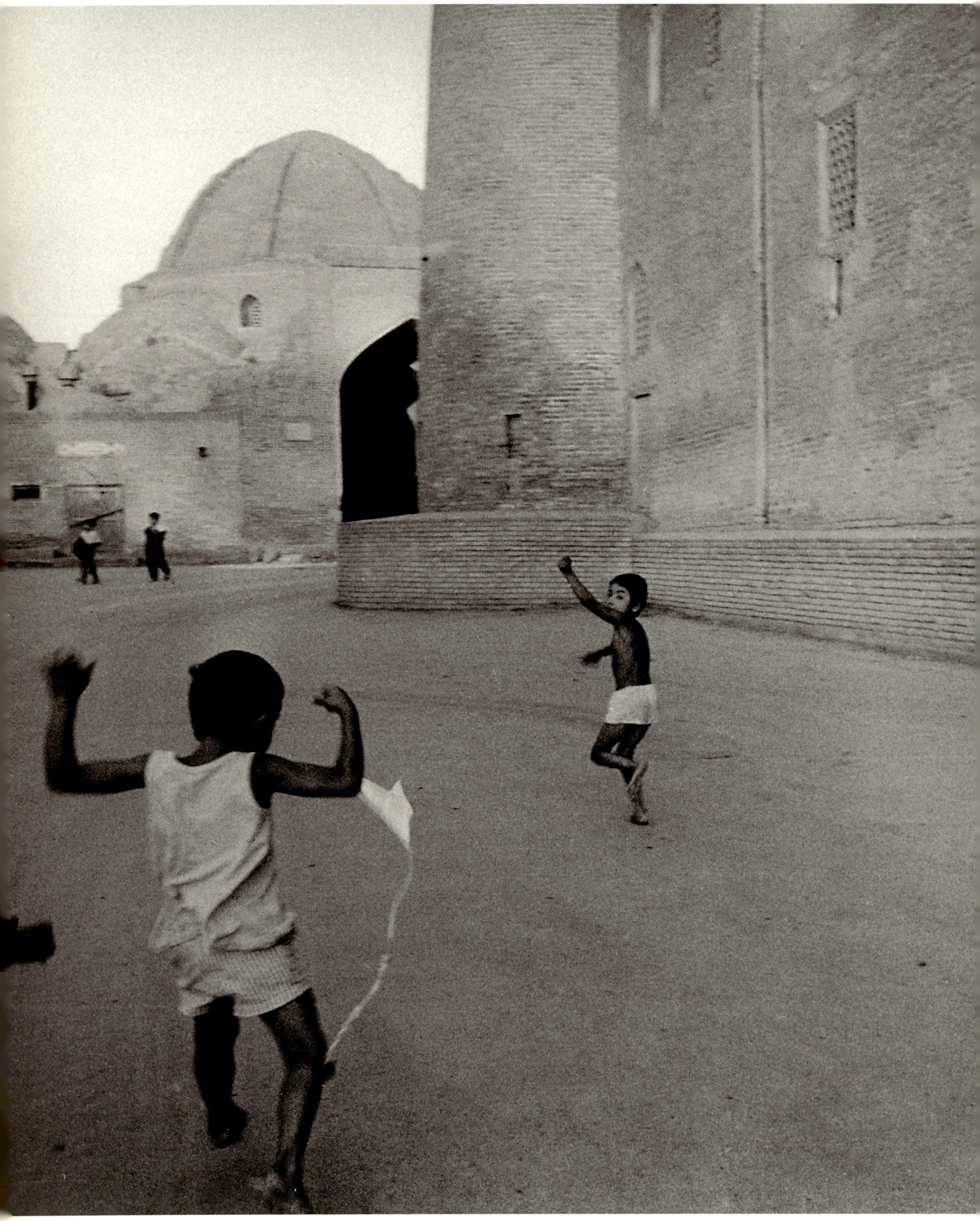

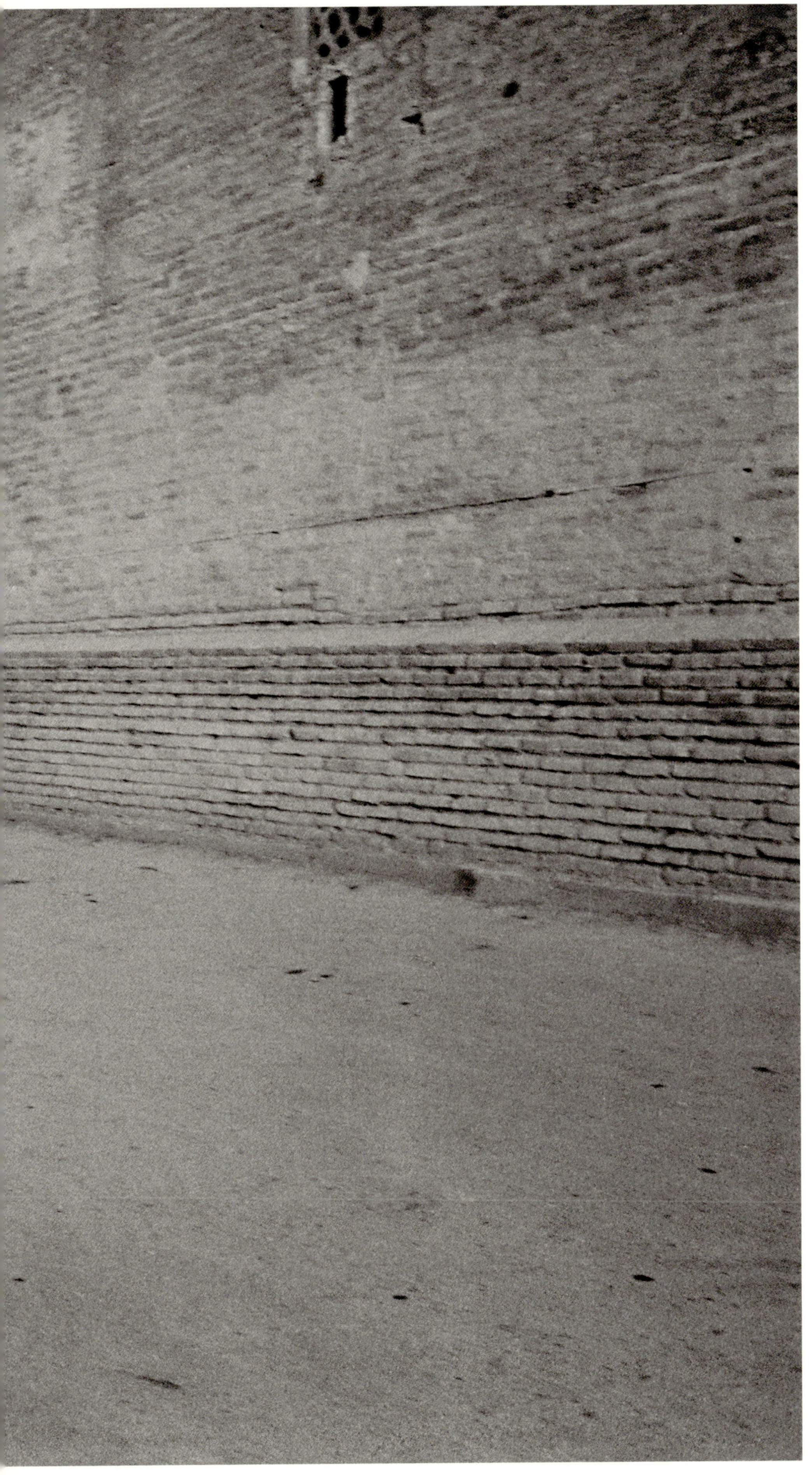

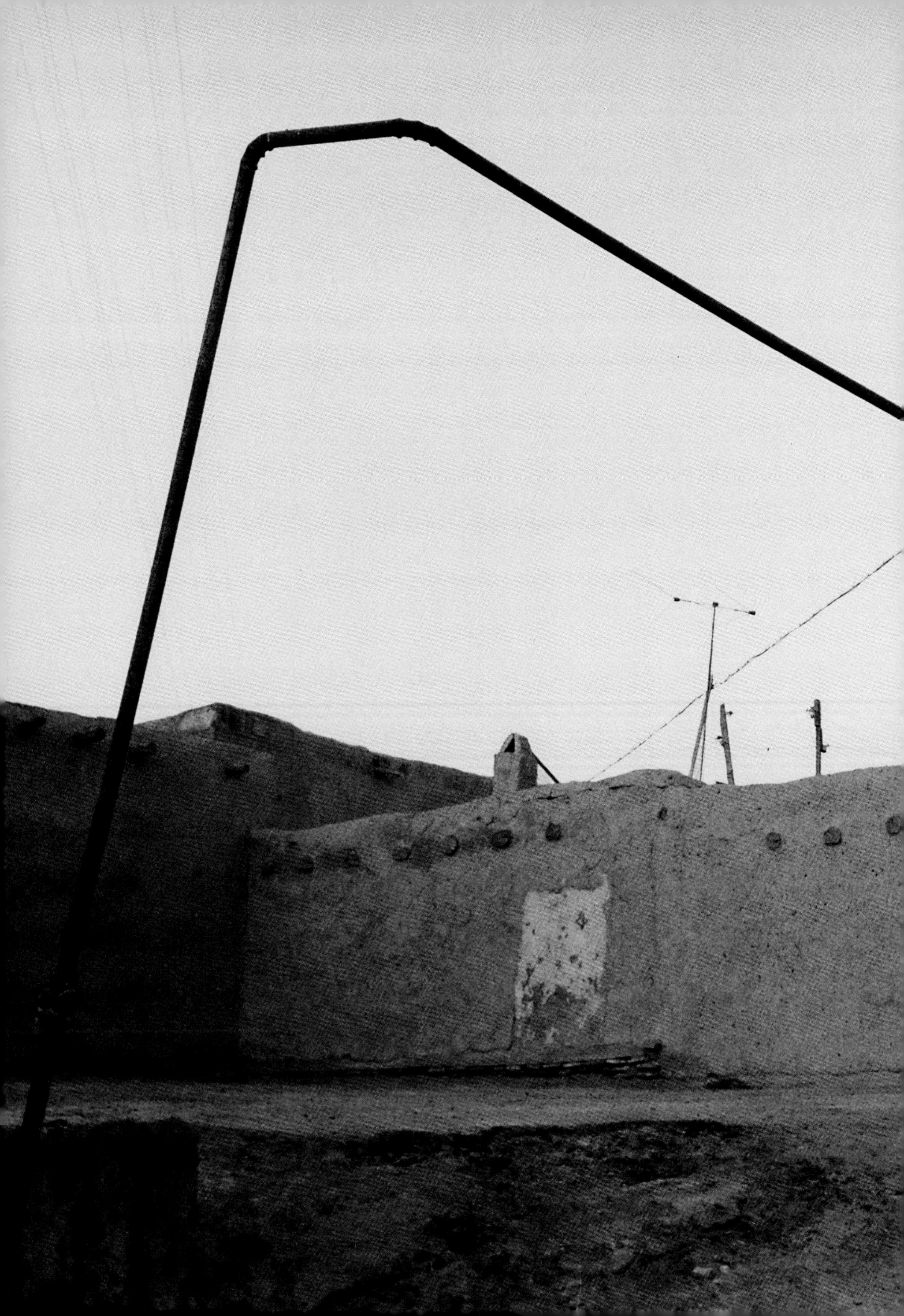

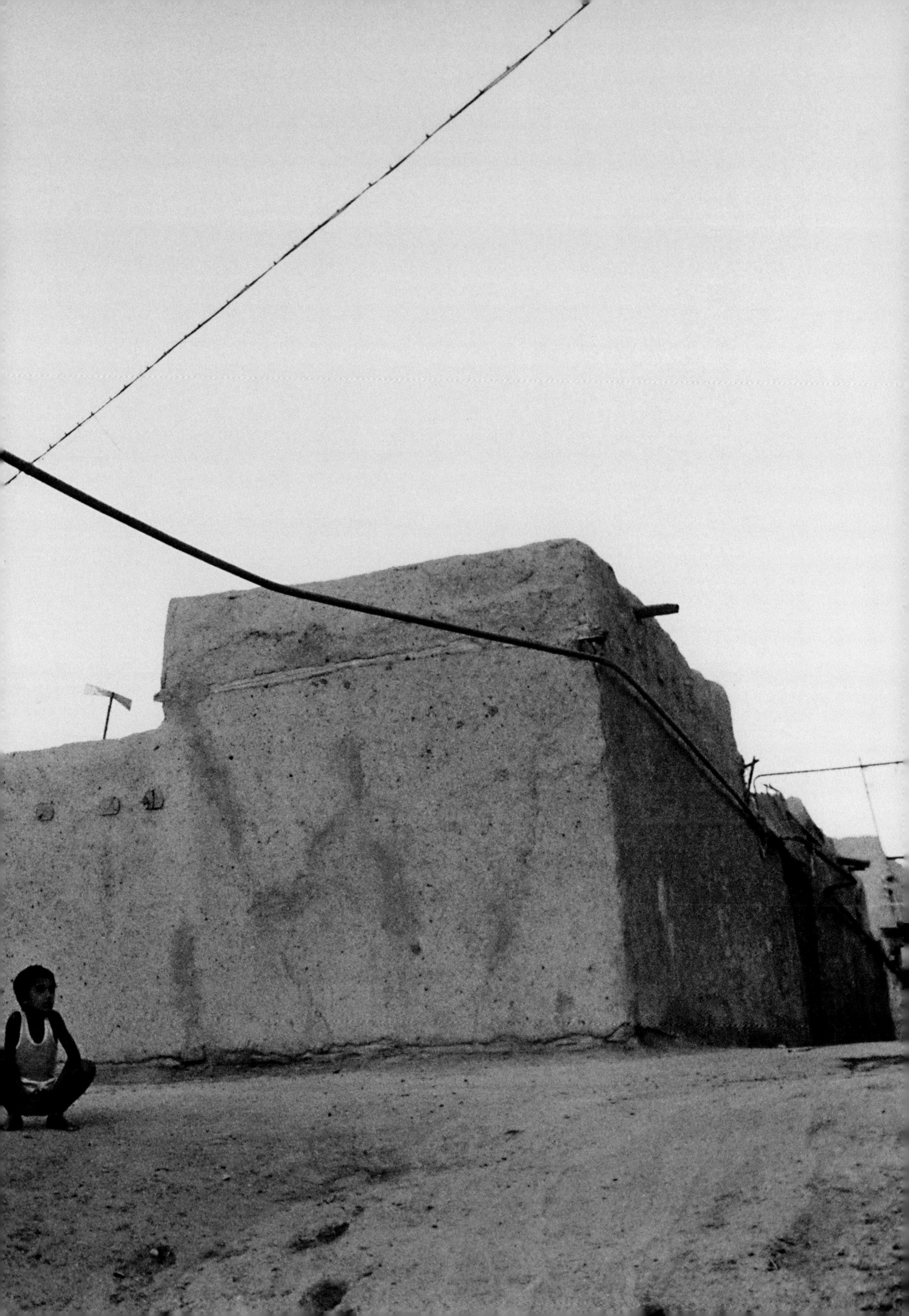

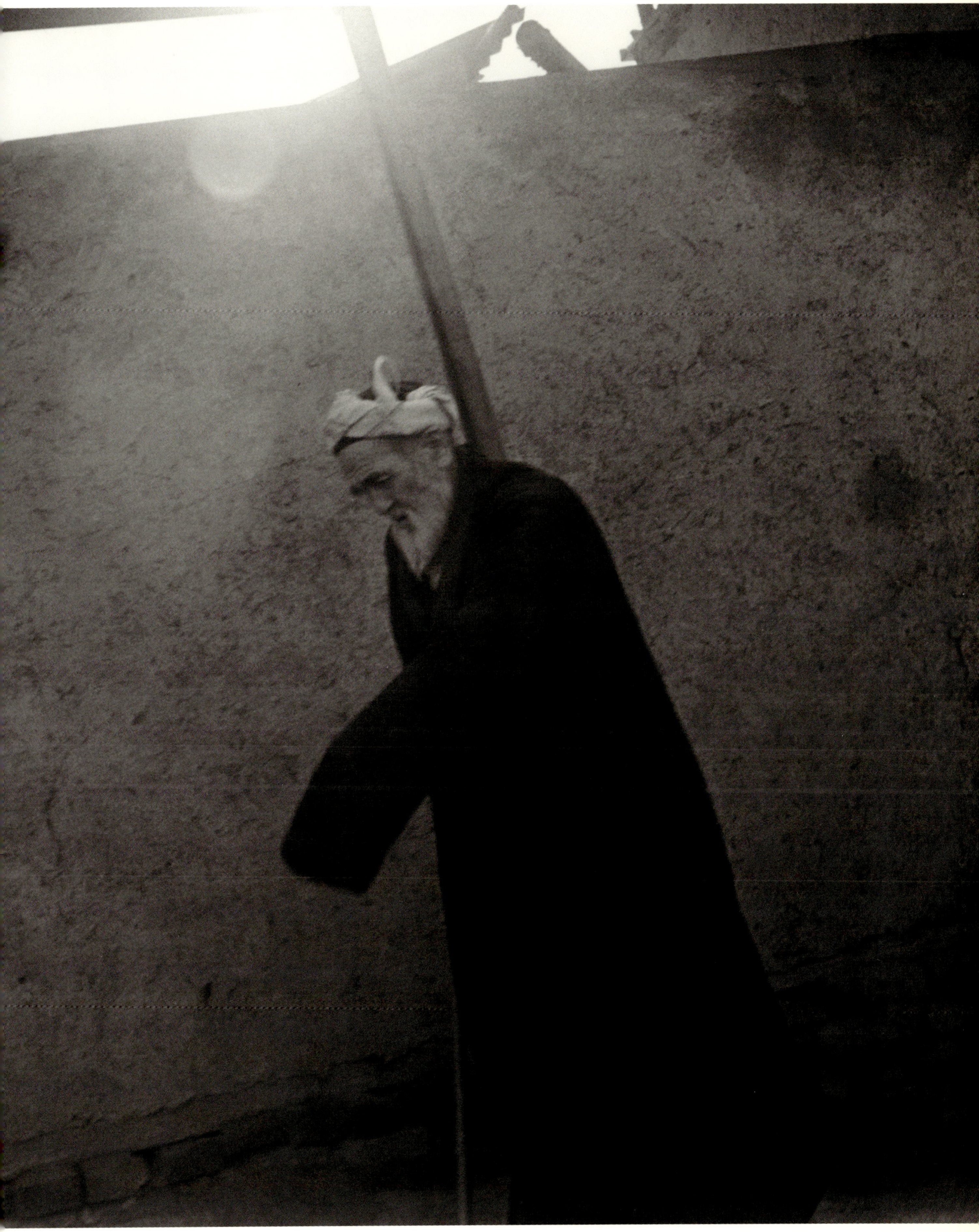

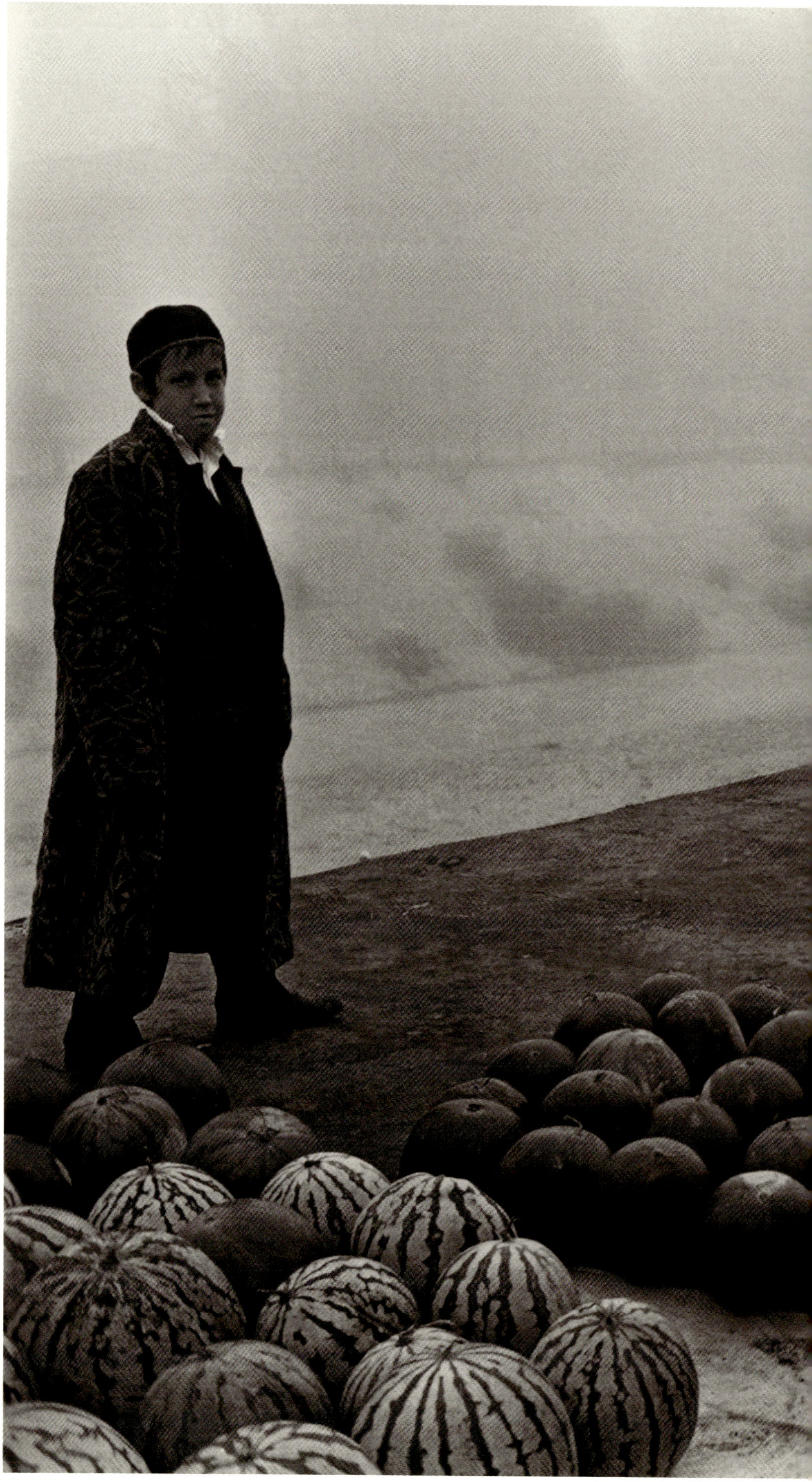

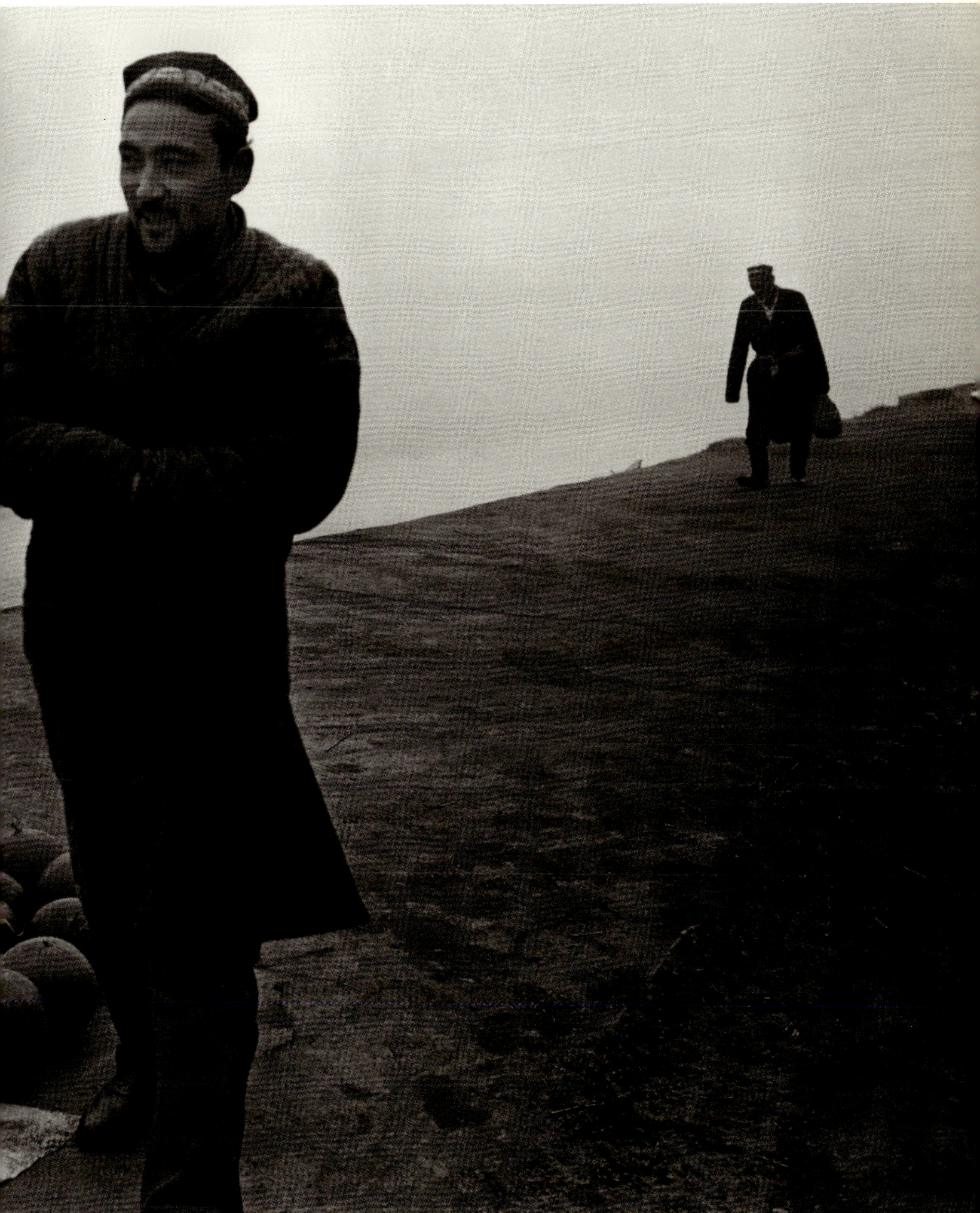

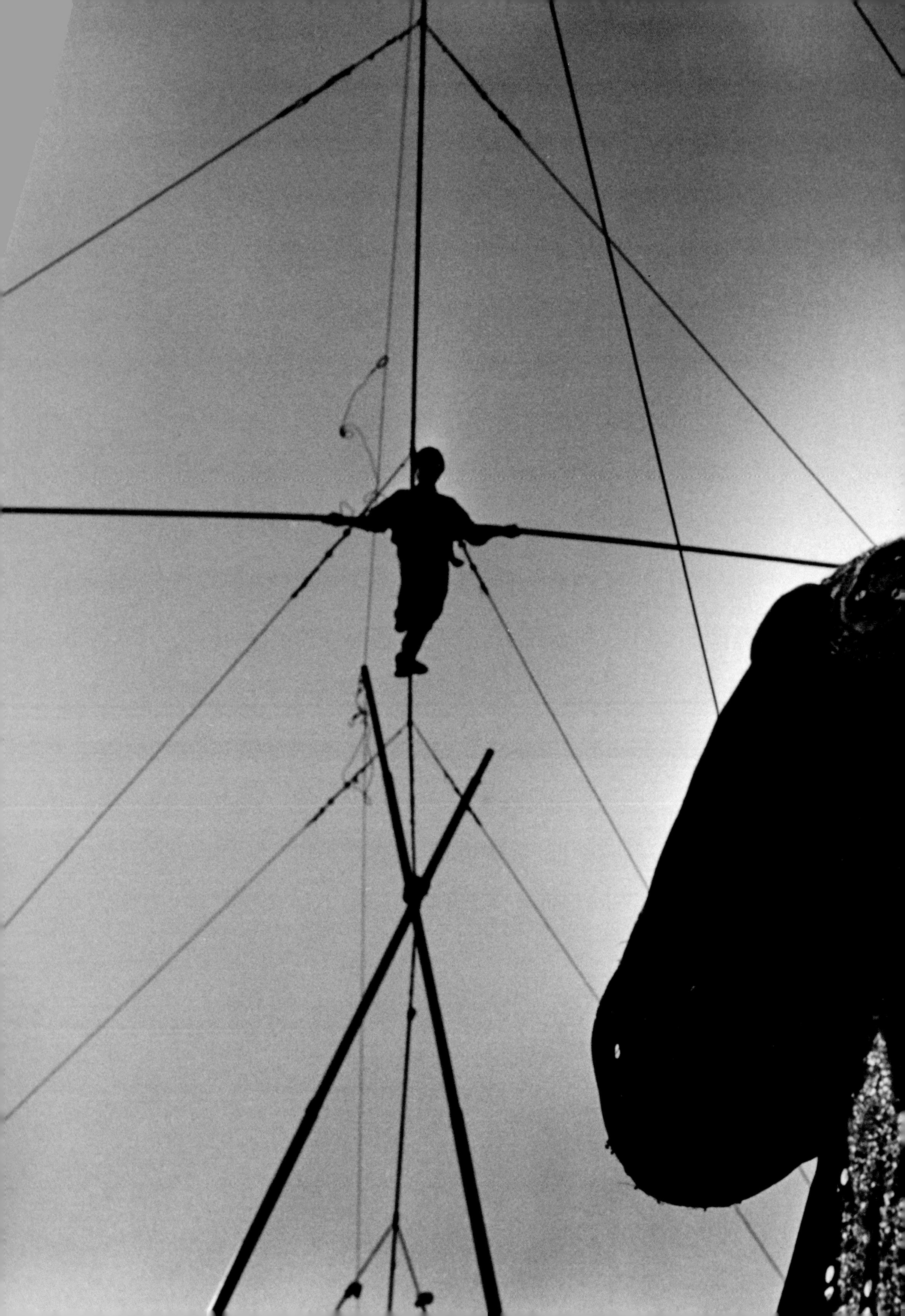

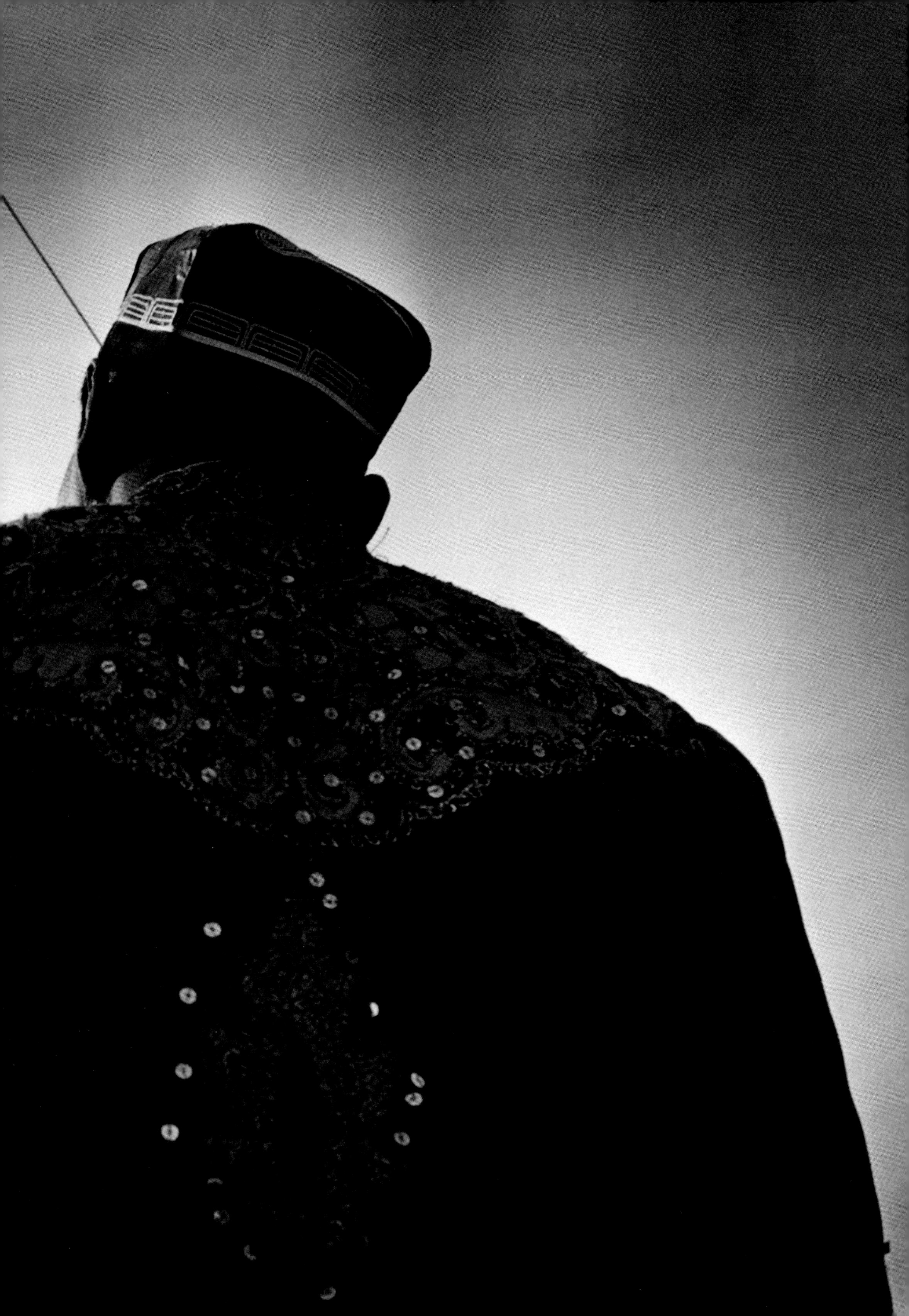

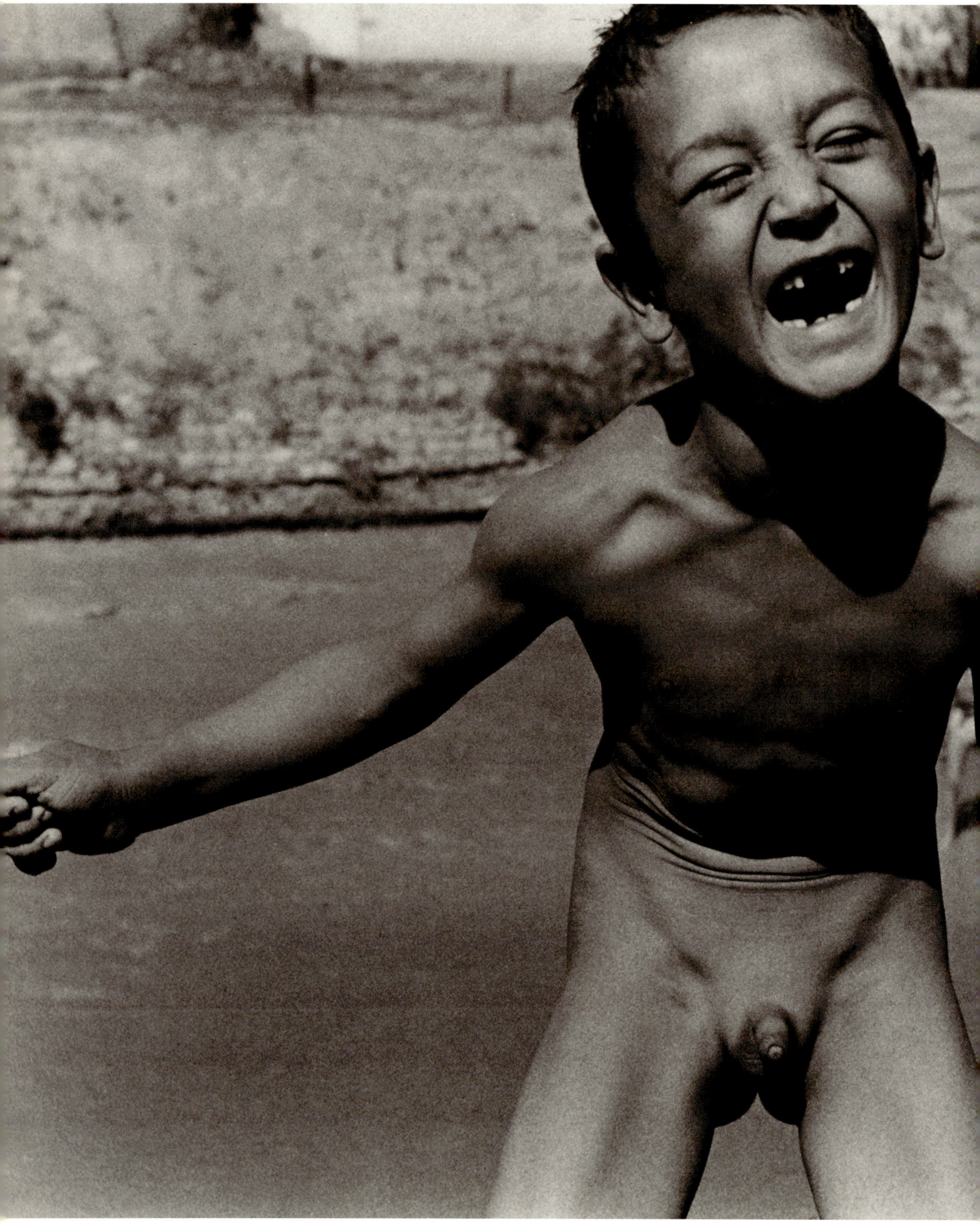

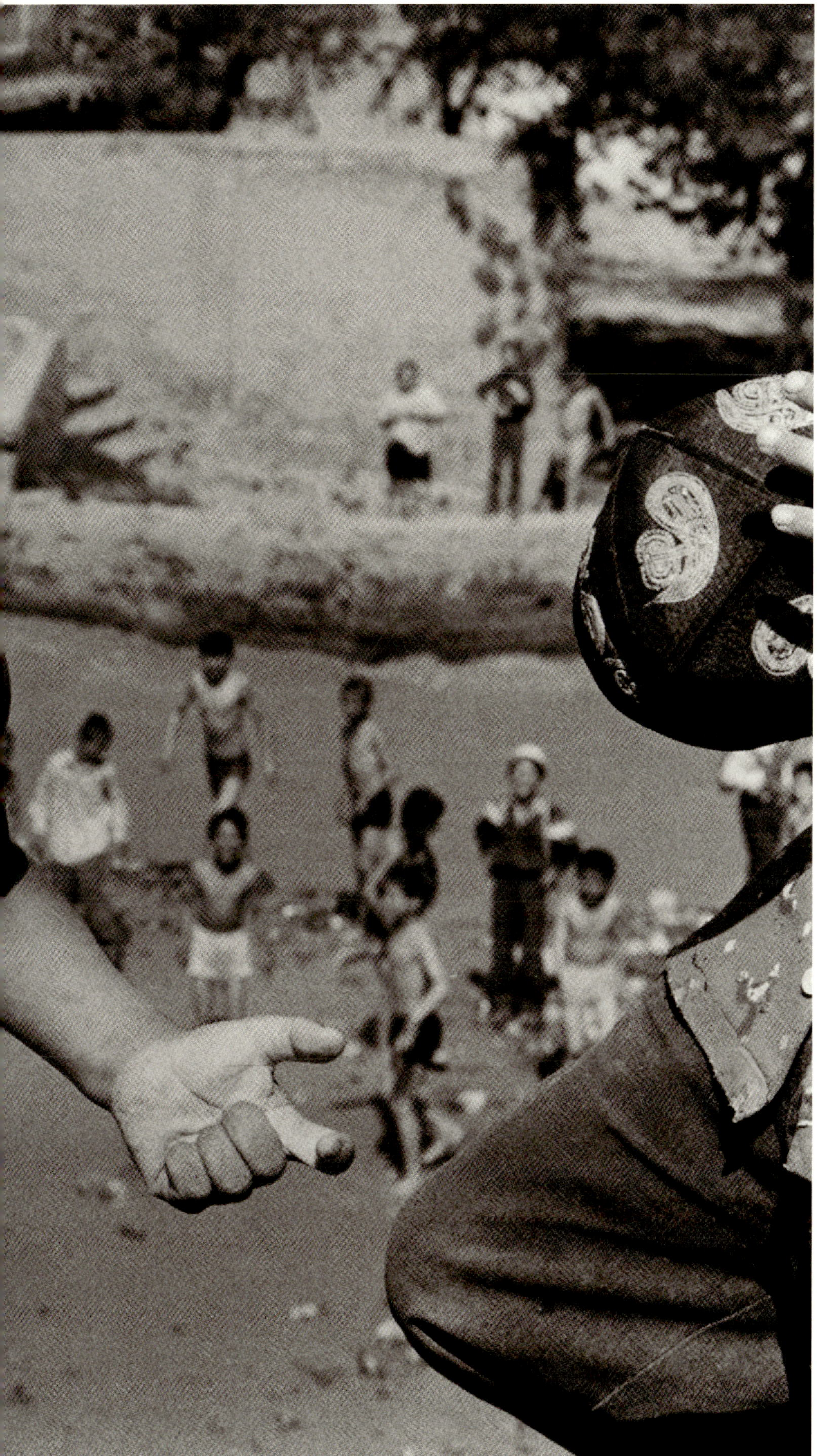

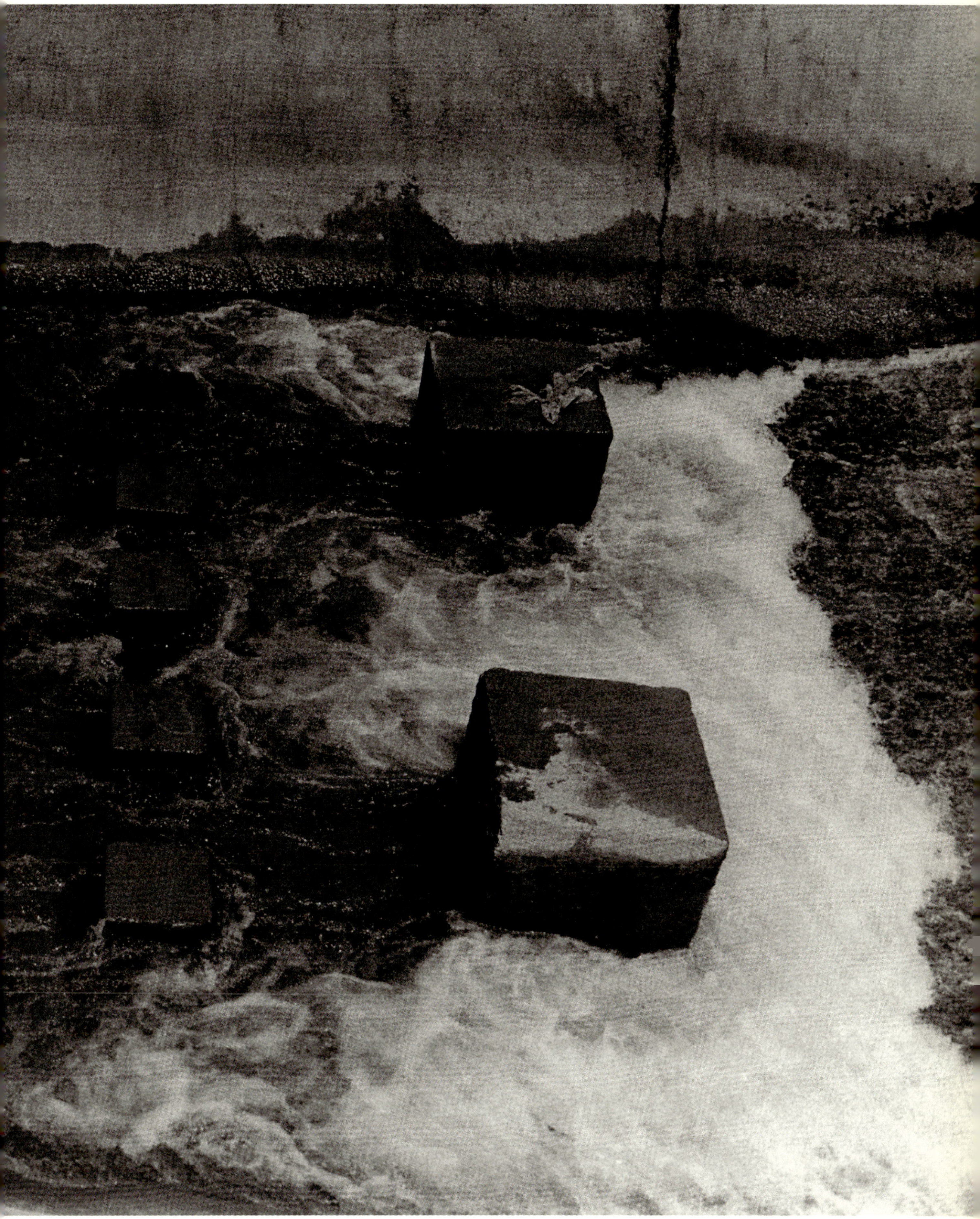

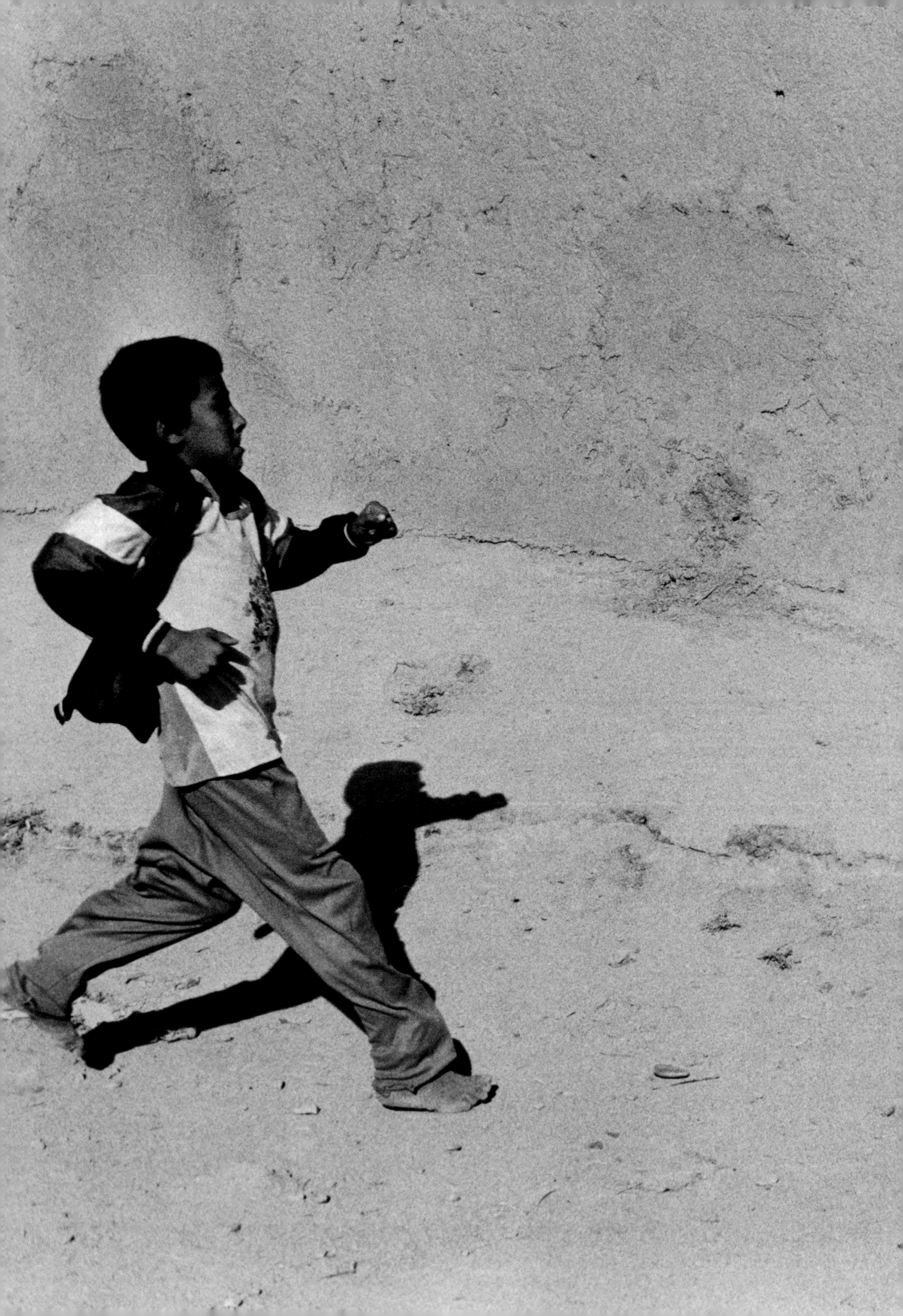

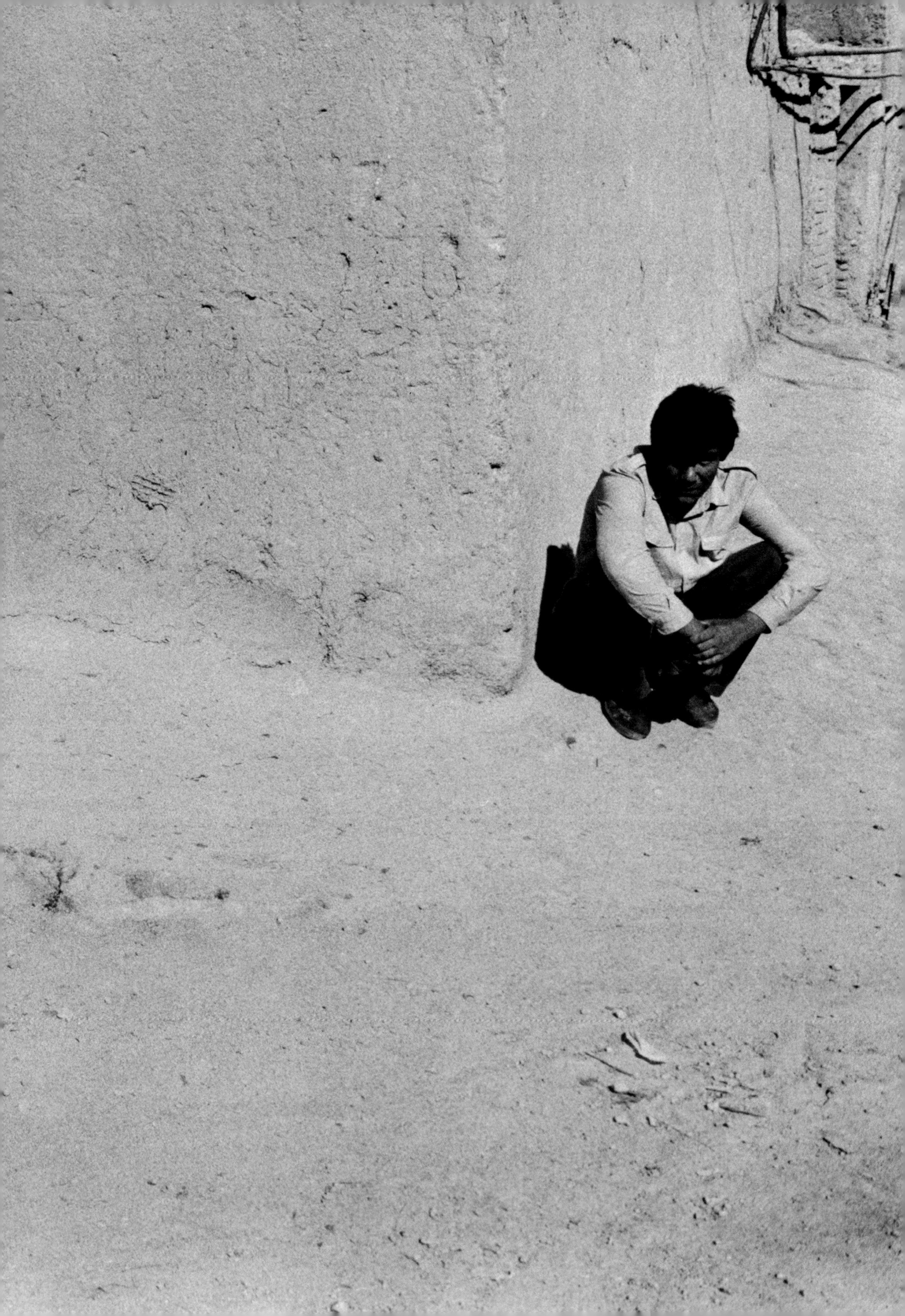

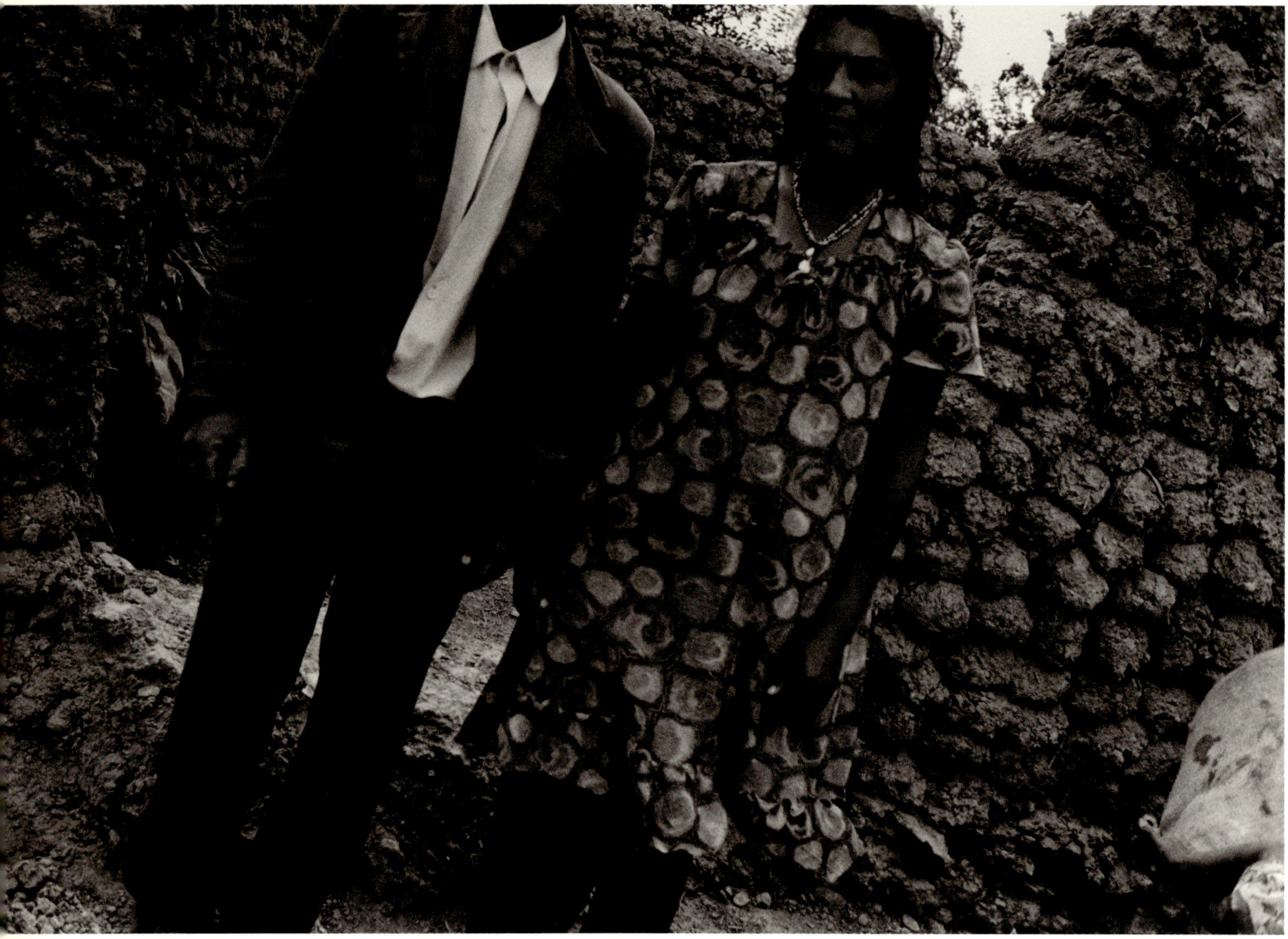

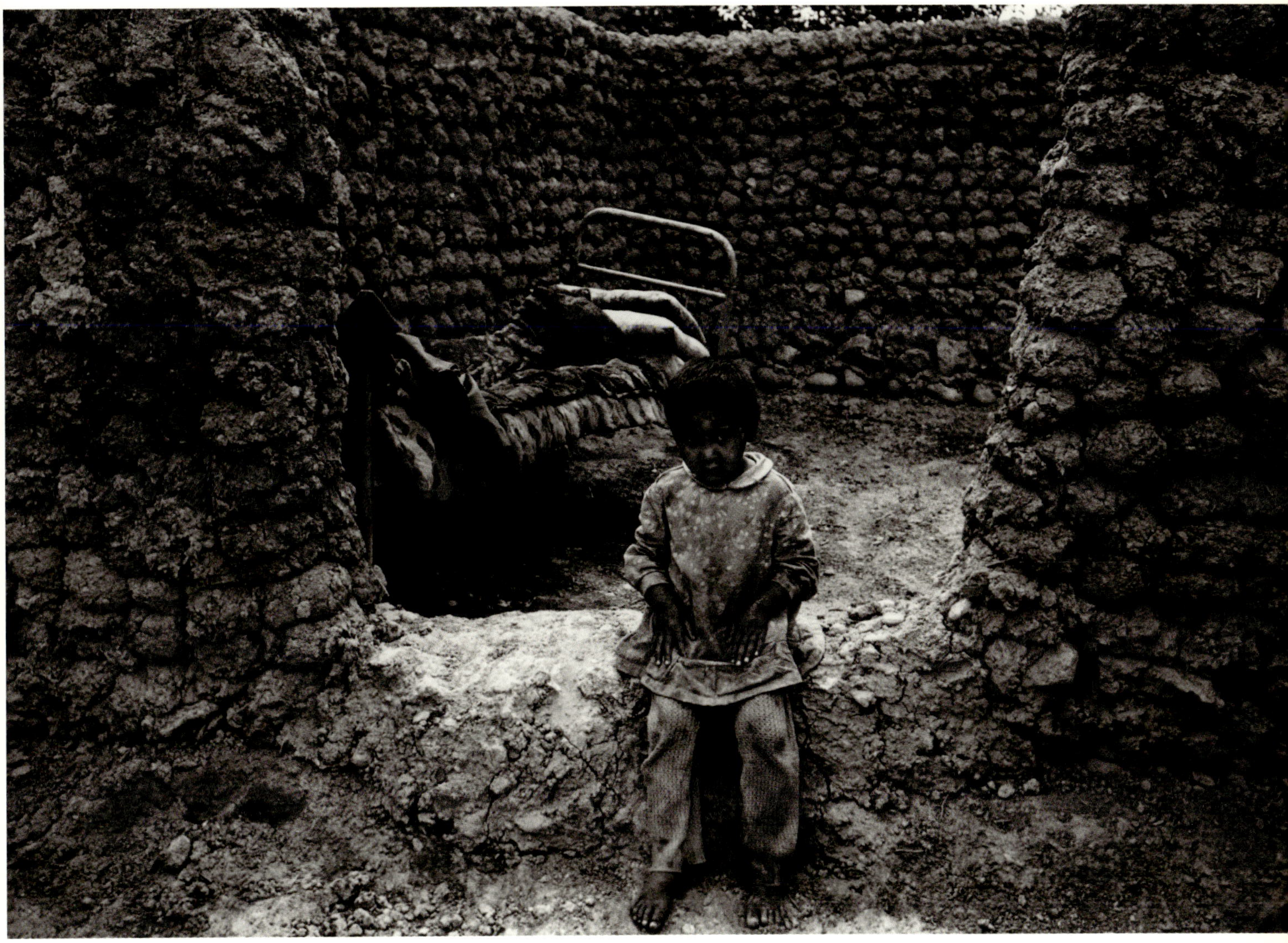

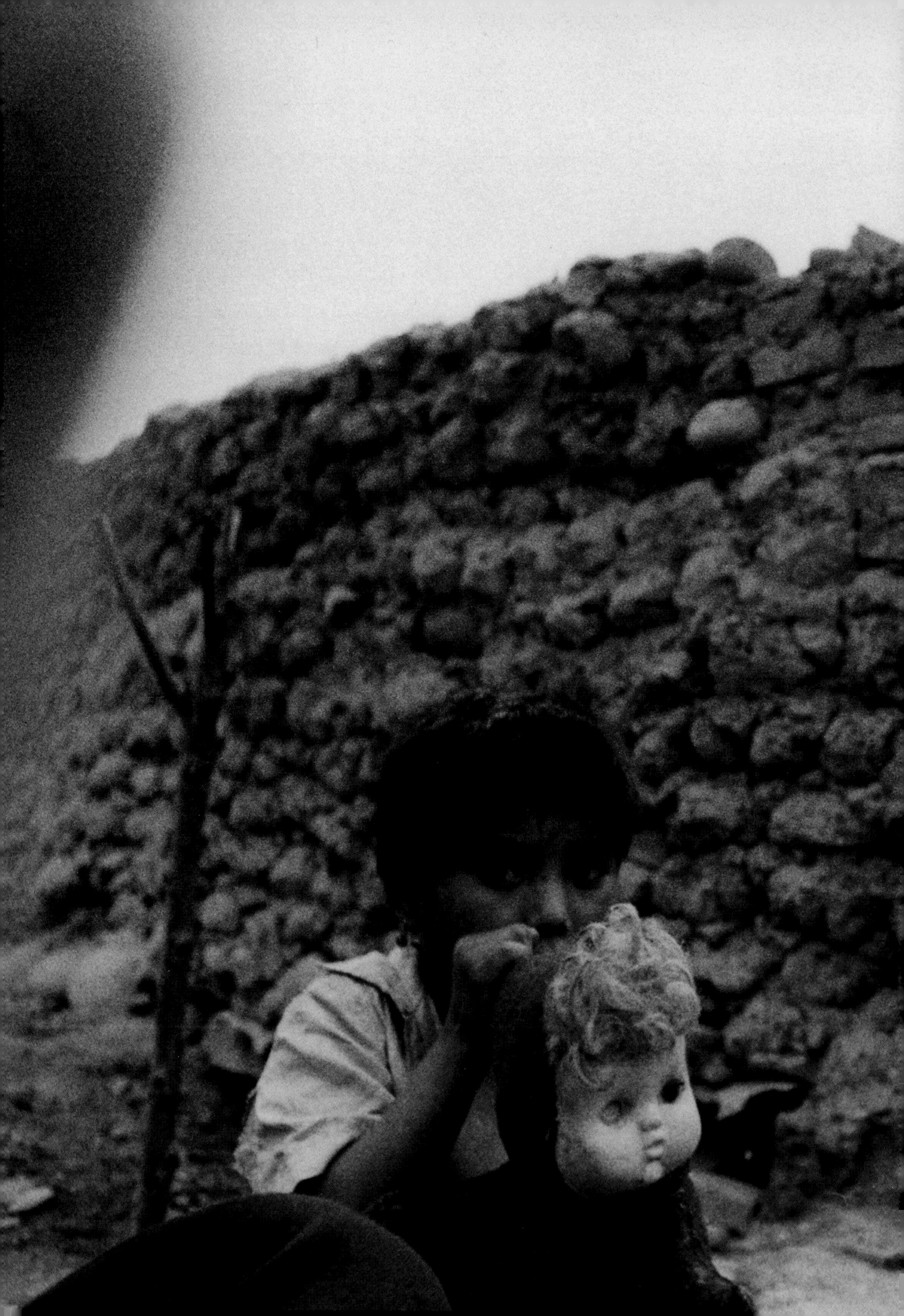

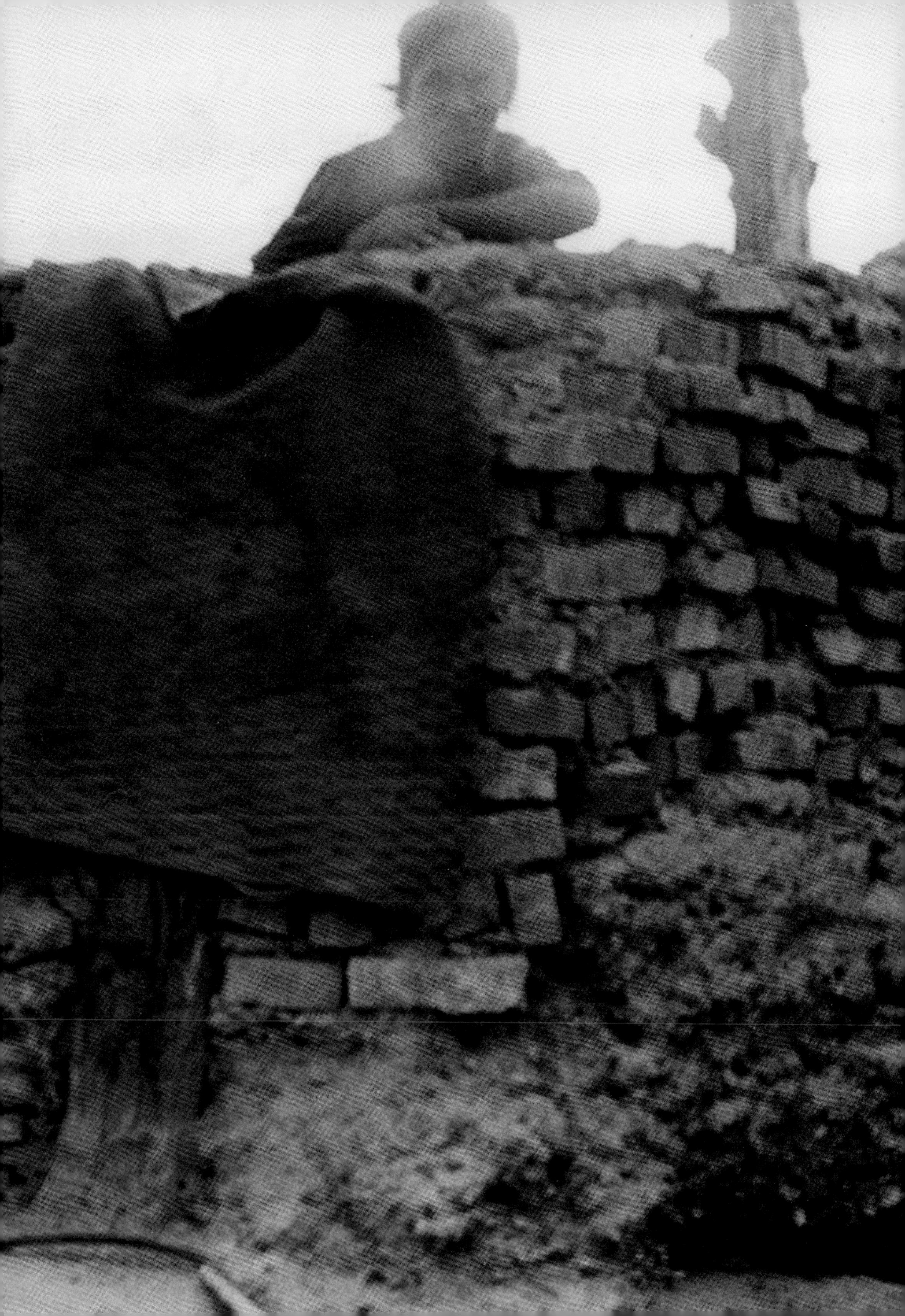

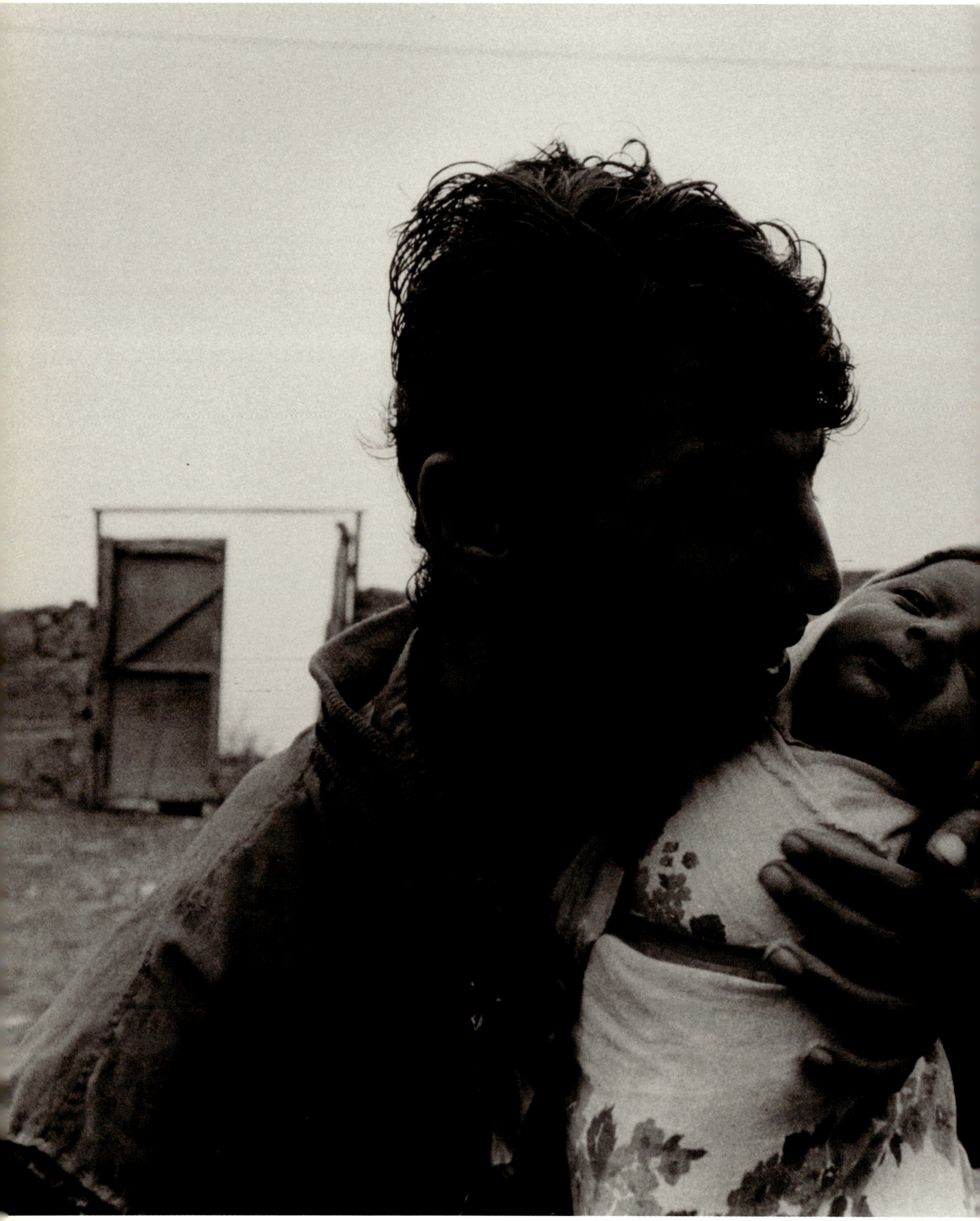

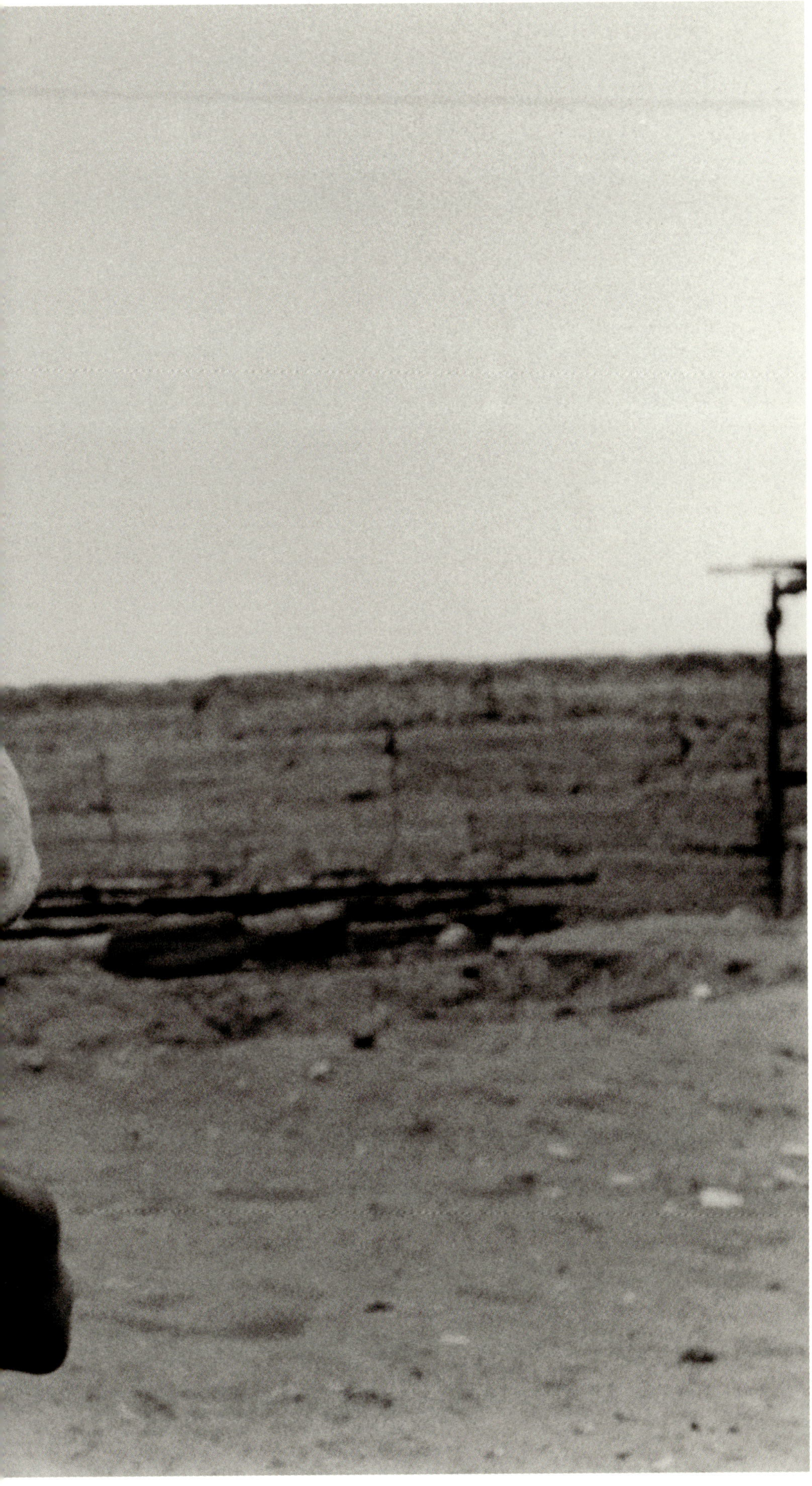

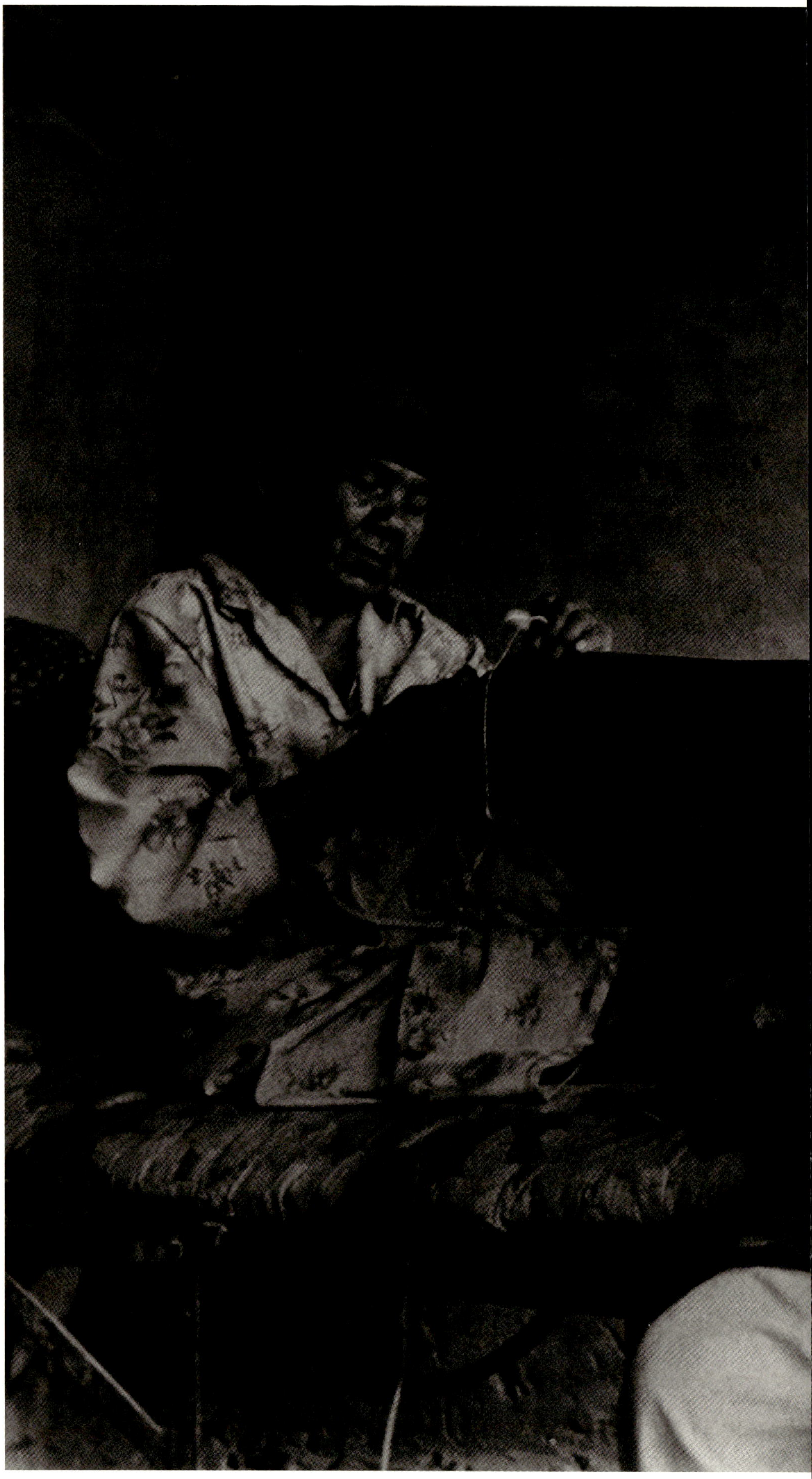

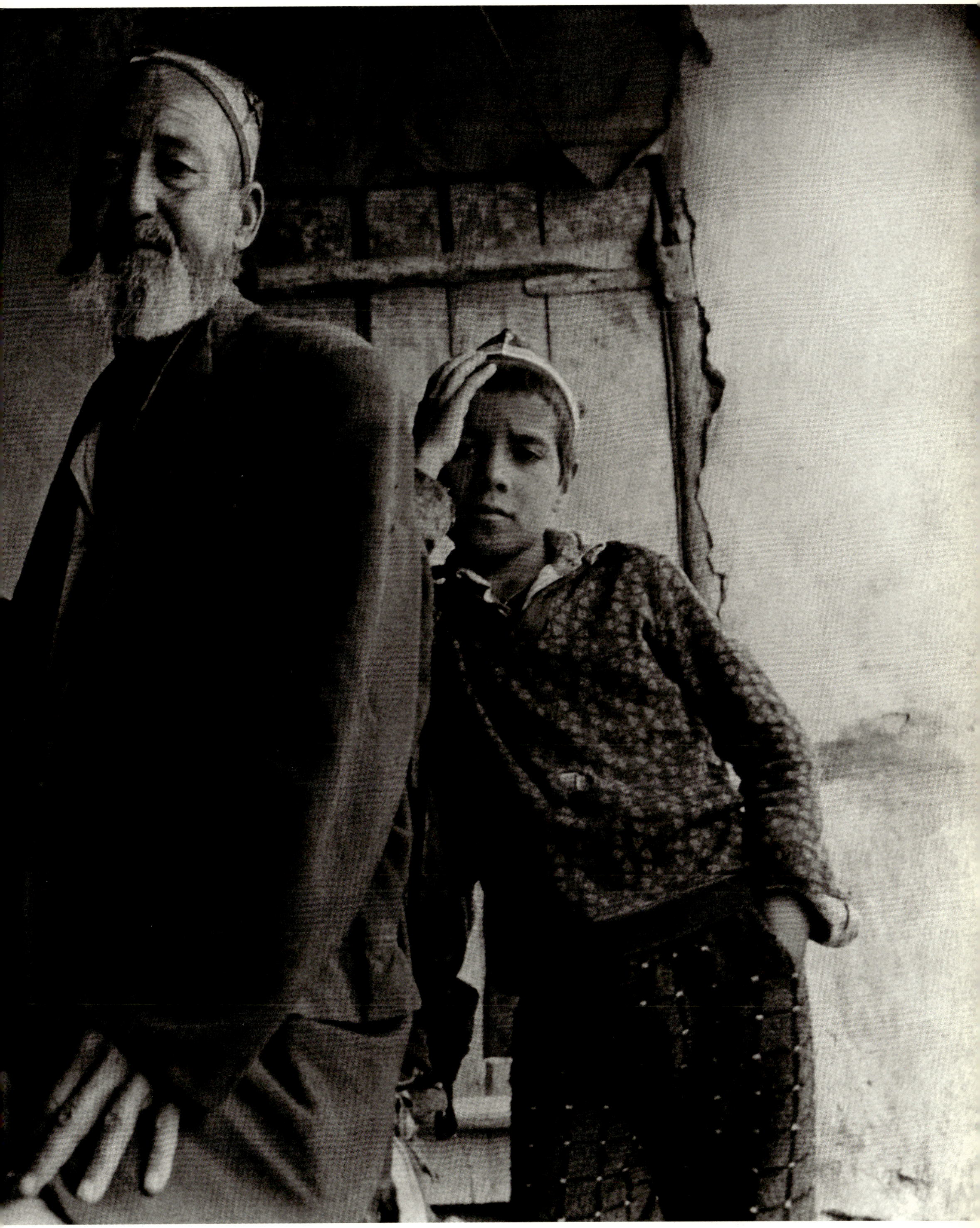

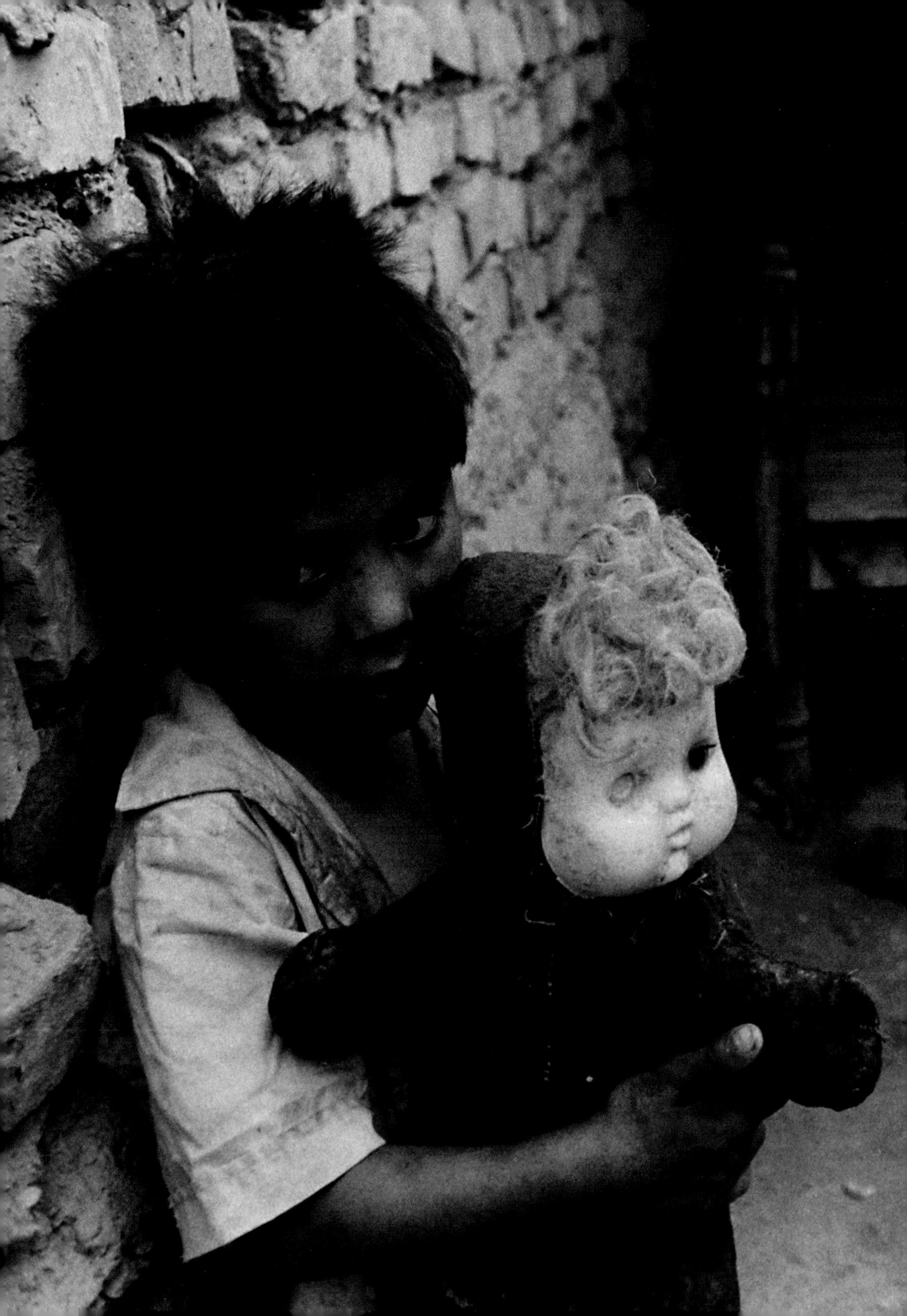

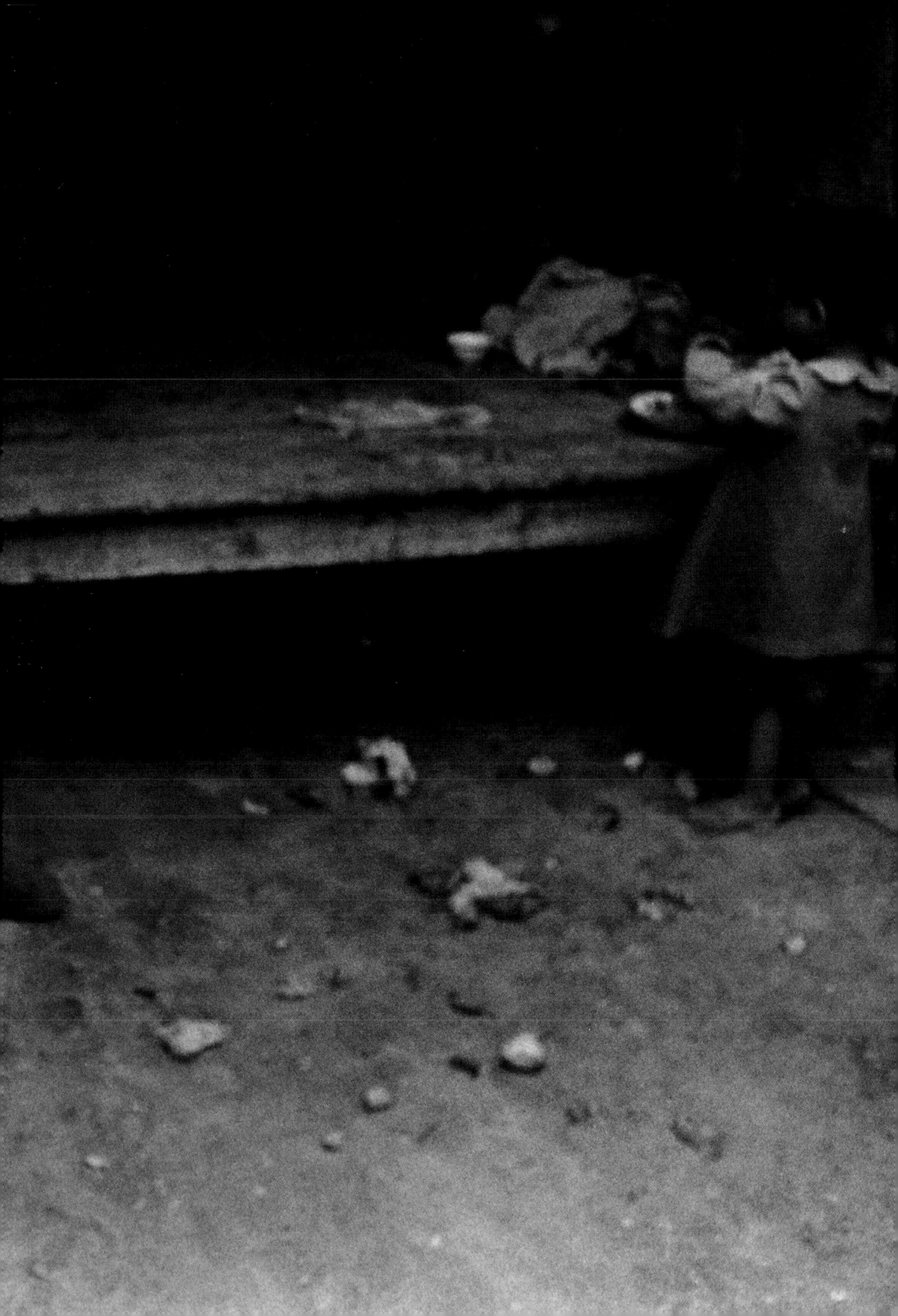

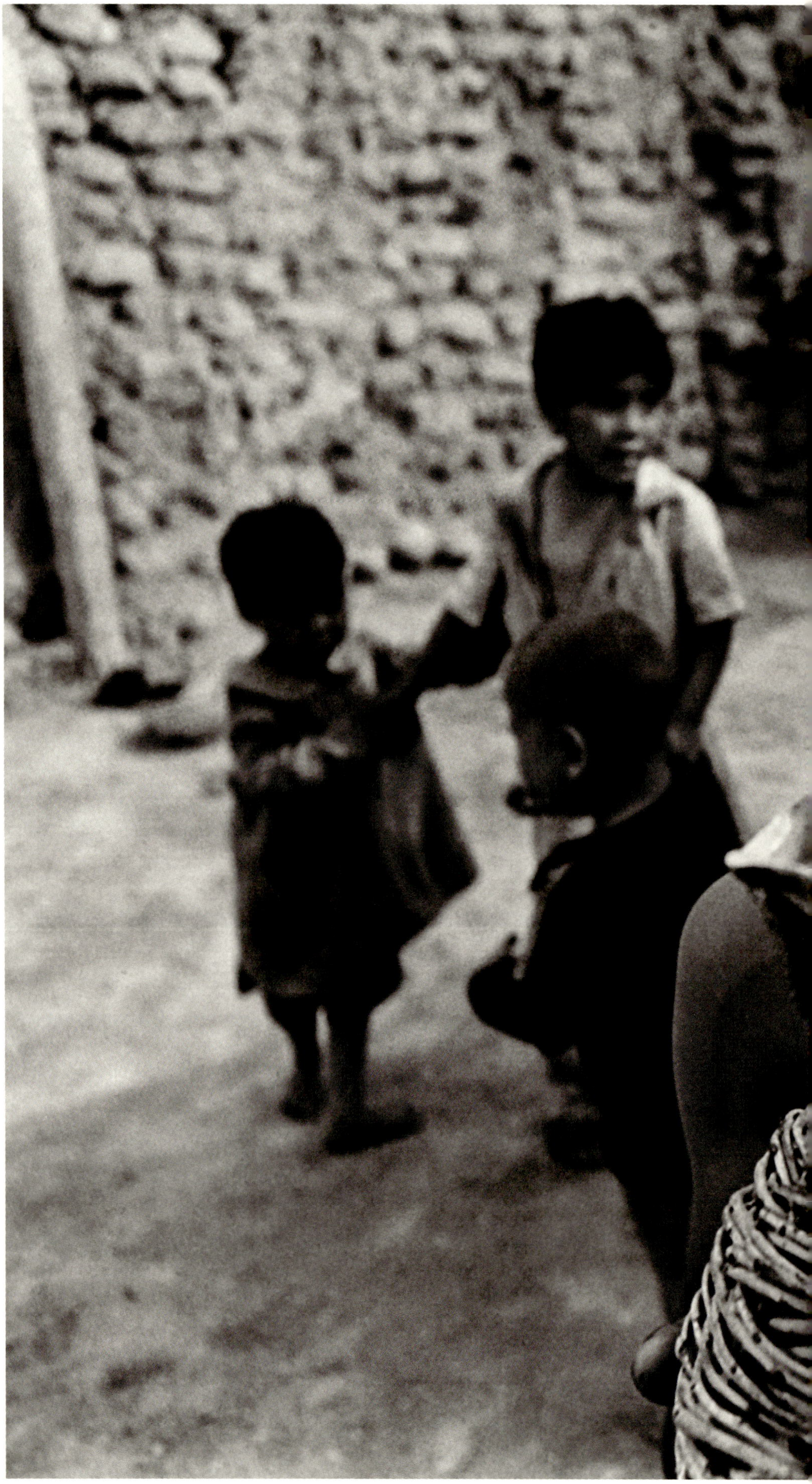

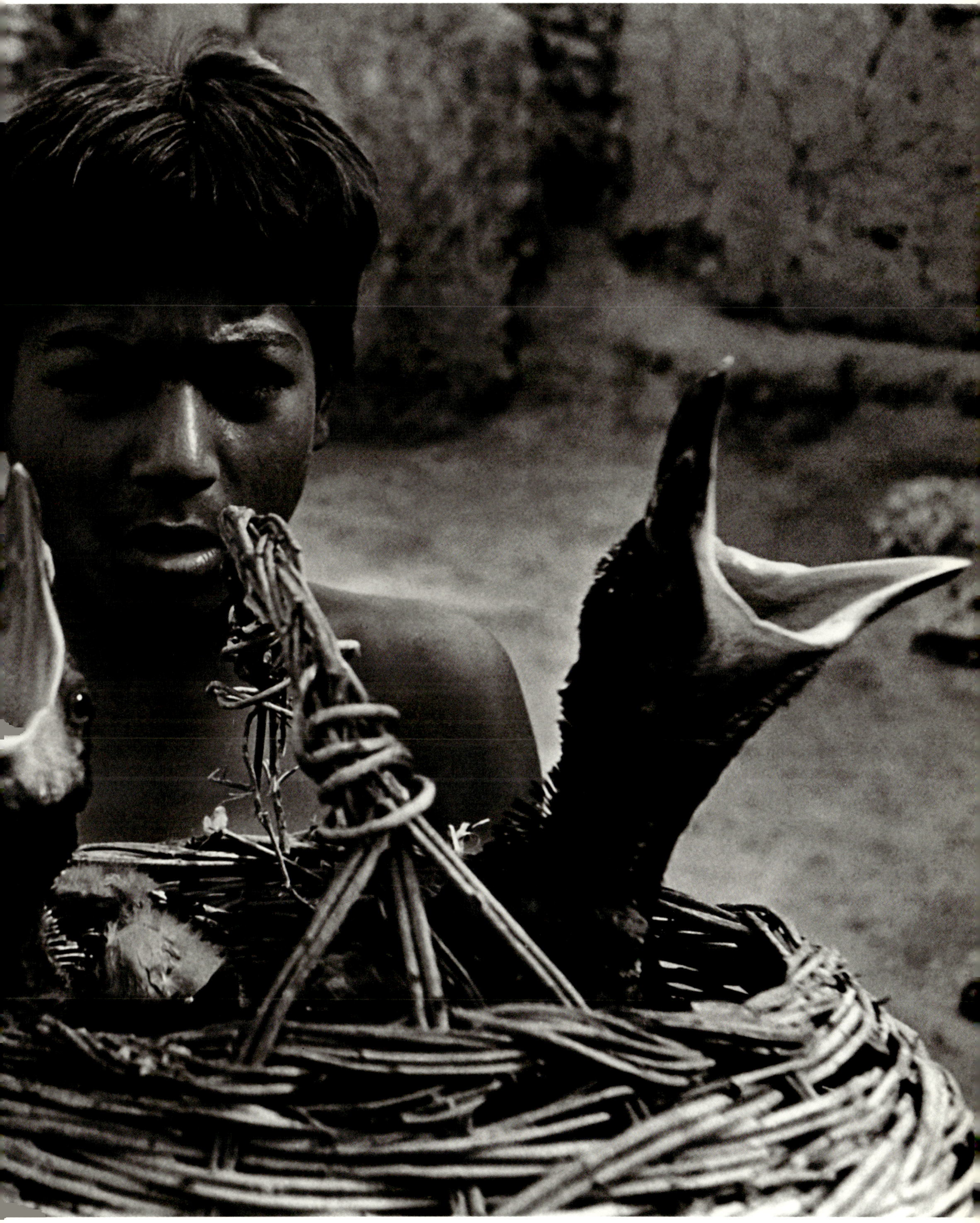

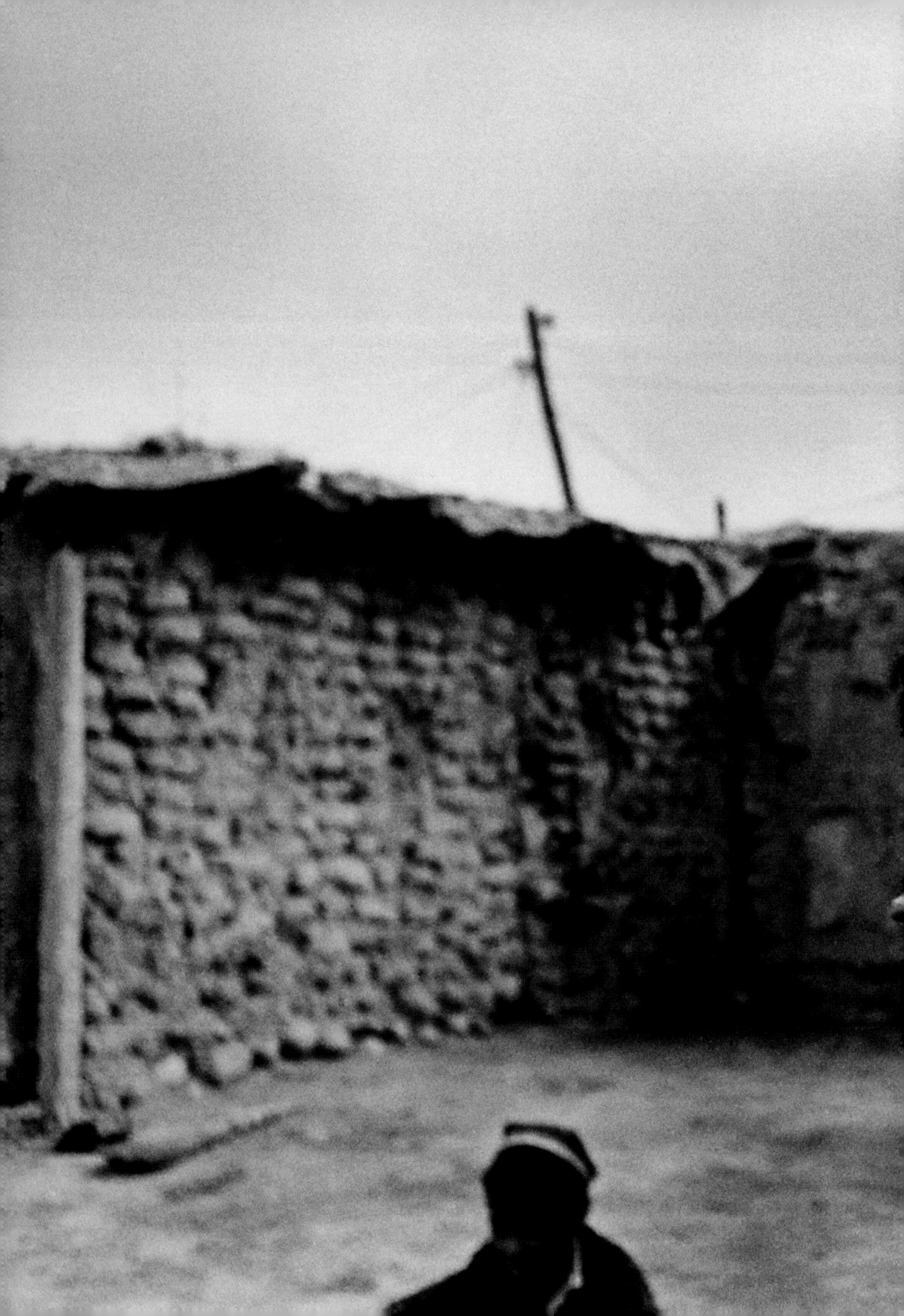

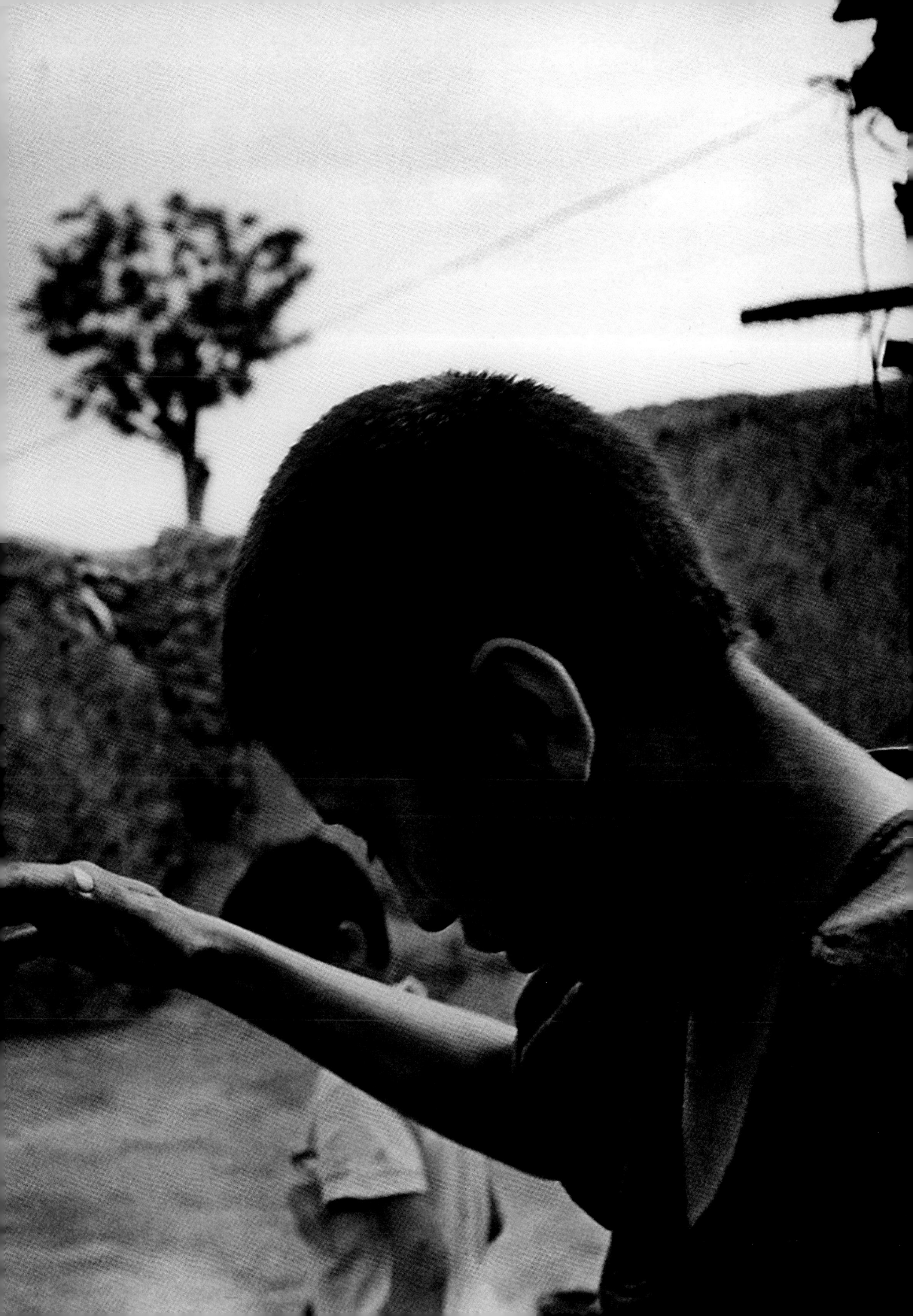

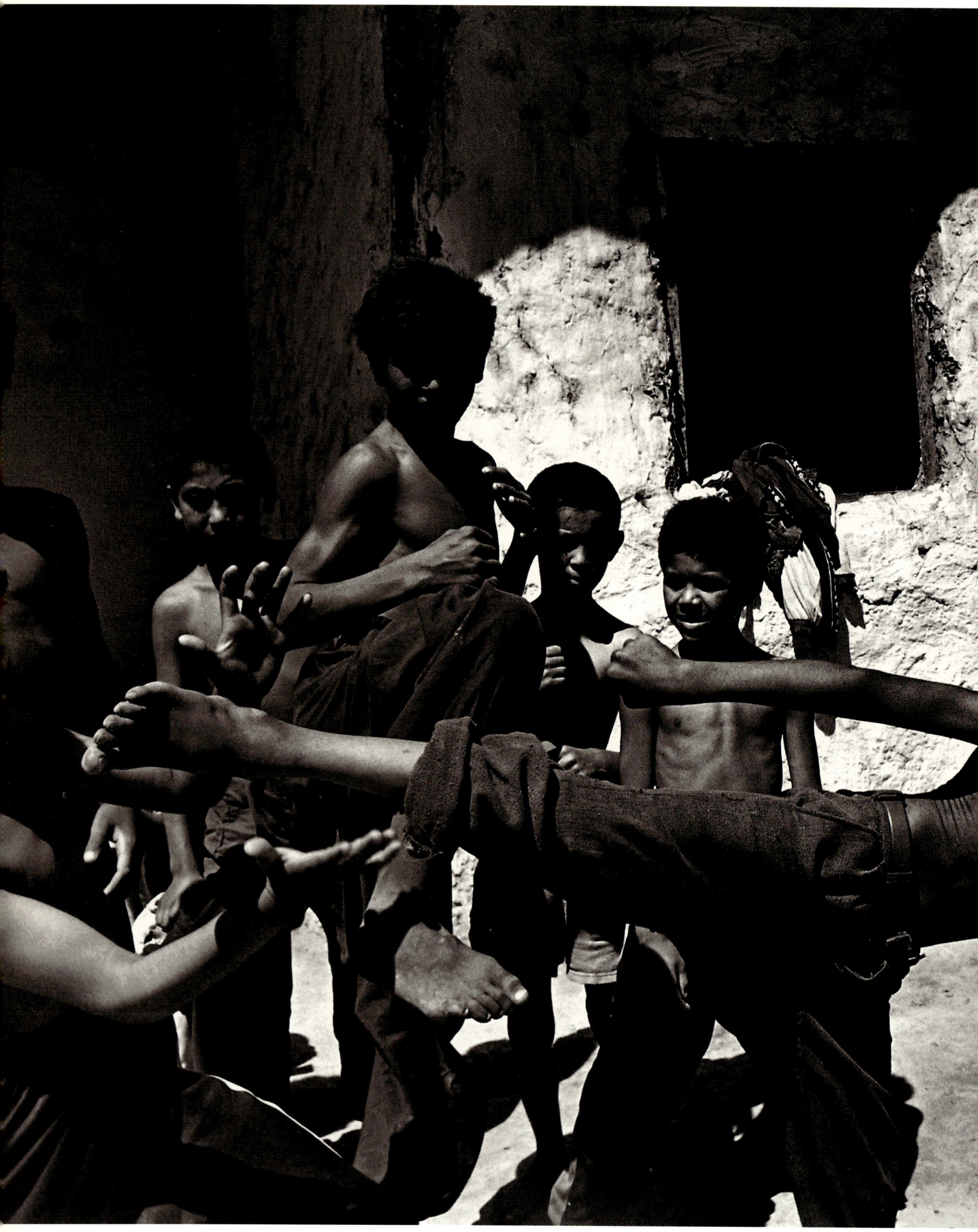

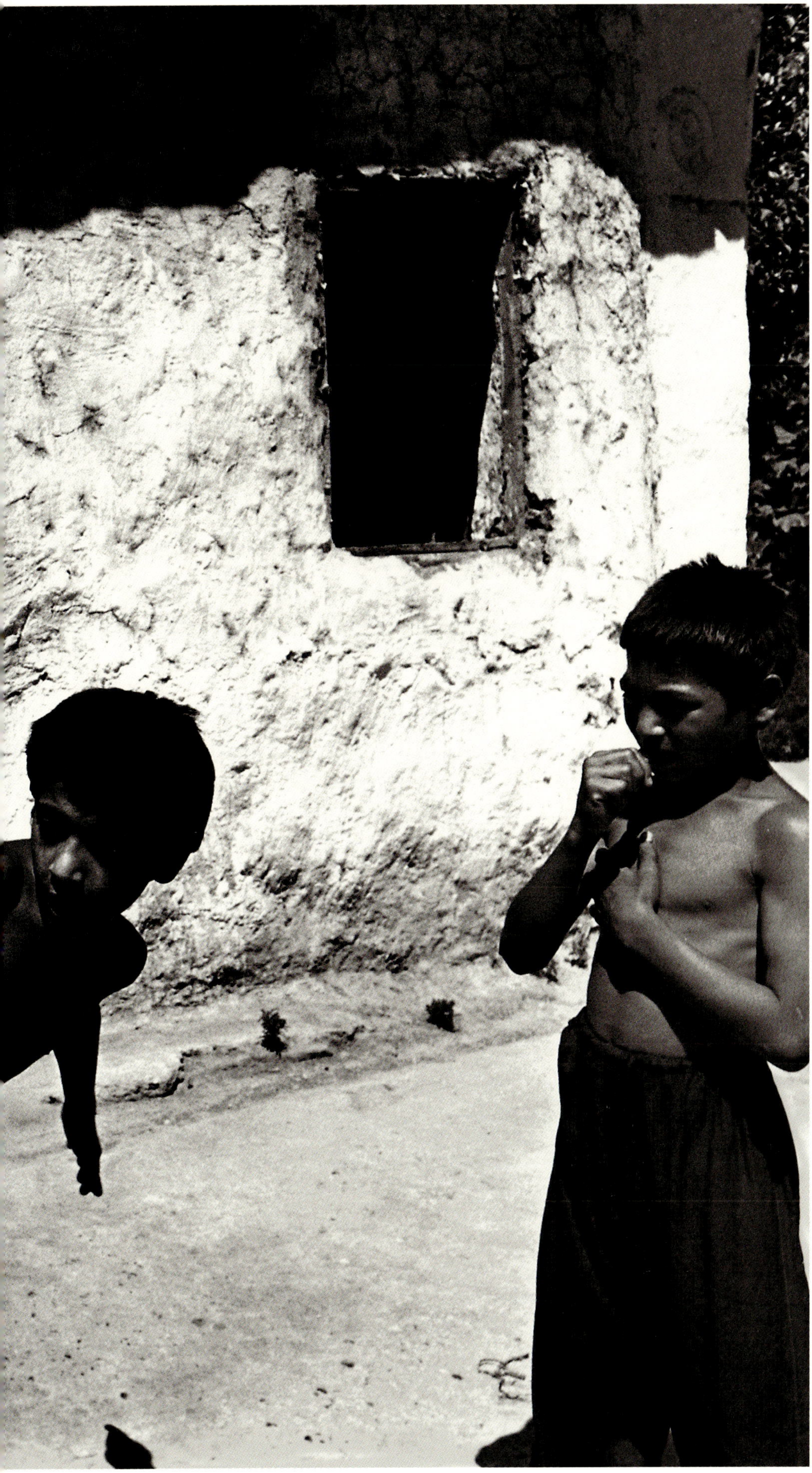

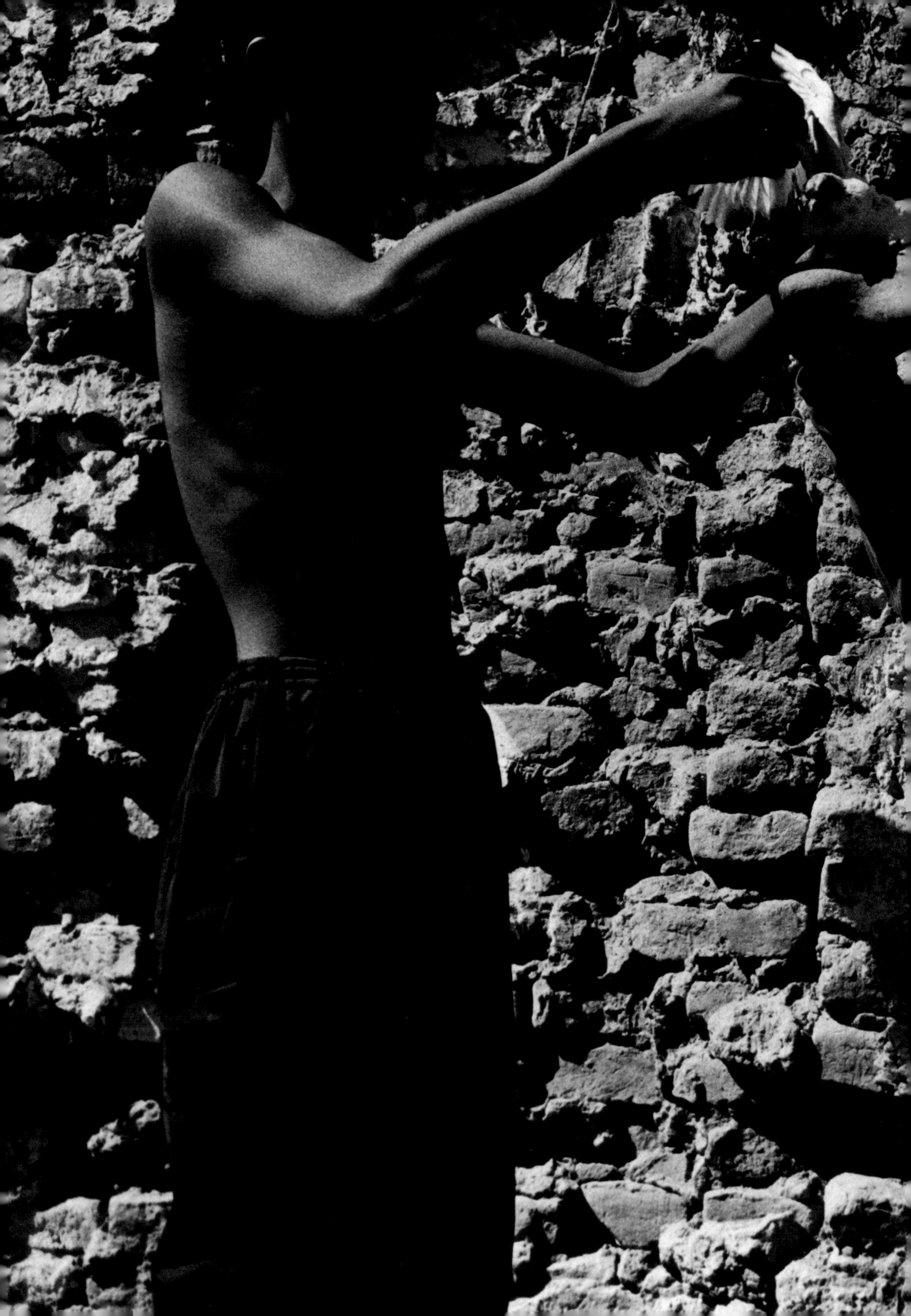

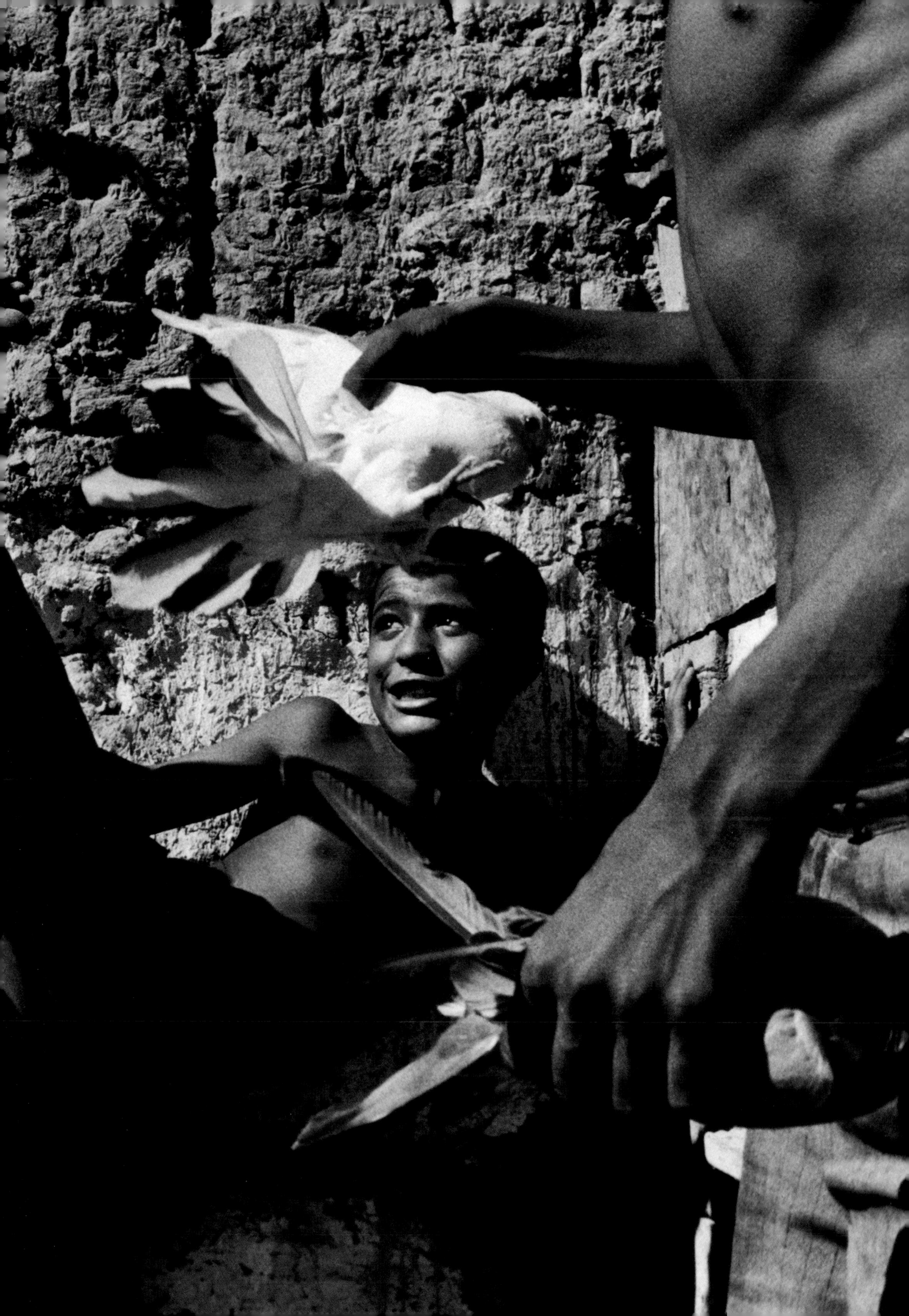

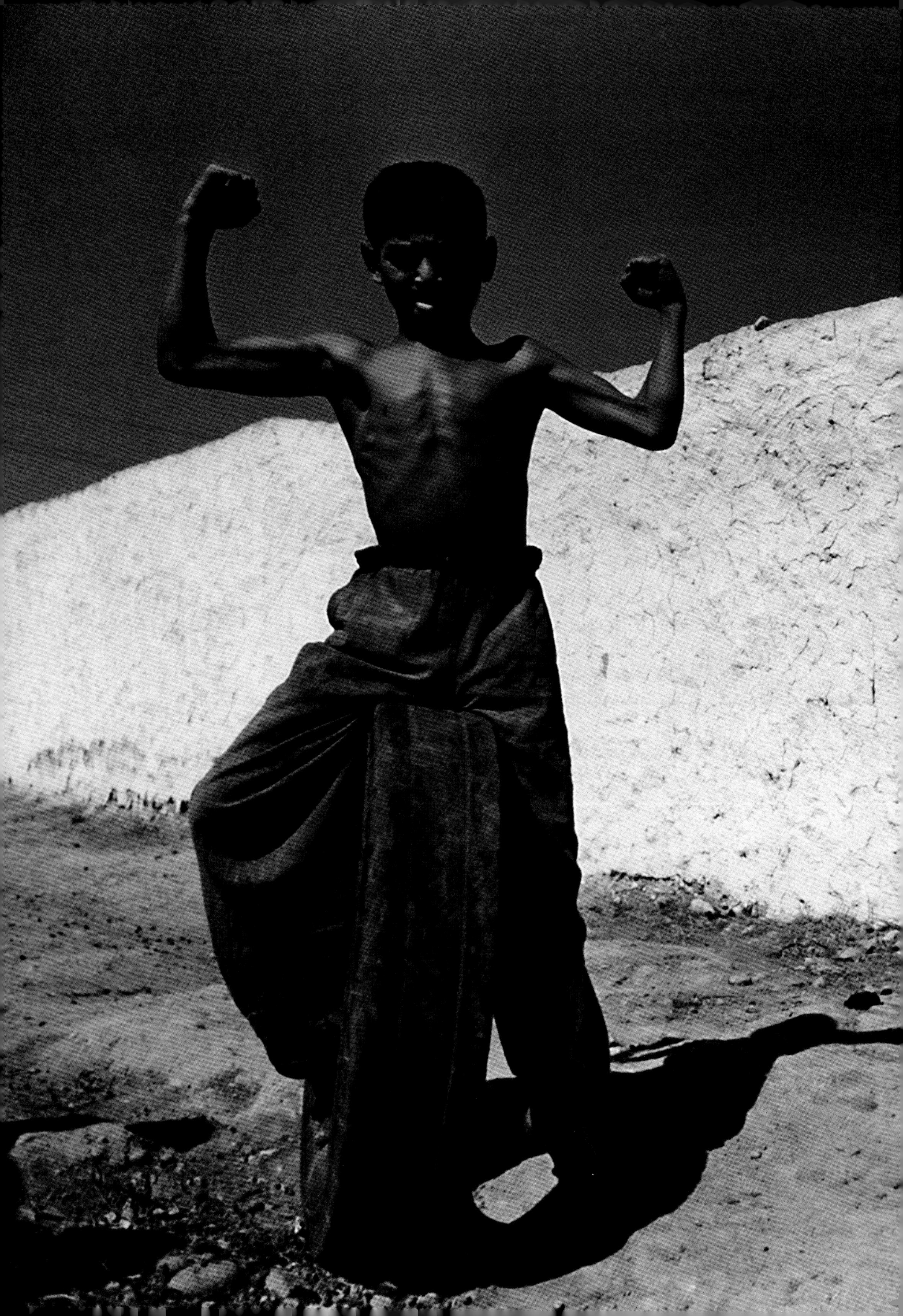

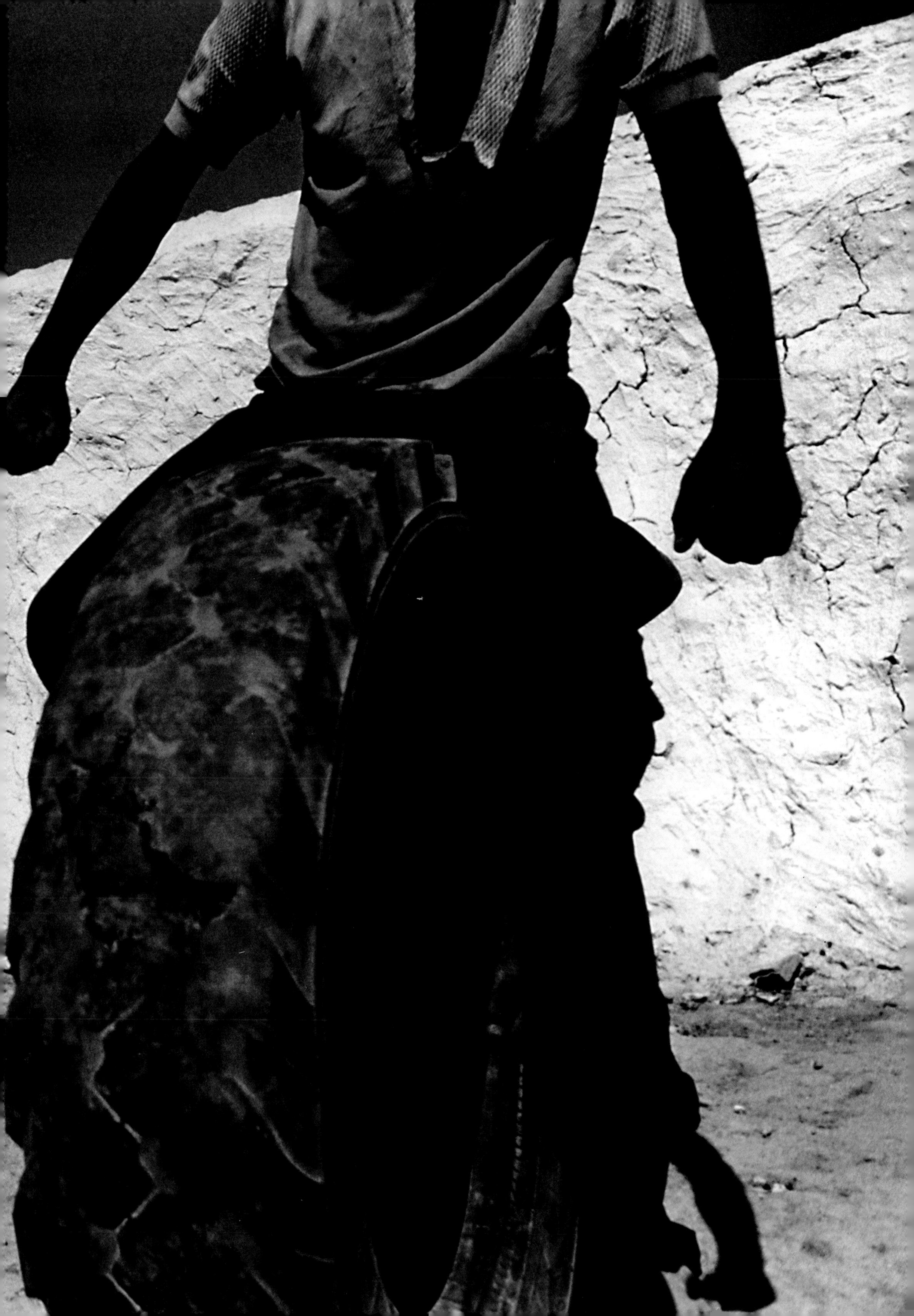

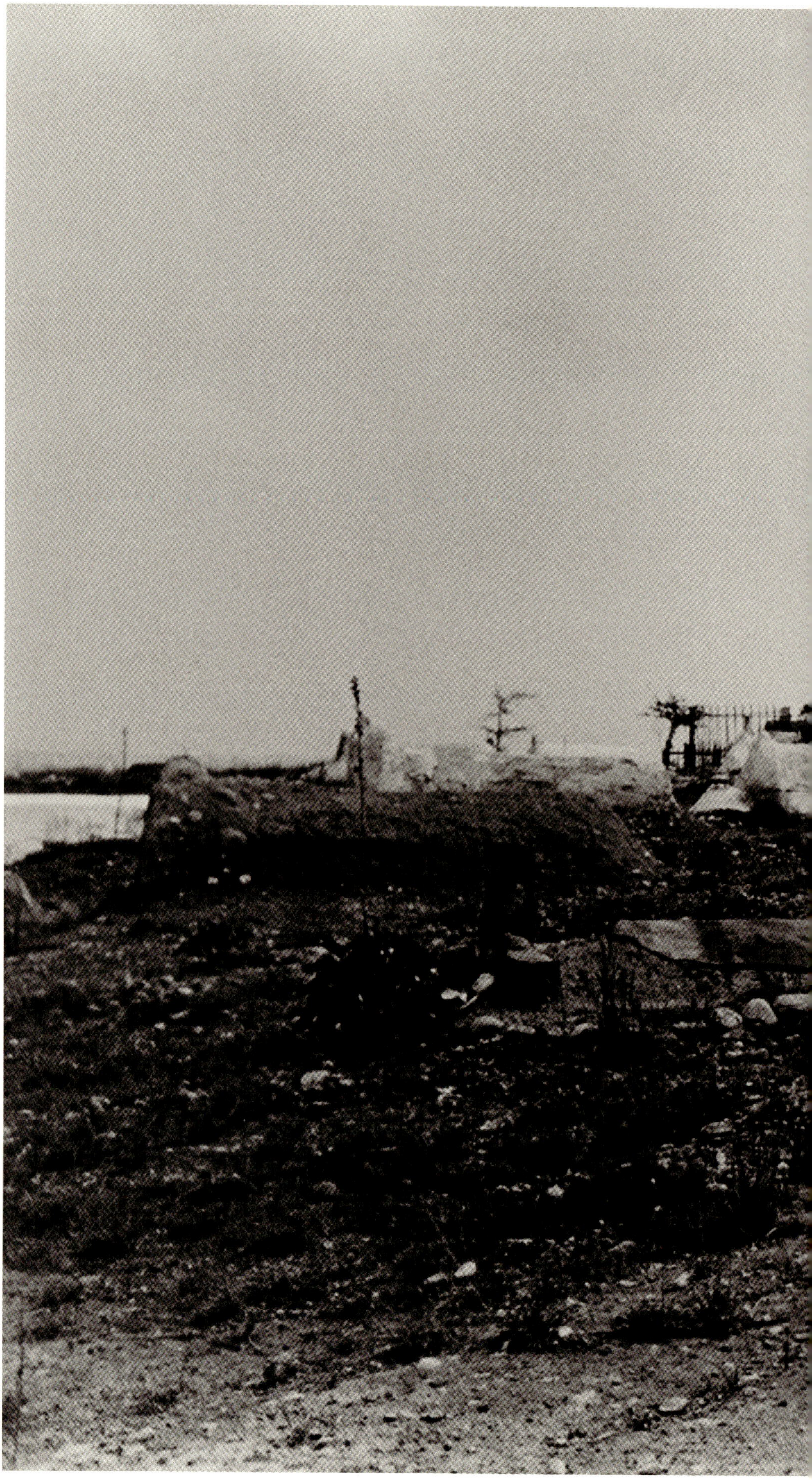

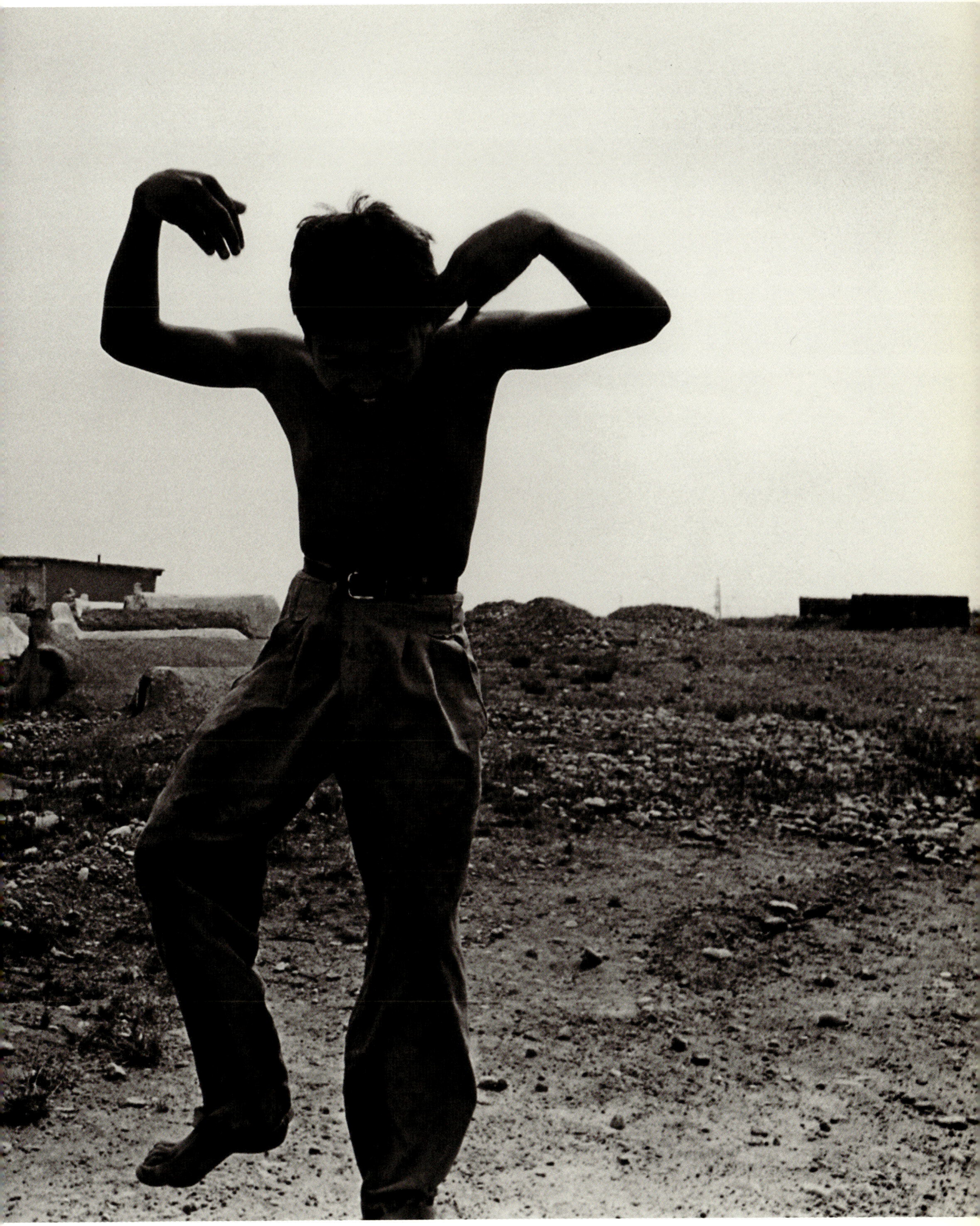

ТУРКМЕНИЯ

Turkmenistan Turkménistan Turkmenistan

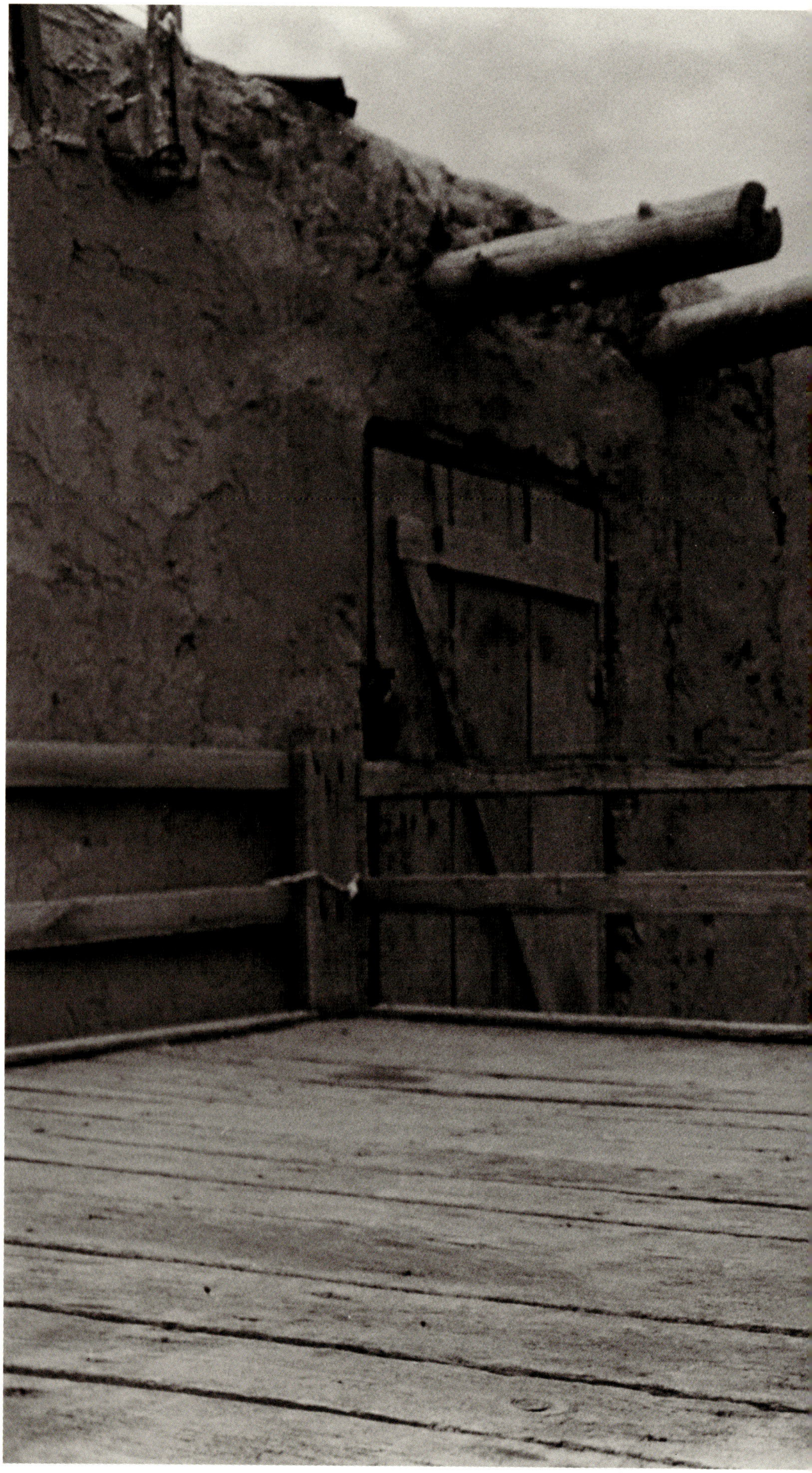

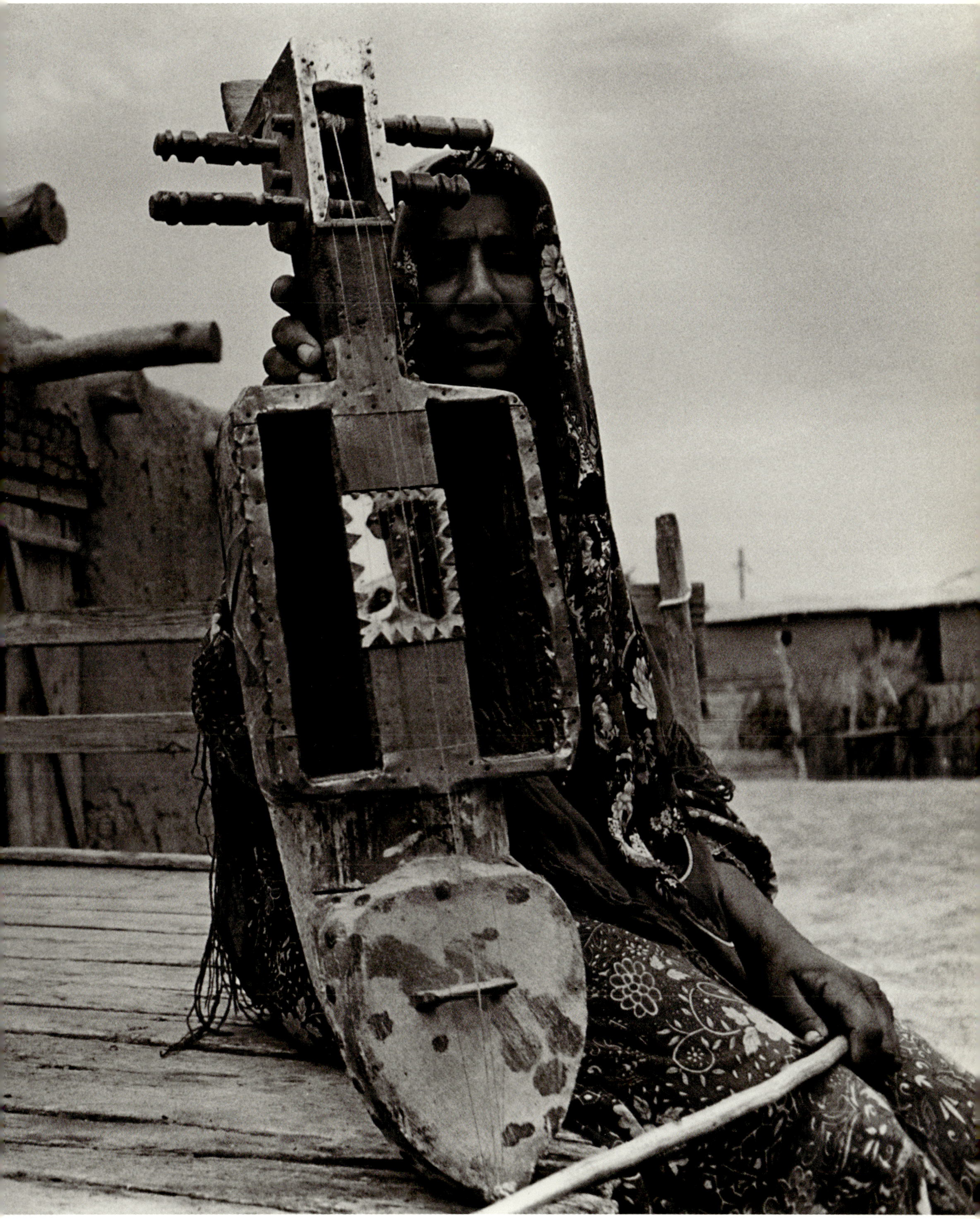

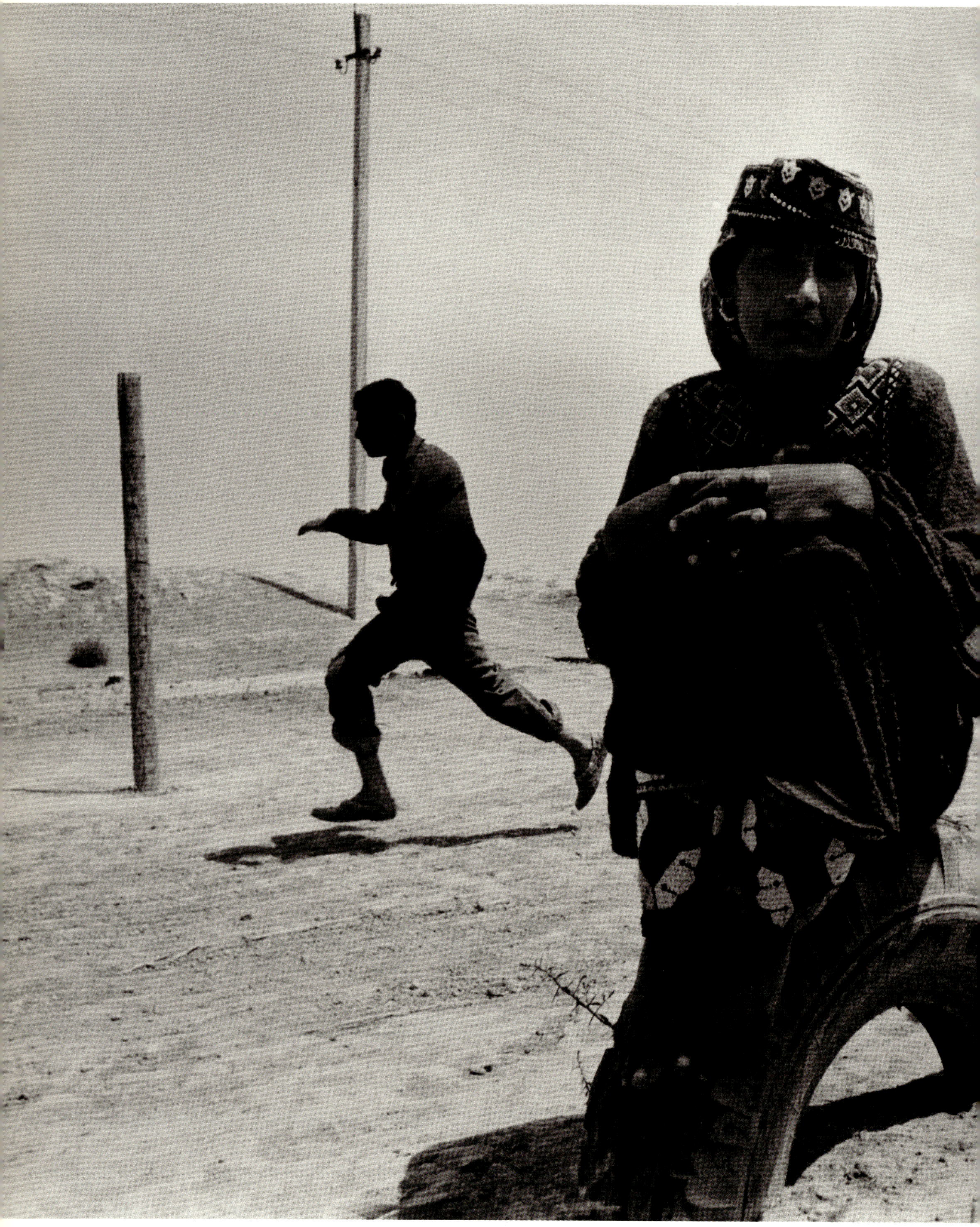

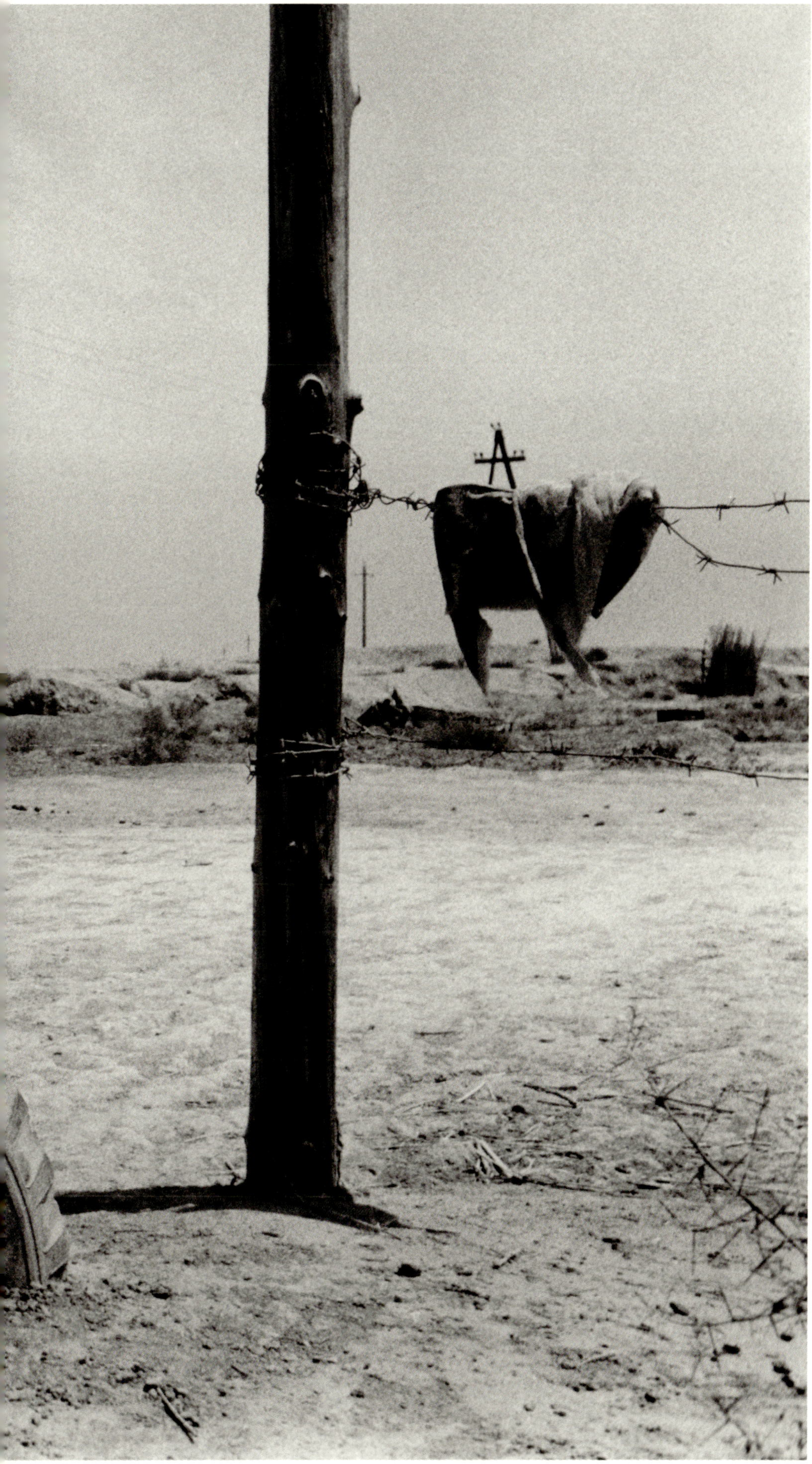

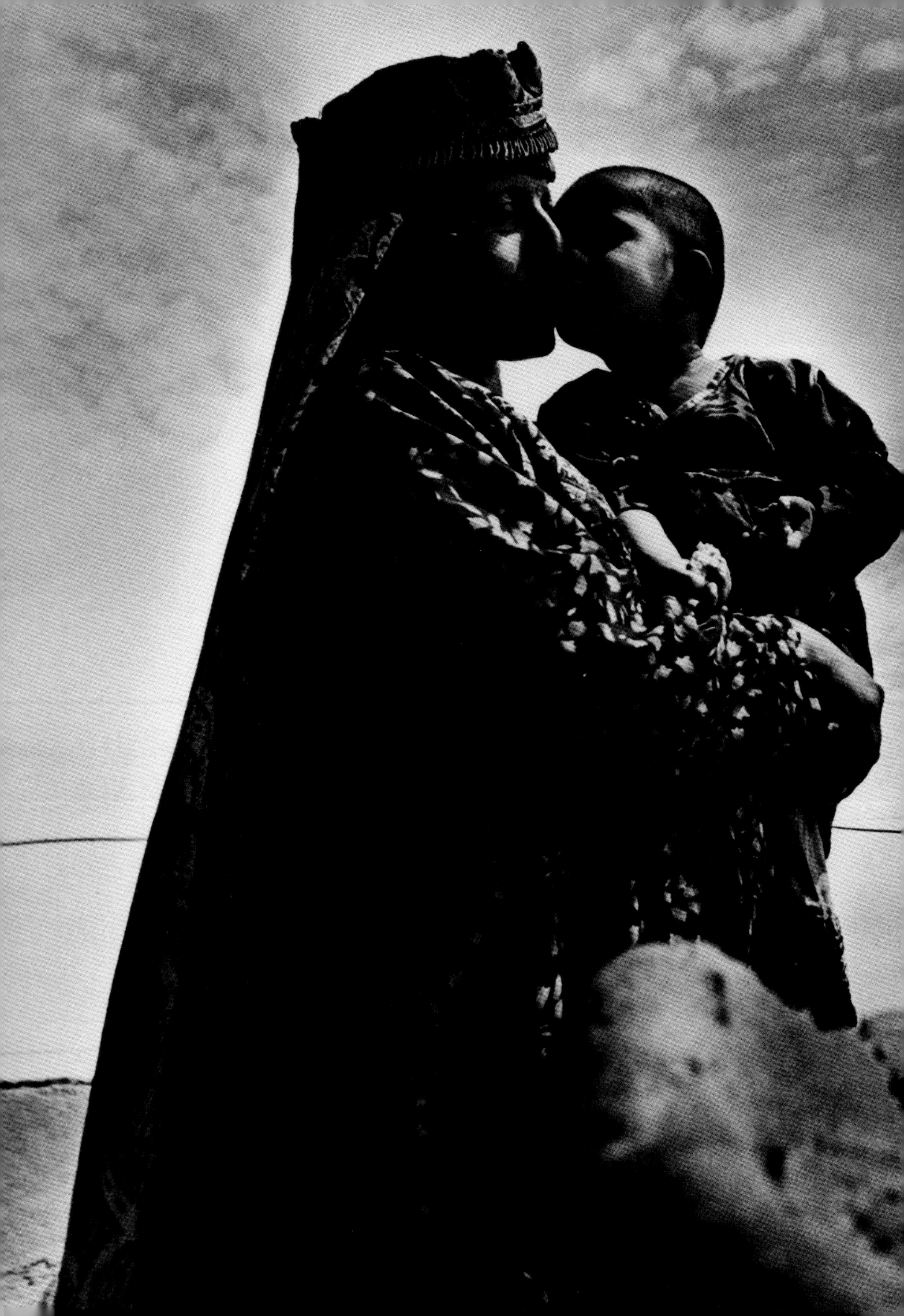

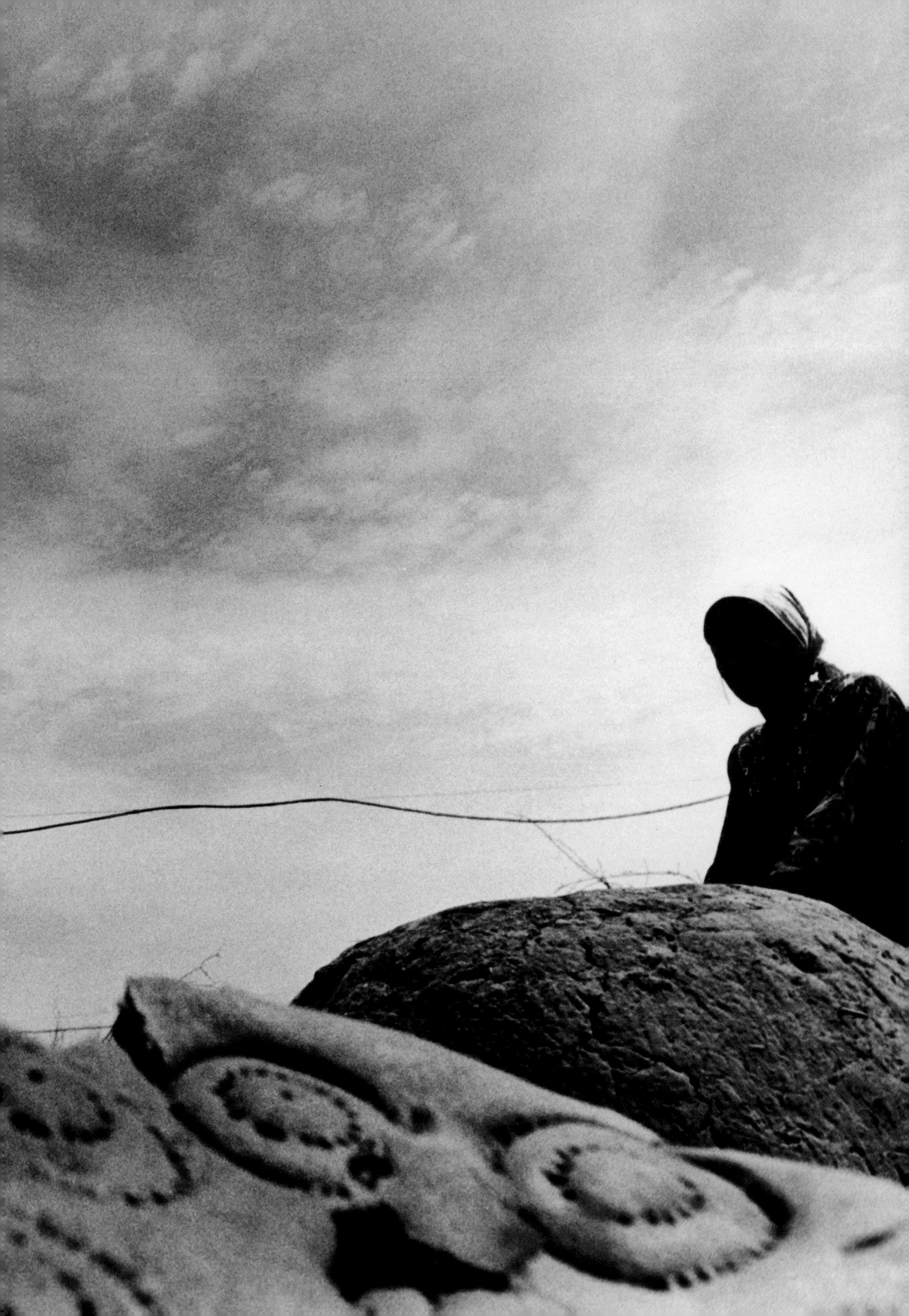

RUSSIA'S SIZE DETERMINES the fate of its people in an almost mystical way. Political systems, family, and upbringing are often just secondary in the life of Russians; much more important are the forests, mountains, seas, and steppes in which they live, and the air they breathe throughout the first years of life.

Marina Rasbeshkina

People Without Frontiers

Ljalja Kuznetsova was born in the small town of Uralsk in West Kazakhstan, close to the Russian border. It was a small multinational Babel where Russian, Tatar, Kazakh and Ukrainian were spoken. The town was in the middle of the steppes, and at night the only light came from the campfires of the gypsies. Nowadays there are very few areas of the steppe that have not at some point been plowed up. But anyone who has traveled across its desolate expanses knows how deceptive the horizon can be there–how it fades into infinity just as you think you are getting closer to it, how heaven and earth become a huge sphere, and the human being shrinks to a tiny speck in the universe.

In Kuznetsova, the steppes have molded an individual who prefers geography to history, the horizontal to the vertical; an individual who neither believes nor accepts that space also means frontiers. She sees the sky as the limit of her own personal space. Until she was thirty she had no idea that she would pick up a camera one day and photograph nomad and gypsy life. Given her strict Islamic upbringing, it seemed until then as though her destiny would embody the patriarchal ideal of Russian fairytales: to live a long and happy life and die on the same day as her husband. But when Kuznetsova's husband died young, she was still full of life, and the campfires of the gypsies were still burning on the steppe near Uralsk.

Kuznetsova took her first photos in the gypsy camp during dark days, days of stagnation, personally and politically, in the Soviet Union of the late seventies. But the photographs, which earned her an international reputation and were included in many photographic collections in the West, depicted an openness in the vast, windy landscape, and in the people living freely there, unbound by the ties of civilization. Kuznetsova had only been taking photographs for a short time, but even then she was more than just a craftswoman–she was an artist who managed to discover independence amid totalitarianism. She did not glorify or rail against the status quo. In her subjects she looked for a common humanity independent of politics, nationality, religion, or social group. Right from the beginning she sought out people who lived in oblivion of governmental changes, technical progress, the invention of the atom bomb, the rise and fall of culture; people who never even realized they were living outside civilization or were simply unaware of civilization altogether.

Far from popular celebrities, Kuznetsova's subjects live obscure, monotonous, mundane lives and, like the endless steppes, know no frontiers. From birth to death, they face an exhausting struggle to survive. Kuznetsova observes these subjects closely and looks for what is good in their lives. She photographs them in those rare instances when they are happy and prolongs those moments in her own way. Time is not frozen, it carries on; but her subjects seem to transcend it. The world of Kuznetsova's characters is eternal and seemingly infinite.

In Kuznetsova's earliest pictures of gypsies, for which she was awarded the Paris Grand Prix, she depicts the Roma as more hopeful than they might be in real life. She always depicts them amid the steppe, where the unlimited vistas seem to represent freedom. Romantic and beautiful, her first gypsy series shows space and liberty, the wild wind, the customs and habits of life in the gypsy encampment. Each picture in this cycle illustrates the Pushkin poem that says "there is no happiness on earth, but there is peace and there is freedom." People from other regions might find happiness easily, but not Kuznetsova's subjects. They are constantly struggling against fate, enjoying only seconds of happiness. The women in Kuznetsova's portraits seem to live in anticipation of joy, as do the Odessa gypsies and the circus artists that she photographs, the tent dwellers, the people with worn, callused hands molded by daily physical training and hard work.

As Kuznetsova has grown older, her pictures seem less romantic, but she continues to love the outcast. The space in her photos has contracted. The horizon has disappeared. Her choice of subject and medium has become more austere. Now she photographs people forced into the narrow spaces between the splendid facades of old cities and cemeteries. Dynamic compositions have given way to the play of light and shade, and there is less and less peace, more and more tension and restlessness. Still, the monuments of Bukhara or Samarkand, the magnificent villas or elegant streets of Odessa, hold no attraction for her. Kuznetsova takes her camera instead into narrow, dirty alleyways, where children play on rubbish heaps between discarded barrels.

Even as Moscow has swallowed up everything that was best in the outlying areas of Russia and its neighbors, Kuznetsova lives in the provinces, loves the provinces, photographs the provinces. Even as other painters, philosophers, engineers, fashion designers, and theatre people flock to the capital because it is so much easier to be noticed, to forge a career, Kuznetsova stays in the background to photograph those whom fortune has not smiled upon. Her gift is that she is able to step into provincial lives without disturbing them by her presence, to remain invisible as if protected by magic.

What happens to human beings in history? Kuznetsova's photos seem to answer, "Nothing happens. The world changes, but things remain the same." Now, just as people did centuries ago, they suffer, have children, and die. And then the whole process is repeated from the beginning. In her photographs Kuznetsova presents us a reminder, so to speak, of the eternity within those moments in the lives of the gypsy, the Uzbek, the Tatar, the Russian, the artist in the Shapito circus, the model, and the tramp.

There are not many people who have been able to speak so clearly about the worth of all human beings. There are not many of us for whom humans are so sublime and significant that even their bad qualities seem deserving of sympathy, not hatred. There are not many of us who feel such pain at people's imperfections. I asked Kuznetsova to try and define her role as an artist in her own words. She said, "Finding words is your job. But I'll try: I am definitely a person who sympathizes." In a troubled world she manages to get to the roots of human feeling: love, hope, and trust. That is why she is so interesting and why she is understood all over the world.

Translated from the German by Lorna Dale.

Kuznetsova

Acknowledgments

For their wonderful support and collaboration on this book I wish to thank my daughter Wlada, as well as Minette von Krosigk, Warwara Petrowa, Elena Gram, Alexander Lapin, Donna Ferrato, Inge Morath, Marina Rasbeshkina, Lician Perkins, and Menno van de Koppel.
In Germany I was helped particularly by Joachim W. Schiwy, Gunter Steffen, Christina Glanz, Dorothea Cremer-Schacht, and Barbara Kunzendorf. In France, let me thank Laurence Lombard and Marc Picco; in the Ukraine and in Uzbekistan I was greatly assisted by Sergej Shdanow, Jelena Ladik, Alfija Walifewa, and Rustan Usmanow.

Texts by Ljalja Kuznetsova and Marina Rasbeshkina translated by Lorna Dale

First published in Great Britain in 1998 by Thames and Hudson Ltd, London

British Library Cataloguing-in-Publication Data

A catalogue record for this book is available from the British Library

ISBN 0-500-54220-1

Printed in Germany